WHAT OTHERS ARE SAYING ABOUT *SOUL CARE*

I have heard my dear friend Rob Reimer teach the truth contained in this book hundreds of times. However, as I read each chapter I realized why it never gets old: This is the power of Jesus to set the captives free. This is why we do what we do. I have been privileged to teach alongside Rob at Alliance Theological Seminary and many conferences throughout the years. We have watched Jesus set people free. My prayer is that you too will experience that freedom as you read this book and that you too will join us in helping Jesus set the captives free.

—**Dr. Ron Walborn**
Dean, Alliance Theological Seminary

In Rob's book *Soul Care*, he addresses the deepest issues of the human experience as an invitation to surrender to God's transforming work of healing and freedom. In a helpful, holistic way, Rob speaks truth in kindness and grace as a good friend or a close mentor. He has a keen ability to cut to the heart of the issue, to the motivator that drives us. I was challenged, encouraged, and pressed to deal with the realities that aren't always "fun" to talk about or work through. But, more importantly, I was always reminded to look to Jesus, the patient healer for even more hope and power. This book is anointed, plain and simple. I truly believe it will have a wide impact across many geographical and cultural boundaries and will be used to see many people released from past, present, and future issues as they work through a guided process of life change.

—REV. TIM MEIER
International Director, Envision

Soul Care is a guide for those who have an inkling that there is a longing in their soul to hold and radiate more of Christ. Soul Care is not a programme to be followed. It is the dawning recognition of life and freedom that Christ truly gives to those who seek to dwell with him. This is essential because we cannot Gospel what we do not live.

—TANIA WATSON
Executive Minister
Churches of Christ in Western Australia Inc.

In my younger years I was a bit of a pest. I would often frustrate people with my silly behaviour and so on more than one occasion was challenged with the words, "It is time you grow up!" Author Rob Reimer, in his book, *Soul Care,* not only boldly dares us to "Grow up" but actually articulates a pathway to help us do just that. In his refreshingly open and honest style, the author takes us on a journey into the delicate spaces of our soul. He asks the questions that we must wrestle with if we are going to find our way to maturity and wholeness. He states: "Growing up is a hard business and it is a heart business." However, failure to step into that challenge permits us to grow older in years but stay infants emotionally. The author warns, "Our immaturity always impairs our productivity. Our sinfulness detracts from our fruitfulness." This is a daring book in that it pushes open doors that many of us would prefer to leave closed. The call to walk in the light through engaging in a "life confession" with some trusted friends is a powerful invitation into freedom from toxic shame. This book is also a healing book. It delicately addresses the wounds of the soul and provides wisdom on how to clean up and remove the debris from our past and embrace fresh courage to face the complexities of the present. Don't miss this call to "Grow up!" It is compelling, liberating and worth the journey.

—REV. DAVID HEARN
   President, Christian & Missionary Alliance of Canada

Significant insights on the human condition and the power of the Spirit to restore the soul, Dr. Rob Reimer writes as both a pastor and a practical theologian. His approach has worked from the first stages of faith in the local church to the doctoral program. I highly recommend Dr. Reimer's book to all who want to see transformation in the care of their own soul.

—DR. MARTIN SANDERS
   President, Global Leadership Inc.
   Director, Doctoral Program at Alliance
   Theological Seminary

SOUL CARE

*Seven Transformational Principles
for a Healthy Soul*

Dr. Rob Reimer

Carpenter's Son Publishing

Published by Carpenter's Son Publishing, Franklin, Tennessee

Published in association with Larry Carpenter
of Christian Book Services, LLC
www.christianbookservices.com

Edited by Robert Irvin

Cover Design by John Pepe

Interior Layout Design by Suzanne Lawing

Printed in the United States of America

978-1-942587-45-3

ACKNOWLEDGMENTS

When I was 24 years old, I was alone with the Lord at seminary and heard Him speak to me about my calling. Among other things, He told me I would write books. I told Him I would do anything He asked, but I would never open a door to advance my own cause; I would wait for Him to open doors, and I would walk through them. I felt a release to write a few years back, and this is now my third book. Although I write all alone, writing is never a solo endeavor. The older I get, the more I realize the debt of gratitude I owe to so many. Here are a few words of thanks to those who deserve more than words can convey.

Dave and Barb MacBeth and Fred and Karen White, I couldn't have published this book without your support. Thank you from the bottom of my heart. Fred and Karen, you have supported me and my family in so many ways, so many times, with such generosity. I am deeply touched. Dave and Barb, you started South Shore Community Church with me and a handful of others; you were a major part of the formative years of SSCC, and even though you moved long ago, you continue to come alongside and serve me in our mutual efforts to advance the Kingdom. Thank you for years of loving support.

To all the staff, leaders, and members of SSCC who have labored in the Kingdom with me, and who have stepped up to fill the gaps left by my writing and speaking ministry: Thank you. May you know the pleasure of God and feel the satisfaction of the fruit your partnership in the Gospel has produced for the King's honor.

Andi, what words cannot convey, I pray God's Spirit would

reveal. You have been an integral part of all three books; they are far better off because of your love and sacrifices on my behalf. Eternal thanks!

To my dear friends Ron Walborn and Martin Sanders: I have often stood on the platforms that you two have established for me. Your partnership in the Gospel has been a great joy, honor, and blessing in my life. Thank you for allowing me the opportunities to teach alongside of you. The concepts of this book were birthed in the classrooms that we have shared, because of the opportunities you have afforded. I pray we get to do this Kingdom work together until we die.

To the readers who have read the first two books: Thank you for joining me on the journey! May this book take you to a new depth with God.

And lastly, to my entire family, I love you all, and I am so glad God gave you all to me. You have filled my life with joy and laughter. I'm lucky to have you!

Danielle, Courtney, Darcy, and Craig – I cried when I took you to kindergarten because I knew you would face the pain of this broken world; I cried when I took you to college, Danielle and Courtney, because I knew my precious daily time with you was drawing to a close. Both the tears and the prayers I have so frequently offered on your behalf are expressions of my deep love for you. I'm proud of you all.

Jen, you have played a central role in my spiritual development for the vast majority of my adult life. Your humor has cheered me, your kindness has softened me, your love has moved me, your honesty has shaped me, and your friendship has bolstered me. Your life has impacted mine, and your fingerprints are all over the content within these pages. With all my love and gratitude.

DEDICATION

This book is dedicated to my Dad and Mom. I can remember the day I realized how fortunate I was to grow up in our home. I was away at Christian college, and as I met new friends, I listened to their stories. Over and over, I realized that they had far more difficult family situations and upbringings, and it dawned on me how blessed I was. You are loving and generous people, who taught us how to work hard, and how to have fun. No family is perfect, and we have had our dysfunctions like all human families, but you provided us with a stable, loving home, and a Christian heritage. And you have grown, developed, and matured on your spiritual journey. Like me, you aren't the people you want to be, but you aren't the people you used to be, either. I bless you for that.

Dad, thanks for playing with us as kids and throwing out your arm pitching thousands of baseballs to us as kids growing up. Thanks for your thoroughgoing good nature, and your sense of humor. We have all laughed with you, and maybe occasionally at you, but you have rolled with it all and laughed along with us – to your credit. Your cheerful disposition and good nature have been evident throughout this latest battle with this dreaded cancer. I have sat with you in hospital rooms and doctors' offices for countless hours now, and you continue to tackle this most difficult and trying season with courage and a sense of humor. You have brought joy to your caregivers, and cheer to their weighty work. You've made me proud, and I'm honored to be your son. Now, get well soon, Pop—we've got more games to go to!

Mom, thanks for taking care of Dad through all of this and for modeling the way it should be done with loving tenderness, patience, perseverance, and humor. You have always been an emotional support to all of us, particularly during the hard times in life. I am still grateful for late-night TV growing up, where I processed with you in the wee hours of the night through some of my rough teenage moments. You're a good mom and a good wife, and I love you.

Thank you both for supporting me in ministry all of these years, in spite of all of my flaws, for being proud parents, and for growing and maturing under my ministry – it's a credit to your humility and God's work in your life. You have lived for Jesus and reflected him well. You have been loving parent figures to many, not just me and Ken. You are noble and honorable people, and I love you.

So, with great thanks and heartfelt love and affection, I honor you and dedicate this book to you.

Your son,
Rob

ADDITIONAL RESOURCES FOR PROCESSING *SOUL CARE*

Life change is hard. We want to help
support you in this journey.

Visit **www.DrRobReimer.com** to get the resources below!

- A **FREE guide** that includes additional questions to process the material for each principle covered in the book

- Join our ***Soul Care eCourse*** for shorter, self-paced video lessons taught by Rob. 40 lessons (over 9 hours of teaching) as well as study notes and questions to help you process your journey. Our free mini eCourse, ***Forgiveness***, gives you a great look at what the full eCourse is like. An eCourse for those who are leading others though Soul Care is coming in 2022!

- The *Soul Care Video Teaching Series (DVD or OnDemand Video)* features Rob teaching through the background of Soul Care and each of the 7 principles. Great for individuals, small groups, or church-wide curriculum, the Video Teaching Series will be an invaluable asset to anyone who is going after freedom and fullness in Christ, and to anyone who is leading others along that journey.

CONTENTS

INTRODUCTION:
MY JOURNEY TO SOUL CARE

In June 2015, my wife Jen and I celebrated our 25th anniversary. We went to Italy to celebrate. Italy is a beautiful country, an idyllic, romantic place steeped in rich history. But amidst all these attractive surroundings, breathtaking art, and remarkable architecture, the brokenness of humanity was also starkly present.

I stood before Michelangelo's Pieta, and there was a couple praying for their young child, who was obviously dying of cancer. Jen and I walked the streets of Florence in the midst of historic beauty, and there were homeless people strung out and begging for the means for their next high. We stood in line waiting to see Michelangelo's David, and we struck up a conversation with two lovely British women who had both lost their husbands when they were 57. We spoke with them about grief.

Everywhere you go, no matter how beautiful, no matter how romantic, brokenness grasps for the soul of humanity. Brokenness gets us all in life: rich and poor, black and white, old and young. No one escapes its clutches.

> We are broken—body, soul, and spirit—and we need the healing touch of Jesus.

We are broken—body, soul, and spirit—and we need the healing touch of Jesus. This is why I wrote this book. Jesus is a healer, and He has come to heal us: body, soul, and spirit. This book focuses on the healing of the soul. Jesus can lead us out of brokenness into wholeness,

1

and these Soul Care Principles from Scripture are profound healing tools of God.

Soul Care Principles changed my life. These aren't theoretical ideas to me. These are deeply transformational and transferrable principles. Life change isn't haphazard or accidental. There are some basic spiritual truths and realities we can access that lead us to a healthier soul.

It is somewhat analogous to physical health. If you want to be physically healthy, there are certain principles you have to follow—you have to eat right and exercise. If you violate those principles, then your health deteriorates. It is the same with Soul Care Principles. If you follow them, your soul can be healthy. If you ignore them, your soul suffers.

After I experienced personal breakthrough, I wondered why I didn't learn these kinds of principles in seminary. It would have saved me a lot of heartache both in marriage and ministry if I had learned this stuff before I began. I thought that if I ever got the chance, I would pass along these lessons and help people learn some of these truths to save them some of the pain that I had to endure.

> It takes a healthy leader to lead a healthy church.

I got the chance. My friend Martin Sanders invited me to teach a class with him at Alliance Theological Seminary; this was somewhere back around the turn of the millennium. We taught together regularly from that point on, and after a few years I suggested that we develop a course on Soul Care to help people break through their soul junk so that they could live free, be healthier, and help others get free in ministry.

It takes a healthy leader to lead a healthy church. If on the scale of 1 to 10 you are a 5 in terms of your emotional and spiritual health, the healthiest church you will ever lead is a

5. You have to change to become a healthier leader to lead a healthier church.

It works the same way with relationships. It takes two healthy people to have a healthy relationship. Here's a scary little secret: people marry to the level of their brokenness. If on a scale of 1 to 10 you are a 5, the healthiest relationship you will have is a 5. If you want to move from a 5 to a 7, there is one and only one path to get there. You must change.

When Martin and I were scheduled to teach this new class together, he ended up getting sick, so I prepared this Soul Care material for the course at seminary. I had lived into these principles for years before I taught them to others. Now I've taught Soul Care for nearly fifteen years in a variety of settings—I've taught Soul Care at the master's level, the doctoral level, in the local church setting, and in conferences for pastors and churches. I've taught it with people of all different backgrounds—economically, racially, ethnically, socially, and denominationally.

What I've discovered is that these principles, when packaged together and lived out, lead to freedom and a healthy soul. I've received countless e-mails, texts, letters, and testimonies of the powerful impact Soul Care had on a person. The language and principles of the heart and soul transcend time and culture.

As I have traveled, taught, and had conversations with many people, I have come to realize that a lot of people are stuck in their spiritual journey, and they need freedom. Some are in a marriage crisis and want to get better, but they can't find a path to wholeness. The church hasn't helped enough of these people get healthy enough to have a healthy relationship. Others are stuck in a sin pattern. The church has too often told them, "Don't do that" without giving them the help they need to get free. I've seen people tormented by the power of the enemy, and they didn't know how to access the power of

God to find freedom from Satan's evil grip.

I long to see revival; I long to see the church be the church so the world will believe. I long to see the church walking in the fullness of the Spirit, tasting of deep intimacy with Christ, and experiencing the freedom Jesus' blood affords. This is why I am writing about Soul Care. I write to lay people who long to be free from soul issues that plague them. I write to pastors, leaders, and missionaries who long to live a healthier life, have healthier relationships with God and others, and lead a healthier church or a healthier organization. I write to church leaders who want to make disciples and help others find freedom in Christ. These are the reasons I write.

THE PAINFUL PATH TO LIFE CHANGE

John Maxwell said, "People change when they hurt enough that they have to, learn enough that they want to, and receive enough that they are able to.[1]" This is why a lot of us change— because things get desperate. If I sat down with you and asked you to describe a time of life change in your spiritual journey, there is a good chance that the time you would describe would have been a time of crisis. Many of us change when we hurt. That was true for me.

I was in my early thirties and had planted a church in New England. The church was growing. People were coming to faith in Christ, and lives were being changed. We were witnessing the power of God. It was fun. All the right measurement charts were going up and to the right—church attendance, small group participation, salvations, baptisms, volunteerism, and finances. On the outside everything looked picture perfect, but behind closed doors something was beginning to

---

1. John C. Maxwell, *Failing Forward: Turning Mistakes into Stepping Stones for Success* (Nashville: Thomas Nelson, 2000), p. 156.

unravel. There was an internal problem that was beginning to produce external consequences.

Jen, my wife, was beginning to grow emotionally distant from me. I was trying to reach out to her, but I wasn't making any progress. I could feel something was wrong, but I didn't know what it was, and I didn't know how to fix it. I tried praying, and I tried talking, but nothing was changing; in fact, things were only getting worse. The longer it went on, the more it felt like she was angry with me— really angry, to the point of being shut down completely. It was a frozen rage.

I started to ask her about it. "Sweetie," I said very softly one night. "Are you angry with me?" She said very curtly, "No." Lies, I thought! But I said, "Are you sure?" She said, coldly, "No. I'm not angry." But I persisted. I kept coming back to the question, "Sweetie, are you angry with me?" "No," was the consistent reply.

We did this dance for a while, until one day Jen picked up a book that I had been reading by Bill and Lynne Hybels, *Rediscovering the Church*. Jen lifted it up off the coffee table, randomly opened it, and read one paragraph where Lynne described a time where she got to the place where she couldn't stand Bill anymore. Jen put the book down and said, "I am angry with you." I said, "Good. I'm glad you admitted it. Now we can work on it." I had no idea what I was in for.

> You can't fix the problems of the soul with a change in behavior only.

The reality was that my wife didn't like me anymore, and this wasn't going to be a quick fix or an easy solution. There were some deep-seated issues; these weren't surface problems—these were soul problems. You can't fix the problems of the soul with a change in behavior only.

At first I thought it was her issue only, or at least mostly.

God needed to help her. I prayed those "God, change her!" prayers, but God doesn't seem to answer those prayers as much as I wish He would. Slowly I began to realize that the problem wasn't just her; I was the problem, and it wasn't just an external problem. It was an issue of the heart and soul.

She had her own set of issues that she needed to address, but even if she addressed those issues, it wouldn't have resolved the problem. It takes two healthy people to have a healthy relationship. I needed to change, too. She didn't like me because I had hurt her emotionally. I wasn't trying to hurt her. I was unaware of what I was doing and why I did what I did. That is a dangerous combination!

We entered into these conflict resolution conversations every night for months. It was painful. Most days it didn't feel like we were making much progress; at times it felt hopeless. Most days it felt like things were never going to change, but we kept saying to each other, "Divorce is not an option. We will figure this out with the help of God." And I am so grateful to say that we did, but it didn't involve merely tweaking our marriage interactions. It involved deep soul change.

In the meantime, while I was having these painful conversations with Jen at home, I was also having a conflict with one of my staff members at work, Randy. And sadly, Jen and Randy were telling me some of the same things. They weren't even talking to each other, so this wasn't coordinated—except by God. He was after my heart and soul—not to hurt me, but to heal me.

They were both saying things to me like, "My opinion doesn't seem to count. You don't listen to me. Your opinion always rules the day." I didn't like what I was hearing, but I couldn't continue to ignore it. And the question I had to address was, "Why? Why did I behave like that? What was underneath that?"

I went to a John Maxwell conference when I was in my

mid-twenties, and I heard him say, "When Tom has a problem with Dick, and Tom has a problem with Harry, and Tom has a problem with Sue . . . Can I tell you something about Tom? Tom is the problem." I loved that line when John said it. I laughed. I had taught it to others, because they needed it! I thought it was great . . . until now. Cute little truth slogans are marvelous tools when they can be proverbially shared to help others, but it didn't seem nearly as funny when the truth was turned on me. I had a problem with Jen. And I had a problem with Randy. I had to face up to the fact that I was the problem.

> Growing up is a hard business, and it is a heart business.

I wasn't the sole problem, of course. But praying that they would change wasn't the answer. Focusing on their problems wasn't the answer. If you are reading this book to fix someone else, that isn't the answer, either. You have to deal with your own issues. Growing up is a hard business, and it is a heart business. I realized that if I didn't change, I was never going to have a happy marriage, and I was never going to bear as much fruit as I could or should in ministry. More importantly, if I didn't change, I wasn't ever going to grow up to be like Jesus. Our immaturity always impairs our productivity. *Our sinfulness detracts from our fruitfulness.*

Choosing Maturity

It is often the issues of the soul that keep us from intimacy with God and others. Many people come to me because they want to get closer to God, but they can't. What they fail to understand is that it is often soul issues that keep them from drawing near to God. Praying, fasting, and memorizing Scripture cannot help us draw near—unless we address the soul blocks. We have these unconfessed, unprocessed, undealt-with issues, and they hinder us from experiencing the fullness of God. Think of your soul like a container. These things fill up the container of our souls, and unless we deal with them, we don't have any more capacity for God.

D.L. Moody, a 19th century evangelist and pastor, wrote in his book *Secret Power*: "Before we pray that God would fill us, I believe we ought to pray Him to empty us. There must be an emptying before there can be a filling; and when the heart is turned upside down, and everything is turned out that is contrary to God, then the Spirit will come, just as He did in the tabernacle, and fill us with His Glory."[2]

We live in a celebrity culture. People are enamored with our abilities, our gifts, and our talents. People will evaluate our maturity based on our capacity, but God examines the heart. People are impressed with our gifts, but God isn't. He gave them to us. Our gifts are a given, but growing up to know and be like Jesus . . . that is a *choice*.

Maturity is a choice we have to make and a price we have to pay, and all the talent in the world can't compensate for immaturity. It is the development of our character and the depth of our intimacy that impresses God. Salvation is free. Maturity comes at a cost.

Immaturity is costly, too. The difference with maturity is you pay up front, but with immaturity, you pay for it on the back end—with interest! Pay whatever price it costs for maturity; it's worth it. I knew I had a price to pay to change, and if I didn't pay it, I was going to pay a greater price in marriage and in ministry and in my relationship with the God I loved. Before I could change, God had to break through my defenses so He could get to the heart of the matter.

---

2. D. L. Moody, *Secret Power: The Secret of Success in Christian Life and Work* (New Kensington: Whitaker House, 1997), p. 32.

Defensiveness

The first area God had to address was my defensiveness. I wanted to be a man of God. I wanted to know Jesus deeply, not just know about Jesus. But I had some stuff in my soul that was keeping me from growing up. And unless I saw and admitted it, I couldn't become the man I wanted to be. I wasn't sure what the issues were, and I didn't know how to fix them. But I was determined to figure it out with the help of God. I had to. I was desperate to change. I was in soul pain.

I would go to church on Sunday mornings, and I would often find myself crying my way through the worship. I would pray, "Lord, if you give me strength to stand, I'll give the talk that you have given me." I'd have strength, and I would get up and give the talk, but then I would go home and collapse on the couch, emotionally exhausted. I couldn't keep living life like that.

Life change is often a slow and painful process. I was not ready to change right away. God is patient, and He was trying to help me grapple with the real issues of my heart, but I was slow to admit the truth. But there can be no transformation where there is no revelation. We cannot overcome that which we will not admit.

> There can be no transformation where there is no revelation. We cannot overcome that which we will not admit.

When Jen and I first started talking about why she was angry, I would defend myself. We would put our little ones to bed, and then we would enter into a dialogue to try to solve the conflict. I would ask, "Why are you upset with me?" She would say something like, "I feel like you don't listen to me." And I would say, "That's not true!" Of course, as I defended myself, I realized that I was proving her point. I wasn't listening. This went on for quite some time.

She would say, "I feel like the church is a mistress in our relationship." I would retort defensively, "Come on! How?" She said, "On our day off, you answer the phone, and you'll rob us of two hours together on one phone call."

I would argue, "What do you want me to do? Not answer the phone?"

"Yes," she said, as if that were simple and plain enough.

Actually, it had never occurred to me that this was a possibility. She would tell me why she was hurt, angry, and upset, and I would defend myself at every turn. Defensiveness only escalates conflict. She didn't feel listened to, so she felt like she needed to make her points a little more forcefully. I would feel more hurt, and I would defend myself with a little more passion.

Finally, one night I went upstairs to my study to be alone with God after one of our unproductive conversations; I was really worked up inside. The Lord spoke to me. I figured He would take my side, but I was wrong. He wasn't interested in sides; He was interested in mature followers with healthy souls. I was interested in the alleviation of my pain; God was interested in the transformation of my heart.

He said, "I don't want you to defend yourself anymore." I thought, *Really? That is one of my best tools!* The problem was that defensiveness was preventing me from life change. I couldn't admit the things that God was trying to address. But as God convicted me that night, I was determined to listen to Him, because I was convinced that He had my best in mind, that He alone could help me out of this predicament and lead me to a healthier soul.

So I surrendered. I am convinced that most life change occurs alone with God—but only if we will listen and surrender.

Blame

Though I surrendered my defensiveness, I still wasn't ready

to change. I had protective layers in place to keep God and others from getting to my heart issues. I wasn't aware of these protective measures, but God was.

Jen and I resumed the conversations again each night, and I resolved just to listen and not defend. But though I listened without defending, I still wasn't ready to change. I now wasn't defensive outwardly, but neither was I open inwardly! There is a big difference.

Jen would tell me what she was upset about, and I would listen and repeat back to her what she said in my own words until she finally agreed that is what she meant. I would end the conversation by sighing and saying, "It's always my fault." This went on for a couple of weeks.

> Most life change begins alone with God. If we give Him access to our hearts, He will do an inner work of transformation.

Of course, Jen still didn't feel listened to. Even though I wasn't defending myself, I wasn't receiving what she was saying into my spirit. I could repeat what she was telling me, but I wasn't open to *owning* what I needed to own.

Fortunately, I continued to spend time alone with God every night after our conversations, and every morning when I got up. Most life change begins alone with God. If we give Him access to our hearts, He will do an inner work of transformation. But God is a gentleman, and He will not force us to change. What He asks for is access; what He longs for is the pierced heart that gives Him room to go deep inside and do the work of transformation.

One night I was alone with God after another unproductive conversation with Jen, and the Lord spoke to me again. He said, "Read Ephesians 5." I knew the passage, and I was a little suspicious of where He was trying to take me! I said, "I know that passage." I heard Him whisper, "Read it."

I read the familiar passage urging husbands to love their wives as Christ loved the church; it goes on to say that He presented the church "blameless." That was the word that leaped off the page at me that night. When the Spirit breathes on a word in Scripture, it stirs within you, it leaps off the page at you, and this is the moment when God is coming near. This is the moment of divine breakthrough. This is the moment, if you'll let it, when the piercing of the heart can take place, and the deep work of transformation can begin. Every time you pick up the Bible, you are one Holy Spirit breath away from a fresh encounter with the living God.

> Every time we pick up the Bible, we are one Holy Spirit breath away from a fresh encounter with the living God.

As the Spirit breathed on that word, I heard Him whisper, "I present my bride blameless, but you blame yours. I don't want you to blame her again. Every time you sigh and say, 'It's always my fault,' you are blaming her." I felt convicted, but I have to admit, I also felt a bit cornered. I was running out of options. I couldn't defend. I couldn't blame. What did I have left?

Bargaining with God

I played my last card: I started bargaining with God. This wasn't a calculated decision; it was an act of desperation. It was just another protective layer keeping God from penetrating my heart. The one thing God wants most is access to your heart, and I still wasn't ready to let Him have full access. I began to pray, "Lord, you have to change Jen. If you don't change her, I am not going to be able to stay in ministry. I am in too much pain. I cry my way through every service, and I barely have enough energy to survive. You have to do something.

You have six months to change her, Lord. Then I'll have to opt out of ministry because I can't keep doing this."

Believe me: I really wasn't trying to be belligerent. That prayer was motivated by pain and emotional exhaustion. But also, down deep, I knew the bargaining had to go.

And yet, I prayed like this for a quite a while. Then one day I was alone with God, and He spoke to me again. He said, "The law of the harvest." I knew He was referring to Galatians 6. A person reaps what they sow. So I turned there and studied it. As I mulled over the passage, I sensed the Spirit stirring within me with that old familiar stirring: "A person reaps what they sow. You can blame Jen if you want to. You can blame Me if you want to. But you are standing in a field of weeds because you have been sowing weed seeds. You have been sowing seeds of anger and selfishness. If you want to stand in a field of fruitfulness, you have to sow new seeds."

Surrender: Full Access to God

That was the day I ran out of options, and that was right where the Lord wanted me. That was the day I stopped defending, blaming, and bargaining, and I started tak-

> A person gets to be a grown-up when they take responsibility for their life.

ing ownership of my life. A person doesn't get to be a grown-up when they are 16 and can drive a car, or 18 and can go off to war, or 21 and they can drink legally, or 25 and get married, or 30 and have their first child. A person gets to be a grown-up when they take responsibility for their life. I stood there that day in my study, and in my field of weeds, and I surrendered to the shaping hand of God. I gave Him access to the deep recesses of my heart. My heart was pierced and accessible to God—but I still didn't know how to change.

Shortly thereafter, I was standing in my study again and prayed, "Lord, I am willing to change, but I don't know how to change. There are some deep-seated things inside of me that are broken. I can see that. The problem is, I don't know what they are; I don't know what the roots are, and I don't know how to change them. I need your help. Can you lead me to a path of change?"

God answered that prayer. It wasn't immediate; there was no one encounter that changed everything. But there were some very important encounters along the way. There was no one secret principle that unlocked a treasure chest of life change, though there were vital principles that I was failing to apply.

> You will never rise above your level of self-awareness. The things we deny about ourselves are the very things that deny us from the fullness of God.

I desperately clung to God, and I discovered that He was enough. I knew God loved me, but on this journey toward wholeness, I experienced the revelation of the love of God in healing power like never before.

I understood that we have to confess our sins, but now I experienced a level of the penetrating light of God that I had never been willing to accept before, and it freed me. I read Jesus' words about forgiving others, but I discovered I had bitter roots that were like shackles on my soul, and the Lord showed me how to break those chains. It was liberating.

I discovered that fear crippled me. I didn't even know I had fear; I was living in complete denial, but the symptomatic expressions of fear were creating havoc in my life. I should have known: the number one command in Scripture is "Fear not." That surely isn't an accident, but I was so completely oblivious to fear in my life that I was allowing it to wreck my relationships. I didn't know that underneath my need to be right was a hidden fear. It was a journey of self-discovery, a journey of healing, and a journey of freedom. You will never rise above your level of self-awareness. The things we deny about ourselves are the very things that deny us from the fullness of God.

THE PROCESS OF LIFE CHANGE

The process of change involved a lot of time alone with God. Most life change begins alone with God. It also involved a lot of books. I am particularly indebted to the writings of Leanne Payne and David Benner. So many of the books I read in those days helped me come into self-awareness, and I couldn't have gotten there without them.

The life change journey also involved some critically important God encounters. I could only overcome some of the issues that I was facing with the presence and power of God.

And community played a vital role in my maturing process. I am so grateful for Martin Sanders and my friend Rich Schmidt, who journeyed with me in those early days; we talked, prayed, and opened our lives to each other. My staff also played a critical role in the self-discovery of those early days. Ron Walborn became a dear friend later on in the journey, and my friendship with him has also been used by God to shape my life. And I would not be who I am becoming without Jen—it was our early conflict that became the impetus to my soul healing journey. Her words forced me to grapple with issues of my heart and soul that I would not have discovered without the gift of truth she offered, and our relationship has been a great source of strength, help, support, and love to me all along the way. There were so many others, and I am grateful for the family of God.

In this book I am going to explore seven principles of Soul Care that can lead to transformation. You can read the book straight through, but simply knowing the principles won't change you. I would encourage you to read it and work through it. You may need to go back and read through and work through sections of the book multiple times. Giving God access to our hearts often occurs over time, in layers. We peel back a layer, and make some progress, only to discover later on that there is yet a deeper level still to uncover and process through. Don't read this book like a novel or a textbook. Read it like a life change workbook.

Life change is an interactive, roll-up-your-sleeves, and get-messy process. It is a journey of self-reflection, Holy Spirit inspiration, deep wrestling, and surrender. It is a process of discovering ourselves in true community, and discovering God as He pierces through the layers of the heart. Give Him access. Go deep. It's worth the trip.

Some people would call this process spiritual formation, and others discipleship. I prefer the phrase *soul care*. I think the word "Soul" communicates even to a secular world. I stay in a hotel in New York when I teach at seminary, and I am there about thirty nights per year. One night I arrived at my home away from home, and the woman behind the desk, who is often there, greeted me by name: "Dr. Reimer, it is so good to see you. Welcome back." I returned her greeting cheerfully, and as she was checking me in, she asked, with her thick Russian accent, "What do you teach at the seminary?" I said, "I teach a lot of things about how to have a healthier soul." She said, "Have you written any books?" I said, "I am writing about it." She said, "I want to become your pupil." I laughed and asked, "Why?" She answered: "Everyone needs a healthier soul."

That's why I wrote *Soul Care*. Everyone needs a healthier soul. Let's lay out a path to get there.

GATEWAYS TO LIFE CHANGE

Many people want to experience life change, and many times our circumstances motivate us to want to change. You may be in a painful marriage situation like I was. You pray and hope that you will change, that your partner will change, that your marriage relationship will change . . . but nothing changes. You feel hopeless. You read books, attend church, pray, read your Bible, and resolve to get better—but still you remain stuck.

You may have a destructive or shameful pattern of behavior that you know is unhealthy and needs to change. You want to change, you pray you will change, but the pattern continues unbroken. You have brief moments of reprieve, but you keep reverting back to this old pattern of behavior. You feel defeated.

The Bible teaches us that when someone comes to faith in Christ, they are changed: "Therefore, if anyone is in Christ, he is a new creature; the old things passed away; behold, new things have come" (2 Corinthians 5:17, New American Standard Bible). So if we are new creatures in Christ, why is this old sin habit still hanging around? In order to experience life change, we need to learn how to access the transformation that Jesus won for us on the cross. How do we access life change?

GATEWAYS TO LIFE CHANGE: THE HEART OF THE MATTER

Sometimes we don't experience the new life that Jesus promises us because we are focused on symptoms and not the disease itself. If a doctor simply treated you for symptoms, but didn't ever address the underlying disease, the disease would persist in its destructive course, even if the symptoms went away. A good doctor wouldn't simply address the symptoms; he or she would go after the disease itself.

Too often in the church we are focused on behavior management or sin management. For example, imagine someone is struggling with a pornography addiction. They feel bad about it, because every time they fall into this sin, they are filled with shame. To make matters worse, their spouse catches them looking at pornography, and now they are in a marriage crisis. So often the focus becomes overcoming the pornography addiction. The addiction is treated as if it were the problem, the enemy that must be defeated. But in reality, most often the pornography is a symptom; it is not the disease.

When the church falls prey to sin management, we usually resort to telling people moralisms. "Just stop that." "Get accountability." "Pray more, and read your Bible." "Memorize Scripture." Don't get me wrong, none of this activity is necessarily bad. Some of these things are even vital to our spiritual development. But there is something more that needs to be done to address the real disease.

Jesus taught that the root issues of our sinful words and

actions lie in the heart. In Matthew 12:34, 35, Jesus said to the Pharisees: "For out of the overflow of the heart the mouth speaks. Good people bring good things out of the good stored up in them, and evil people bring evil things out of the evil stored up in them."

But it isn't just our words that flow from the things in the heart: our actions do as well. A few chapters later, Jesus explained this concept in a little deeper way to the disciples. In the context, the Pharisees harassed Jesus because the disciples ate without ceremonially washing their hands properly. Jesus explained to the disciples that it wasn't what they put into their mouth that made a person unclean; it was a matter of the heart.

In Matthew 15:18-20, Jesus said, "The things that come out of the mouth come from the heart, and these defile you. For out of the heart come evil thoughts, murder, adultery, sexual immorality, theft, false testimony, slander. These are what defile you; but eating with unwashed hands does not defile you." (My take is that doing so, though, may displease your mother and the religious people around you!)

> If we are going to experience true transformation, we must deal with the issues of the heart and not simply external behaviors.

It is out of the overflow of the heart that the mouth speaks and the person acts. Notice Jesus didn't limit the flow of the heart to our words, but he includes actions in the list—like murder, adultery, and sexual immorality. Good and bad flow from the heart. If we are going to experience true transformation, we must deal with the issues of the heart and not simply external behaviors.

Often in Scripture, agricultural imagery is used for matters of the heart. I'm not much of a gardener, but in watching others, I've learned a few things. One of the things I know is that if you want to remove weeds from the garden, you cannot simply chop off the head of the weed. You have to hoe it up or somehow pull it out by the roots. If you only combat the leaves of the weed, you will not kill it. The weeds return until you pull them out by the roots.

It is the same with the matters of the heart. You must get to these root issues in order to experience true transformation. Behavior management is focused on the leaves of the weeds that grow up in your life. You have to get down below the surface and deal with the issues of the heart that are motivating your actions.

People come to me all the time when they are struggling with a sin pattern. They feel bad about it. They want to change. But they are obsessed with the behavior. What they really want is for God to fix them; they want God to change their behavior. God is far less concerned about our behavior than we think He is. He is much more concerned about our hearts than we'll ever know. God knows if we get our hearts healthy, and rightly aligned with Him, our behaviors will follow. But if we get our behaviors in line without dealing with the condition of our hearts, we will become Pharisees at best. We will be left with dark places in the soul and a life full of judgment, not love.

> God is far less concerned about our behavior than we think He is. He is much more concerned about our hearts than we'll ever know.

The key is to look at the heart. What is underneath your behavior? Why do you do what you do? What is driving this? When you get to the heart level, you deal with the disease and not the symptoms, you deal with the roots and not the leaves, you deal with the heart and not just the behavior—and it is then that true transformation can begin to take place.

In this book we will look at seven different issues of the heart that need to be addressed in order to experience freedom.

GATEWAYS TO LIFE CHANGE: CULTIVATING THE SOIL OF THE SOUL

In gardening, there is an environment that you need to cultivate so the garden can produce and bear fruit. If the soil is rocky, hard, weedy, too dry, or too wet, the crops won't grow. But if the right conditions are cultivated, the plants will produce a harvest—in time. It is equally true with life change. There is an atmosphere that best allows life change to occur over time.

There are three essential components that comprise an atmosphere where maximum life change can occur. These three ingredients cultivate the soil of the soul and create an environment where fruitful life change can result. If you are a church leader, you need to cultivate an atmosphere in which these three components are accessible to the people. If you are a church member and your church does not have these three components, then you need to find other avenues to access these indispensable keys to life change.

Anointed Teaching

First, you need to experience anointed teaching. If teaching is based on the truth of God's Word, there is an anointing in the truth that is being taught. There is also anointing in the spiritual gifting of the teacher. But if the teaching is *lived into* by the teacher, then the anointing of the truth and the anointing of the gifting carries greater weight in the heart of the listener.

Lived-into truth expands the authority of the teacher and gives greater weight to his or her words. That greater authority is able to pierce the ready heart. And only the pierced heart—the broken, humble, and contrite heart—is accessible to God and ready for transformation.

As a teacher, I only have authority over that which I walk in victory. My spiritual authority and capacity to set a context where others can get free is limited by my life. Jesus sent His disciples to proclaim the kingdom of God and set the captives free, and He told his disciples, "Freely you have received, freely give" (Matthew 10:8). We can only give away what we have.

Scripture has infinite depth, and the more revelation that the teacher has received, the greater insight the teacher can convey. The greater freedom a teacher walks in, the greater authority that teacher carries to set others free. The more access the teacher gives God to his or her heart, the more the teacher can access the deep recesses of the heart of others. When a teacher writes or speaks from a place of deep revelation and transformation, he or she can convey truth that doesn't just land on the mind, but it *pierces the heart*. This creates an atmosphere for deep change.

And, of course, it isn't enough just to teach truth. We must teach the truths of the heart that allow for freedom. But if a teacher simplifies the message to behavior modification, they will not create an atmosphere of freedom. We need teachers who have insights into the soul, who preach with a spiritual weightiness that leads to breakthroughs.

True Community

Life change occurs in an environment of true community. In true community, people live open, honest, and confessional lives in a culture of grace. There is no hiding or pretending. Secrets are toxic to the wellbeing of the soul. If you are going to experience breakthroughs, then you must resolve to live confessional lives with no secrets.

When I was in college, I struggled with lust. The church I grew up in never talked about these issues. Confessional living wasn't part of my upbringing. I had surrendered my life to God, and I desired to walk with Him. Yet I still struggled with lust, and no one knew. I felt defeated and ashamed.

One day I was praying about it, and I sensed the Spirit of God leading me to confess my struggles to one of my college buddies. The very thought of talking about it turned my stomach, because confession was so foreign to my way of life. I was afraid to come clean; I was afraid of what people would think of me. But I summoned the courage and one night, in the dark, I confessed my struggles with lust. My college friend immediately shared that he too was struggling.

At that point in my life, because I hadn't lived in an open, honest, and confessional community, I thought I was the only one who struggled with lust. It was a great relief to know I was not alone in the struggle. More than that, though, confessing that sin broke the shame I felt and helped me begin to overcome the sin pattern, as long as I continued to walk in the light.

Church leaders, we must create a grace-filled atmosphere where people can confess their sins. I was preaching in a conference one day and had a sense that the region in which we were teaching was covered with secrets. The Spirit of God was allowing me to feel the weightiness of the secrecy. I called people to confess their secrets and get out from under the weight of their sin, guilt, and shame; I modeled it by being open, honest, and vulnerable. People came forward and confessed all sorts of secret sins, and breakthroughs came. The healing of the Spirit flowed.

As leaders, we have to live in the light with God and others. We have to be vulnerable with our own shortcomings. And we have to allow the grace of Jesus to penetrate and permeate our own hearts so we can extend his grace to those who come out of the darkness into the light.

As followers of Jesus, we must all choose to live in the light with God and others. Only light can set us free from darkness. No one ever discovers ultimate freedom by protecting dark corners of secrecy in their soul. Even if this is not part of your current church family, you can create a small group of people who will live this way with you.

Presence and Power

Finally, in order to create an atmosphere that allows for life change, we need the presence and power of God. In the end, only God can change the heart.

When we come to faith in Christ, we are given a new heart (Ezekiel 36:26, 27). God gives us a heart that wants to follow Him. He puts his Spirit within us, empowering us to live this new life in Christ. We need to access His presence and power in order to change and walk out this new life that is within us. We need the presence of God to heal our hearts from past trauma and hurt. We need the power of God to deliver us from Satan's grip.

> We need the presence and power of God. In the end, only God can change the heart.

Too often in the church we talk about the presence and power of God, but we don't actually see any demonstration of it. This wasn't true in the early church. Paul wrote, "My message and my preaching were not with wise and persuasive words, but with a demonstration of the Spirit's power, so that your faith might not rest on human wisdom, but on God's power" (1 Corinthians 2:4, 5). I wonder if the same could be said of many of our churches today. We need the authentic presence and power of God being demonstrated in our midst again today. It is often in our theology, but not in our reality. When the presence and power of God are part of our belief system, but absent from our practice, there are significant gaps in the integration of faith into our lives.

> When the presence and power of God are part of our belief system, but absent from our practice, there are significant gaps in the integration of faith into our lives.

I can trace all of the life change I have experienced back to the presence and power of God being manifest. God spoke to me; God revealed Himself to me; God encountered me; God filled me. It was these God-moments that produced transformation.

This is why I have made time with God a nonnegotiable commitment in my life. I spend time with God when I feel like it and when I don't. I engage in spiritual practices like reading Scripture, meditating on Scripture, praying, listening to the voice of the Spirit, worship, solitude, and silence, because I know I need God. I need His presence.

John said that "when Christ appears, we shall be like him, for we shall see him as he is" (1 John 3:2). This is an end time principle: when we see Him face to face, our transformation will be complete; we shall be transformed into His likeness. But there is also a present day principle in this passage: His presence is transformational. We need to engage in spiritual activities that allow us to access His presence if we are going to experience life change.

My first two books, *Pathways to the King* and *River Dwellers*, both emphasized this point of intimacy with God being essential to life change. Normally, when I teach Soul Care, I spend a lecture or two just talking about intimacy with God and accessing his presence. Don't bypass this point. This book will emphasize some key principles of the soul that need to be appropriated in order to be changed. But it all begins with your relationship with God. Most life change occurs alone with God. Don't miss this. Only God changes the heart. Only God heals the soul. Only God sets the captives free.

Many churches today have one of these components in their culture: anointed truth, true community, or the presence and power of God. But it takes all three to create a culture of deep change. It is equally true of inner healing ministry. The practitioners I have observed who have the greatest, most lasting impact on people they serve have combined all three of these components into their ministry. All three are necessary for life change. If you are a leader in the church, one of your primary jobs is to create the right kind of culture. Create a culture where all three components are accessible. If you are a church attender, and all three are not readily visible in your church, then you may need to go to other places to access some of the tools and resources you need for life change.

ACCESSING THESE AREAS IN SOUL CARE

I have been reluctant to write this book because I realize a book can only operate in one of these three areas. Hopefully, I can write with the anointing and revelation of the Spirit. But anointed truth alone is not sufficient for deep change. Again: you need all three areas. You need anointed teaching, which I hope to offer in this text. But you must willingly engage in the true community, and you must eagerly seek God's presence.

That's why I urge you to read this book in a community of friends with whom you commit to being totally honest. Hold no secrets. I know the very thought of this makes many people sick to their stomachs. I get it. Many people have carried around a long history of secrets. But there is no transforma-

> There is no transformation without confession. There is no victory in hiding. There is no breakthrough in secrecy.

tion without confession. There is no victory in hiding. There is no breakthrough in secrecy. You must walk in the light with God and others in order to be free.

You also should commit to applying these principles and really working through this book. Pause for time alone with God so his presence and power can come. Take time to be still and listen for his transforming voice. Go to events, places, and conferences where the presence and power of God is notably experienced.

Whenever I teach Soul Care, I incorporate all three components. It isn't just a lecture time. At the beginning of a class or a conference, I call people to break into triads. I exhort them upfront to be open and honest, and then I have them break into groups of three to tell their stories, to open their lives to one another.

Over the years, hundreds of times, people have come clean with secrets and confessed things they have never told anyone before. There are many tears and there is much love and grace—and there are many significant breakthroughs. Often the triads that are formed stay connected with each other because of the deep bond that occurs. These are people who often do not know each other coming into the class or conference, but they take a bold risk and willingly open their lives to each other. I have had people come to me and say, "I can't open up to these people. I've done a lot of bad things, and I have never told anyone." I say to them, "You don't have to open up. But if you want to get free, I would encourage you to. You'll never get free with secrets." Over and over I have watched those people open up, confess their secrets, share their stories, and come to dramatic and significant breakthroughs. Take a risk.

Please, form a triad, and go through this book with others. Determine to be open, honest, confessional, and gracious with one another. Make a resolution to live without secrets. I've taught Soul Care classes and conferences for a long time, with thousands of people, from all sorts of cultures, ethnic groups, and church backgrounds and experiences, and it is my observation that a very low percentage of people are living in true community, one that is both confessional and gracious. And such a community is critically important for life transformation.

When a plant gets the right environment, it bears fruit. It needs the right amount of sunlight, water, and nutrients in the soil; if it gets what it needs, it will become healthy and grow. The same thing can be said of the soul.

When we get the right mixture of anointed teaching, confessional, grace-filled community, and the presence and power of God, then life change happens. The soul will absolutely flourish in that type of atmosphere.

Pastors and church leaders, we need to learn how to cultivate these atmospheres. This is one of the reasons I began offering Soul Care Equipping Conferences. I speak with many pastors who attend a Soul Care class, and they experience significant life change and freedom. When I see them several months later, I ask if they started a similar ministry in their church context. The vast majority of times they say, "No. I didn't know how." Or: "No. I was afraid to implement some of these things in our context."

These pastors have written me letters that detail their life change experience, but they didn't bring it back home to their churches. So I started the Soul Care Equipping Conference as a tool to help them create this kind of atmosphere in their local church. The conference is designed for them to attend along with their leaders, so that, as a leadership team, they can experience these three elements of the atmosphere of life change, and we can equip them to bring it back to their ministry setting. Many leaders have come through the Soul Care Equipping Conference, and many settings now have a culture for life change.

I have often created these cultures in classroom settings and conference settings in just five days. We can certainly create such a culture in our churches. True transformation depends on it. We must create the kind of Kingdom culture where life change can occur—cultures of anointed teaching and confessional community where the power and presence of God are demonstrated.

GATEWAYS TO LIFE CHANGE: SELF-AWARENESS

You've heard the expression: "What you don't know won't hurt you." But when it comes to the soul, that is a dangerous lie. What you don't know is already killing you.

Self-awareness is a gateway to life change; it doesn't guarantee it, but you can't get there without it. 1 John 1:5 says, "God is light; in him there is no darkness at all." God shines light into our souls; He reveals the truth about us. Our job is to stand in the light with God and admit the truth.

> We cannot heal that which we will not admit. God cannot cleanse that which we will not confess.

We must learn to embrace the light God offers. It is a gift. It is not an intruder. Jesus taught that the enemy, the prince of darkness, tries to kill, steal, and destroy; darkness is an intruder. But not so with God: He shines the light to heal the soul, to bind up the brokenhearted, to release the captive, to give victory to the oppressed.

When we reject the truth, we miss out on the freedom God affords. We cannot heal that which we will not admit. God cannot cleanse that which we will not confess. We are often reluctant to admit the ugly, broken, and sinful parts of our self. But to the degree that we deny these realities, we live in bondage to them.

Let me provide an example. Imagine Sally is a worship leader. Each week, Sally gets up to lead people into the presence of God. People come up to her afterward and say, "Oh, Sally, when you lead, I can just feel God's presence. I love when you sing and lead us into worship." Sally is very humble and bashfully says, "Oh, thank you. It's just the Lord."

Then one day a new singer joins the worship team. Jane has an outrageous voice, and she is anointed. Not just talented, but anointed with the Spirit of God to lead people into worship. The same people that used to come up to Sally now come up to Jane, in Sally's presence, and they gush, "Ooh, Jane, when you sing, it's like I'm in the throne room of God!" Sally feels something inside of her, and it's not a good something. She thinks that it must be discernment. She thinks to herself, *Something isn't quite right with Jane. She's showy; she's a little performance-oriented.* And she begins to share this assessment with people when they make comments about Jane. But this isn't discernment; it's envy.

Envy starts with the question, "What about me?" and ends with the accusation, "God isn't fair." Because of Sally's lack of self-awareness, there is now divisiveness on the worship team and conflict that has gone underground between Sally and Jane. Sally is gossiping against Jane with others, though she does it under the guise of prayer requests and concerns, and others are now beginning to get a little suspicious of Jane as well.

What you don't know can not only hurt you, it can hurt

others and the cause of God. It is vitally important that we live in the light with God. Only when we live in the light with God can we be filled with the Spirit and walk in step with the Spirit. Christians filled with the Spirit are dangerous to hell. If you're not dangerous to hell, then you're dangerous to the church.

> Christians filled with the Spirit are dangerous to hell. If you're not dangerous to hell, then you're dangerous to the church.

There were many things in my life that I was unaware of, and they were hurting me and the people around me. Jen— and others—felt stomped on by my strong opinions and lack of emotional sensitivity to them. But I often was not aware that they were being stomped on, nor was I aware why I was doing it.

Jesus said the most important thing in all the world is to love: love God and love people. But my lack of self-awareness was preventing me from loving the way God wanted me to love. I had soul issues that were interfering with my loving God and loving people, but I didn't know it.

I eventually became aware of the destructive patterns in my life. But I still didn't know what was underneath them. Exploring this is what led me to understand some Soul Care Principles—principles that can deeply affect life change when you earnestly seek to walk through them. I had to learn to connect the dots in my life; how did I become like I was? Why did I do what I did? The more self-awareness I gained, the more freedom I walked in.

SOUL CARE PRINCIPLES

I had to get to the heart of the matter. I could have puttered around tinkering with my behaviors, and it wouldn't have led to deep change. It wouldn't have saved my marriage. The principles that I discovered through the Scriptures and the Spirit got to the heart of the matter and helped change my life and the lives of many others.

These are the key Soul Care Principles we will examine in this book.

1. **Identity** – Your identity in Christ is the foundation of a healthy soul. Who you are determines how you behave. What you believe about yourself influences your level of maturity, peace, and soul health.

2. **Repentance** – You must repent and receive the forgiveness of God in order to be free. Secrets rob you of soul health. When you confess, but still carry around shame in your soul, it is toxic to your well-being. It isn't enough to know you are forgiven; you must experience release.

3. **Breaking Family Sin Patterns** – Family sin patterns have unusual pull on our lives. They are hard to break. You must deal with them severely before they deal severely with you.

4. **Forgiving Others** – You need to forgive those who sin against you. The single greatest mark of maturity is the capacity to love your enemies. Bitter roots create weeds in the garden of your soul. They must be uprooted before you can be healthy.

5. **Healing Hurts** – Unprocessed wounds leave you with festering soul sores. You need the healing presence of Jesus to free you from the ill effects of your soul wounds.

6. **Overcoming Fears** – The people of God make more mistakes in times of fear than any other time. This is why the number one command of Scripture is "fear not." You must overcome your fears to be spiritually healthy.

7. **Breaking Demonic Strongholds** – We have a real spiritual enemy who can get a foothold in our lives. You need the power of God to free you from his grip and deliver you so that you can have a healthy soul.

These seven Soul Care Principles are the seeds that can lead you to transformation if they are cultivated in an atmosphere of anointed truth, true community, and the presence and power of God.

Life change is hard. But it is possible in the right atmosphere. So gather a small group of comrades in arms, read and process together, open your souls to one another, and access the presence and power of God together. Let's journey together into the freedom and fullness of Christ.

SOUL CARE PRINCIPLE #1
IDENTITY

There is a new building going up in the town where I live. I drive past it frequently. When the foundation was being laid, the building progress seemed extremely slow. Each day I would drive past, and there was hardly any noticeable progress; there was a big hole in the ground. Slowly, the foundation was laid, but then after months of laying the foundation, the building started going up. And once it started going up, it went up in a hurry.

If the foundation of a building is improperly laid, the building is doomed. It doesn't matter how slowly you construct it or how carefully you build, or if you use the best material, or if you have the best builder. If the foundation is faulty, the building is in jeopardy.

What you believe about yourself is the foundation of your life; it is your identity, and a faulty foundation will create

What you believe about yourself is the foundation of your life; it is your identity, and a faulty foundation will create cracks in the soul.

cracks in the soul. If you are going to construct a healthy life, it begins with what you believe about yourself.

Ephesians is a captivating book. In the first three chapters, Paul mainly focuses on who we are in Christ. As a matter of fact, the phrase "in Christ" or "in Him" is the key expression used throughout; it is used 11 times in the first chapter and 30 times in the book. That phrase is talking about our relationship with God, our union with Christ, and it is about how we are given this relationship with God through Jesus and who we now are in our Father's eyes.

Paul says that we are chosen "in Him." Read Ephesians 1, and look at who the Father says you are. The Father chose you in Christ before the foundation of the earth. It wasn't dependent upon what you did or who you are or what you have. The Father chose you in Christ to make you holy and blameless in his sight. You are adopted into the family of God. In the Roman Empire, the adopted child had the full privileges of a biological child and also was completely released from control of his biological parents. Adoption implies belonging and freedom. "In Him" you have been redeemed by His blood, and your sins have been forgiven because God lavished His grace upon you. You are forgiven according to the riches of His grace, not according to the poverty of your life. His grace is greater than your sin; His rich grace is infinitely greater than the poverty of your sin-stained soul.

In Him you have been called for a purpose of eternal significance. You have received an inheritance from God, and you are God's inheritance, His lot. You have been included in Christ and marked with a seal as a family member when you received the promised Holy Spirit. This is who you are in Christ, and this is only the beginning of your identity, the foundation of your well-being.

Paul describes who we are in Christ across three entire chapters, emphasizing how much God loves us, and how God's love is not dependent upon our best efforts. God's love for us is rooted in God's grace to us. God doesn't love us because of who we are or what we do. God loves us because of who He is and what He has done, which makes God's love, and our foundation, unshakable.

> God doesn't love us because of who we are or what we do. God loves us because of who He is and what He has done, which makes God's love, and our foundation, unshakable.

After three chapters of solidifying the foundation of God's love for us, Paul makes a shift in Chapter 4. He says, "As a prisoner of the Lord, then, I urge you to live a life worthy of the calling you have received" (Ephesians 4:1). Paul wants you to live a life worthy of an identity rooted in God's radical love. Paul calls you to live an integrated life—a life where your identity shapes your destiny, where who you are permeates how you live. If you only understood who you are in Christ, if you only believed what God believes about you, it would revolutionize the way you live.

To really understand your identity, you have to properly divide soul and spirit. Your spirit has been made new. You are a new creation in Christ. You have received a new spirit and a new heart (Ezekiel 36:26). Your spirit has been perfected in Christ. You have received every spiritual blessing you need in the heavenly realms (Ephesians 1:3). You are adopted into the family of God (Ephesians 1:5; Romans 8; Romans 8:15). You are heirs of God and coheirs with Christ (Romans 8:17).

These are all the claims of Scripture for who you are in Christ. Your spirit has been purified, purged, renewed, born again, and transformed. But your soul . . . well, that can still be a bit of a mess.

Your soul can have hurts and bitterness. Your soul can still have sin and demonic strongholds. Your soul can have fears and faulty beliefs about who you are. Your soul can still feel condemnation and shame.

Sanctification, or the process of becoming like Jesus, is simply becoming who you already are. You have to work out in the realm of the soul what has already taken place in the heavenly realms through the work of Christ in your spirit.

Your soul is where your mind, your will, and your emotions still hold sway over the reality of your daily existence. For example, you may know cognitively that you are loved, but because you grew up in an abusive home, or because of your own sinful behaviors, you don't *feel* loved. You don't act as if you are deeply loved. Your soul still feels shame, you may even feel unlovable, and you feel distant from God. Until you deal with the issues of your soul, you will not experience the fullness of God, nor the intimacy with Him for which your heart longs.

Working out your identity is learning to become who you already are. This battle for your identity is a critical part to your spiritual maturity.

RENEWING YOUR MIND

A key problem with our identity is that we often believe lies about ourselves rather than the truth. These lies are like building a house on a faulty foundation, and they leave us with cracks in our soul.

The power of a lie is in our agreement with it. Whatever we agree with, we give power to. If you agree with the truth, and hold on to the truth, the truth will set you free, but if you agree with a lie, its influence will cast a shadow in your life.

For example, this generation has grown up under a Darwinian worldview in public schools. One of my children had a science teacher in the public high school who greeted the students every day with this warming sentiment: "Welcome, cosmic accidents!" If you really believe that you are a purpose-less cosmic accident, imagine how that would shape your life. Is it any wonder that this generation came up with the phrase "Whatever"? Or even worse: "WTF."

If you truly believe that you weren't carefully crafted, but accidentally thrust into being, then you will struggle with meaning and purpose. But if you believe that you are fearfully and wonderfully made by a loving Creator, in the image of God and redeemed by the Savior who counted you worthy of His very life, then your life will be rich with meaning, purpose, and passion. You will be motivated to love others and treat them with dignity and respect because they have inherent worth. They, together with you, bear the image of God. And as image bearers, you matter to God.

What you believe about yourself and others will shape how you live. But it isn't enough to have knowledge of the truth; your life must be built upon this foundation of truth, and it must be deeply integrated into your daily existence. This never happens accidentally.

You need to build your life on the foundation of who God says you are. This is your identity in Christ, and when this foundation is properly set in your soul, your life can be well constructed.

Two Tools to Renewing the Mind

There are two key tools that you can access to renew your mind. They are both vital—you need to *renew your mind by holding on to the truth*, and you need the presence of God. In God's presence, who you are in Christ is revealed to you.

There is a word translated "transformation" in the New Testament; it is a Greek word from which we derive the word "metamorphosis." This word (*metamorphoo*) only occurs four times in the New Testament. It occurs twice at the transfiguration of Jesus. Jesus is "metamorphosed" right before their eyes as they catch a glimpse of Him in His glory. The other two times it occurs both involve our personal transformation.

In 2 Corinthians 3, the apostle Paul is talking about our access to the presence of God in the person of the Holy Spirit, and there he tells us that in the presence of God we can be transformed. We aren't like Moses, who accessed God's presence on the mountain. When he did, his face shone, but he couldn't remain in God's presence, and the glory faded. Rather, we have full-time access to the presence of God because the Spirit of God lives within us.

The presence of God is transformational. This is why you need to spend time alone with God, developing intimacy with Him as you journey toward wholeness. God is a healer, and His presence is life-changing. I often spend time alone with God in silence. I don't say anything; I don't come for what God can do for me. I don't seek His hands. I just come to be with Him. In his presence, God can do deep things in my soul, things that I am not even aware need to be done. His presence accesses the deep places in the basement of my soul, and He changes me. God whispers about His love for me, and the revelation of His voice in His presence is transformational. These are identity-forming moments that are critically important for setting a firm soul foundation under a well-constructed life.

The last passage where this word "metamorphosis" occurs is in Romans 12. Paul said in Romans 12:2, "Do not conform to the pattern of this world, but be transformed by the renewing of your mind." In this passage, Paul tells us that we are also transformed (metamorphosed) by the truth. We must combat the lies of this world that seek to rob us of our inheritance in Christ with the truth. Only when our mind is renewed with the truth and transformed in His presence can we live the life we were born to live. Only when the truth forms a firm foundation under our feet and His presence bears revelation in our soul will we walk out our faith.

Renewing your mind with the truth is not a passive activity. For years I have heard people misquote, or only partially quote, Jesus: "You will know the truth, and the truth will set you free." The assumption is that if we only know the truth, we will experience freedom. But knowledge does not produce freedom—and that isn't what Jesus said.

Look closer at what Jesus actually said in John 8:31, 32: "If you hold to my teaching, you are really my disciples. Then you will know the truth, and the truth will set you free."

It is an if/then promise. If we hold to the teaching, *then* we will know the truth, and the truth will set us free. It isn't in knowing the truth that freedom comes; it is in *holding on to* the truth that we are set free.

This is the way you renew your mind so that it transforms your life: you must hold on to the truth, precisely at the moment that the lie is vying for position in your heart and in your soul and in your behaviors. The truth of who you are in Christ,

> The truth alone will not set you free, but holding on to the truth in the face of the lie, over and over again, will set you free.

in your spirit, must be tightly grasped precisely when the lies of your soul are threatening to prevent you from becoming who you already are.

For example, if you grew up in a home where you were abused, you will most likely struggle with the lie that something is wrong with you, that you aren't lovable. You may have acted out sexually when you were in your teen years and early twenties in an effort to secure love. But sadly, your promiscuity only left you feeling more used and more unlovable. It left you with guilt and shame.

But this isn't actually who you are in Christ. In Christ you are forgiven. You are adopted. The Father chose you out of a heart full of love to be holy and blameless in His sight. He accomplished this through Christ; your spirit is, in fact, holy and blameless. Your blamelessness is not dependent on your getting your act together; it was graced to you before the foundation of the earth. It is a fact in your spirit. You must hold on to this truth when you are most tempted to feel unworthy, unlovable, sin-stained, and irreparable. The truth alone will not set you free, but holding on to the truth in the face of the lie, over and over again, will set you free.

All of us are affected by lies. They form in us as a result of things we were told, things that happened to us, pains we have suffered, the culture we live in, our own sin, and Satan's dirty work. These lies prevent us from experiencing the health, freedom, and maturity that is our inheritance in Christ, and they can't be ignored any more than a crumbling foundation can be ignored. They must be identified, and then we must reconstruct the foundation of our lives upon the truth by the renewing of the mind.

IDENTIFYING THE LIES

As always, the process of building a healthy foundation of identity begins with self-awareness. You have to know the lies that plague you. You can never rise above your self-awareness. That's why the first step needs to be identifying the lies that shape you.

To identify these lies, you have to pay attention to the symptoms in order to diagnose the disease. David Benner, in his book *The Gift of Being Yourself*, describes the self that is constructed on a foundation of lies as "the false self." It is a common term used by other authors as well. Benner says that our false self always tries to cover up our vulnerability, shame, and inadequacy by reaching for some attachment. It is like Adam and Eve reaching for fig leaves to cover the shame they felt in the garden. We have our own modern-day fig leaves that we grab for, and underneath these outward attachments lies our inward lies that we believe.

The problem is that we are often not aware that we are even grabbing for these things as a means of covering up the lies we believe. Benner writes, "While other people's excessive attachments and personal falsity often seem glaringly apparent, it is never easy to know the lies of our own life." As I give some examples, ask yourself, "What are some of the fig leaves I grab for?"[3]

Symptoms of Lies: Defensiveness

One symptom that reveals the lies you believe is your defensiveness. When you are standing on the faulty foundation of a lie, you become more defensive. Benner said, "Because of its fundamental unreality, the false self needs constant bolster-

---

3. David G. Benner, *The Gift of Being Yourself* (Downers Grove: InterVarsity Press, 2015), p.76.

ing. Touchiness dependably points us to false ways of being."

In my relationship with Jen, she often said she felt like I never listened to her. I immediately felt defensive. I said, "That's not true. I listen to you." And I began to give specific examples of recent times when I had listened to and valued her opinion. It would have been easy for me to dismiss the light God was offering me in this moment, because I could think of real examples where I did listen. But this defensiveness was a like a "tell" in a poker game. It was a giveaway that kept hidden something buried that I was covering up, and I sensed the Spirit probing me to go deeper.

As Jen and I continued to talk after the Lord told me to stop being defensive, I began to hear what she was really saying. She felt like every time she shared an opinion that differed from mine, I stomped on her opinions with the forcefulness of my own viewpoint. I didn't belittle her, demean her, or yell at her, but I powerfully expressed my opinion in such a way that she felt crushed under the weight of my passion.

As I wrestled with God, I asked Him what was underneath that action. Why did I have to win? Why did I crank up the power gauge when she disagreed with me? Why was I more interested in being right than I was in being in a right relationship?

> We cannot overcome that which we will not admit: light is a gift, it is not an intrusion.

The answer came over time as I waited on the Lord and continued to dialogue with Jen. The lie I believed was that if someone didn't agree with me, they didn't love me, or at least I felt threatened that they wouldn't love me. Somehow or other I felt invalidated by my wife's disagreement. When I said it out loud, it seemed ridiculous, but I was living my life off that faulty foundation in such a way that it was creating all kinds of cracks in my soul and my marriage, and until I repaired the foundation, I couldn't fix the building. We cannot overcome that which we will not admit: light is a gift, it is not an intrusion.

Symptoms of Lies: Pettiness

Pettiness is another symptom that reveals the lies you believe. The things that annoy you point to your own false ways of being. For example, if the laziness of others bothers you, perhaps it is because performance is a false way of establishing your value. Rather than receiving your sense of identity and worth from the love of God, you seek to achieve it through your doing—and thus lazy people annoy you.

If you are standing on the faulty foundation of performance, you may also be highly irritated and annoyed with people who are critical of you. This is because their criticism is chipping away at the foundation of your worth—of course, this isn't actually true, but if you believe it is true, then you will be shaken by their critical comments.

Symptoms of Lies: Compulsive Behavior

Another symptom that points to your faulty foundation is your compulsive behavior. We are compulsive about the things that we believe we need most; we grab and clutch to the things we feel are lacking in our souls, things that we believe will help us overcome feeling "less than" or inadequate. We fill our deprivations with our compulsive activity.

I have ministered to people who grew up in extreme poverty. There were times in their formative years that they didn't have enough—not enough food, money, or heat—and out of this deprivation grew a false attachment to stuff. They collected stuff, gathered stuff, held on to stuff; sometimes it was money, and at other times certain possessions. They grew up lacking, and it formed a lie that still shaped them: "There will never be enough." So they tried to fortify their sense of security by what they possessed and accumulated. They became attached to image and appearance because it made them feel secure, "covering" the shame they felt from not having enough in their early years.

The truth was that they were living in plenty, but they still felt like there wasn't enough; they had a poverty mind-set. They were still living off the false foundation long after their reality had changed, and it shaped their decision-making.

An external change cannot alleviate an internal torment. A change of circumstances will not overcome the power of a lie. You must renew your mind and reconstruct the foundation of your soul upon the truth of who you are in Christ, or you will not experience deep change. If you grew up feeling insecure, only the security of Christ's eternal love revealed by the Spirit can set you free.

> An external change cannot alleviate an internal torment. A change of circumstances will not overcome the power of a lie.

Other people are compulsive about a sin pattern, like pornography or an addictive behavior. Underneath this compulsion is a lie. We often try to get people, even ourselves, to change by saying, "Just stop that. Just don't do it anymore." We add a little accountability and hope for life change. But a behavioral change and some accountability won't repair what is broken on the inside. If the foundation is in disrepair, the only way to construct a healthy life is to repair the foundation. Ask yourself: What is the lie that is underneath this compulsive behavior?

At the root of all addictive behavior is shame. You feel unworthy, unlovable, vulnerable, or inadequate, and you grab for the object of your addictive affections as a self-medicating means to numb your internal pain. If you can get to the heart and bring freedom and healing there, then the behaviors will follow.

Reflection Exercise

In order to discover the lies that are impacting your life, you will have to engage in some Spirit-led reflection. I recommend journaling.

Take some time to reflect with the Spirit's insight about the following questions.

- **What were the things that your parents said to you regularly?**

    You may have been told that you will never amount to anything. Or you may have been told that you were a child of destiny. Either statement can form lies in you that shape your life.

    For example, if you believe you are a child of destiny, you may internalize that in a way that makes you proud. You could begin to view others through the lens of your "destiny" and see them as objects to help you advance your cause. If you were told you would never amount to anything, it could affect you in a variety of ways. It could become a self-fulfilling prophecy. You live out what you were told you were. Or you could live in defiance of the lie, and seek to prove everyone wrong. You become an overachiever. The reality is, both the person who surrenders to the lie and the person who defies the lie are *bound* by the lie. Only when you hold on to the truth can the truth set you free.

- **What family slogans do you remember, either spoken or unspoken?**

    I talked to one young woman who told me that the lie she was wrestling with was that she was a disappointment. I asked her if that was something that her parents told her. She said, "No, but often at the dinner table my father would just shake his head and make a *tsk* sound when he was disappointed with something I had done." That simple shake of the head, repeated often enough, had formed the lie in her that she was a disappointment. He didn't need to say it; he demonstrated it. For many people it wasn't merely demonstrated; there were actual phrases that were said, and they stuck. They became like labels on the heart that became limitations to their life.

- **What are the shaping experiences of your life? Pay special attention to repeated experiences, because lies often get reinforced here.**

  If your father abandoned the home when you were a toddler, and then you were rejected by your friends when you were in grade school, and your first boyfriend or girlfriend cheated on you, and your spouse left you, that is going to leave a significant hole in your foundation. You may end up feeling unlovable, inadequate, or unsafe and believing that no one can be trusted. There will be lies there that must be addressed or the house will be in disrepair.

- **What are the things you catch yourself saying to yourself?**

  Start to track the unfiltered train of thinking in your mind. What are you saying in the imaginary conversations you hold in your mind? These things are like the background noise to your soul, and they are highly revealing.

When Jen and I were in our season of marriage conflict, I had a lot of imaginary conversations with her in my head. I would often prepare for a real conversation with her by having an imaginary conversation with her. I would think about what I would say, and what she would say, and I would have my comeback. Don't lie; you've done this, too! We're all a little sick—that's why we need a healer! In my mind, I was undefeated! No matter what she said, I had a good answer. I was prepared. But when we came to the actual conversation, she said stuff that I wasn't actually prepared for, and I was getting creamed!

These imaginary conversations were incredibly revealing to me about the lies that I believed. They showed me the things I obsessed over, the areas where I felt insecure, the places where I felt the need to prop myself up, and the things I was hurt over and defensive about. I started paying attention to these, and journaling about some of the things going on in my mind so that I could understand the beliefs that undergirded these behaviors.

What are the lies that you believe? What faulty foundation are you standing on? Take time to pray about this and reflect on these questions before you move on.

LIES ALWAYS MANIFEST

Lies are like a disease. Eventually the symptoms of a disease show up, and it is the same with our lies. They manifest themselves in our lives.

Have you ever stood on a shaky platform? We rented a facility one day at church, and they had a makeshift stage for this event. Every step I took, the platform shook under me; it did not feel safe and secure. This is what happens when our souls are standing on the faulty platform of a lie—there are tremors.

The results of standing on a lie will show up in your life. If you see these symptoms, you will be able to identify when you are standing on the faulty platform. The quicker you realize you are on the wrong platform, the sooner you will be able to hold on to the truth, and the truth will begin to set you free.

The most common indicator to me that I was standing on the wrong foundation was anxiety. I began to realize that when I was standing on a lie, I felt low levels of anxiety in my soul. I emphasize that it was low levels of anxiety, because if we catch the subtle symptoms of the soul in the early stages, we can keep ourselves from far more serious soul maladies.

Early on in ministry, someone would come to me on a Sunday and say to me, "I need to speak to you. Can we get together this week?" And I would respond, calm and cool on the outside; I set a date to meet with them. But after this brief interaction, the wheels of my mind started churning, and the imaginary conversations surged in my head. *What did I do to Joe? I wonder what he is upset about. I don't remember saying anything to him. Well, there was that one thing, but he shouldn't have taken offense at that. I didn't mean anything by it. He is just thin-skinned if that bothered him.* Then I would think about what I was going to say to Joe, how he would respond, what I would say next, and so on. And all the while, I would feel this low level of anxiety as I ran through this self-talk. My mind was racing, and I kept coming back to it all week long.

While I was still functioning fine in my job and accomplishing all the things that I needed, I was wasting a lot of internal emotional energy around this self-talk and on these imaginary conversations. The anxiety wasn't crippling, but it was surely revealing a deeper issue that I needed to address.

Then on the morning I got together with Joe, quite often such a meeting would go like this: "Rob, I'm having this problem in my marriage. I'm so glad you took the time to meet with me. I need your help." I felt two things: First, relief. I wasn't "in trouble." Second, annoyance—I had spent four days of my life wasting a ridiculous amount of time obsessing about nothing. Sadly, this was a pretty common experience for me around conflict—or even potential conflict—early on in ministry.

When people had conflict with me, I would feel like a little kid in the principal's office about to get yelled at.

My anxious reaction to the mere threat of conflict revealed to me that I was standing on a lie. When you are on a faulty foundation, you will experience tremors. I had to keep peace with everyone. If someone was upset with me, it must mean they didn't love me, and somehow that threatened my security. The lie was exposed by the anxiety I felt.

Thomas Merton, a 20th century monk and author, said, "A current of useless interior activity constantly surrounds and defends an illusion. . . . Man's intelligence, however we may misuse it, is far too keen and too sure to rest for long in error. It may embrace a lie and cling to it stubbornly, believing it to be true: but it cannot find rest in falsehood. The mind that is in love with error wears itself out with anxiety, lest it be discovered for what it is. . . . The first step toward finding God, Who is Truth, is to discover the truth about myself: and if I have been in error, this first step is the discovery of my error."[4] My mind cannot find peace when I am standing on a faulty foundation.

When your foundation is threatened, your mind will start racing; your soul will feel the internal quaking that results from a life constructed on a lie. Only when you stand on the true foundation of God's love can you feel peace, no matter what circumstances surround you. This is your true identity.

THREE CORE LIES

The lies that you believe are faulty foundations under your feet, and they often affect the issue of your value. You may feel

---

4. Thomas Merton, *No Man is an Island* (New York: Harcourt Trade Publishers, 1955), p. 245.

like your value is dependent on something other than God's love. You likely *know* this is not true, but the lie is so deep in you that you *feel* and *act* as if it were true. And whatever you act on, you reinforce in your soul. Every time you act on a lie, the lie gains power in your life. When you act on a lie, you fail to integrate faith. So you must identify these lies that are often at the core of your foundation.

There are three main lies that people believe. Stop, reflect, and ask yourself if any of these lies are affecting your foundation.

The Performance Lie

The first core lie is that the issue of your value is dependent on your performance. A lot of us gain our value by our performance. This is an American way of life. Think about how many times we have a conversation with someone we just met and this question is asked: "What do you do for a living?" Your life is associated with your doing.

It is often complicated by religious performance. You are valued, you are loved, and you are acceptable if you do certain things, but if you don't perform well, then you are judged, condemned, and shamed. You are applauded in church if you behave well, serve well, give well, and live well. So you serve more, give more, and try to behave better. When you can't behave well, you may even be tempted to hide it, to pretend to be good so that you can try to maintain your image and hold on to the lie.

One day, in the midst of this reparative season of my life, I came home from church and just laid on the couch because I was feeling a bit depressed. I had a coffee and the TV remote and I was watching a football game. The sermon didn't go as well as I had hoped that Sunday morning. I would have given myself a C on it, to be truthful, and I was emotionally exhausted.

As I lay there on the couch, I heard the still, small voice of the Spirit whisper to me, "What are you doing there on the couch?" I said, "Lord, I'm having a hard time. My wife doesn't like me. The talk didn't go well this morning; it was a 'C' talk. I just want to lie here and watch some football and drink my coffee. Please. Can you give me some space?"

He said, "The issue of your value isn't dependent upon whether you give an 'A' talk or a 'C' talk. Now get up off the couch, and don't lie there again."

That was literally the last time I ever laid on the couch after a subpar sermon, because the revelation of God came and I realized in a deep place that my value is not dependent on the quality of my talks or the adequacy of my performance. Now when I give a 'C' talk, I say to Jen on the way home, "What did you think?" She grimaces and says, "It wasn't one of your top ten." And I laugh and say, "Let's go get a cup of Dunkin' Donuts." A good cup of Dunks and the love of God go a long way in healing the soul!

Often when you reflect on your past, you begin to see how these lies were formed in your soul. For example, I remember being in seventh grade when my school switched from letter grades to number grades. I got a 98 in one of my classes on my first seventh-grade report card, and I was hooked on the importance of performance. An A on a report card didn't hook me nearly as much as that high-90s scorecard. Not only did the grade make me feel good, but other people were impressed by it. I got a lot of positive attention and affirmation. Double hooked. These kinds of events solidify the faulty foundations in our lives.

Take a moment to reflect with the help of the Spirit. How does the performance lie affect your life? If you are a public speaker and you get ten comments after a talk, nine positive and one negative, do you fixate on the one negative comment? If you receive a performance review at work, do you fixate on the growth areas that are pointed out? Do you feel discouraged, even a little depressed, after a bad performance or some criticism? Have you ever fallen into sin and felt like you needed to crawl back to God? These are just symptoms of the performance lie. What does it look like in your life? What are some of the symptomatic expressions? Where did it get formed in you?

The good news is the issue of your value is not determined by your performance. God doesn't love you any more when you get it perfectly right, and He doesn't love you any less when you get it all wrong.

The People-Pleasing Lie

The second core lie that people believe is that the issue of their value is dependent on whether certain people love or like them. Some people need everyone to like them. They feel pressure to please everyone, and they run around and try to make everyone happy. They feel the need to serve everyone, care for everyone, solve everyone's problems, and make everyone get along and live in harmony. For others, it isn't everyone; it's just important that a handful of the right people love them.

My problem was that I didn't realize how this lie had woven its way into the foundation of my soul. As a matter of fact, when people disagreed with me, I would even think to myself, *I don't care what people think.* Of course, that was just a way of propping up my false foundation when it felt threatened. I was feeling the tremors in my soul, and I used a lie to reinforce the lie under my feet. Again, pay careful attention to the thoughts that run unguarded through your mind.

I did care what people thought. Deep down, I wanted people to love me, and if they didn't love me, it felt like something was wrong with me—like I wasn't lovable. When people didn't love me, or when they criticized me, I felt like it chipped away at the foundation of my worth. I couldn't have articulated that, but it showed up in my actions, reactions, self-talk, imaginary conversations, and low-level anxiety.

The problem with the soul is that it can't be ignored, and it can't be deceived. If you try to bluff it, and build your life on a faulty foundation, that foundation will manifest itself in some way. The symptoms you are trying to fix in your life right now are likely connected to the lies you believe. Trace the symptoms back to the disease and deal with the real issues. This is the only path to freedom.

> The problem with the soul is that it can't be ignored, and it can't be deceived.

If you believe the lie that you need people's approval to feel good about yourself, then you will feel anxiety when people are upset with you. You will get defensive and hurt by criticism. You will fall into the trap of people pleasing, and you will likely take on too much and say yes too often. The answer isn't to try to overcome people pleasing and "just say no." The answer is to go after the root lie. If you change the foundation, you'll change your life. If you deal with the disease, you will cure the symptoms.

If you build your life on the foundation of other people's approval, you will likely end up resentful. When they withhold approval, you will resent them. When they continually demand more from you, you will resent them. The reality is that they aren't really demanding more; you feel this internal pressure to give more and do more because of the lie that you have to keep them happy and have them like you to feel good about yourself. As you rebuild the foundation of God's love under your feet, you will find freedom from people pleasing and resentment. And you will discover the freedom to say no without feeling guilty.

Take a moment to reflect with God again. How does the lie

of people pleasing affect your life? Think about times when you are defensive. What makes you defensive? Are there times in your life where you feel like people are taking advantage of you, and this makes you resentful? When people disagree with you, do you "power up," voice your opinions more passionately, or tell yourself, *I don't care what people think!* These are just some of the signs that this faulty foundation is under your feet.

Good news: The issue of your value is not dependent on whether people love you. God doesn't love you any more when everyone is on your side and pleased with you, and He doesn't love you any less when you are scorned, ridiculed, maligned, and mistreated.

The Lie of Control

The third core lie is that the issue of your value is dependent on whether you are in control. Some people afflicted with this lie try to control others. The people around them feel manipulated, shamed, judged, condemned, and sometimes bullied. Other people want to control outcomes.

I am a classic type-A personality. An overachiever, driven, in-charge type of person. I want to control the outcome of the things I care about. If I work hard and produce good results, I feel good. But if I work hard and things don't come around, I can feel irritable and angry. What's underneath that?

The issue of my value is somehow connected to my capacity to produce results and control the outcomes that I desire. And if I can't produce results, it feels like it diminishes my worth. That's not true, but there are times in my life I have acted on that lie—more times than I wish to recall. It leaves me feeling an internal pressure to produce results; it is a self-inflicted pressure that comes from standing on the faulty foundation. I have to get off that poor foundation to release that internal pressure in my soul. The stress and pressure I feel isn't the problem; it is simply a symptom that points me to the real problem—I am trying, in this moment, to build my life on a lie, and my soul knows it.

People who have been abused often struggle with control issues. Fear is always lurking underneath the desire to be in control. These Soul Care Principles are connected to each other. We often have root fears that affect our root lies, and wounds that tie into those fears and lies. We have to learn how to connect the dots. People who are abused often give up on the hope of receiving love, but they opt for control so that at least they will not suffer more abuse. It is as if they tell themselves, "You may not love me, but you will not hurt me anymore." So they choose control as a way of creating security and overcoming the fears deep inside. But this is just another false foundation, and it leads to a life full of soul cracks. Unless we stand on the true foundation, we cannot have a healthy soul.

I had a friend who grew up in a home of an alcoholic. Children who grow up in such homes often feel shame. The core of shame that they feel can drive them to do all kinds of things. Many of them repeat the cycle of addiction and abuse. But my friend became an achiever. He was out to prove his worth by his performance; he was building a life on this faulty platform. Whatever he did, he set out to win, whether it was an academic achievement or sports.

There was one event that shaped him and reinforced this need to perform in order to prove his worth. When he was a preteen, his father was in a drunken rage and started yelling at my friend's mother: "I'm going to tell him!" She pleaded with the drunken man not to tell the boy, but this man pointed a finger at my friend and yelled, "You are a f---ing bastard!" That's how my friend found out that this drunken man was not his biological father.

His family disintegrated shortly after that incident. He was left with a void, a father wound. One day when he was a young man, he was competing in a sports competition. He couldn't do what he wanted to do, and he yelled at himself, using the same words his stepfather had used. Shame was his motivator for achievement. He was out to make something of himself, to perform, to control outcomes, to win, to prove his worth. But none of these things can bring us freedom. Even when we win, and achieve, we still worry that someone else will come along and defeat us.

Reflect with the Holy Spirit. Is control an issue in your life? Have people ever said that you were controlling? How does the lie of control show up in your life? Do you seek to control people? Do you seek to control outcomes? When you are not in control, does it make you fearful, angry, or anxious? These are just symptoms telling you that you may be standing on this faulty platform. The good news is that your value is not determined by whether or not you are in control.

Strengthening a faulty foundation only reinforces a doomed building. Your value is not determined by your performance or whether people love you or whether you are in control. These are all core lies that can create cracks in the foundation and damage your soul. You need to replace them with the truth.

THE TRUE FOUNDATION

Here is the truth that can set you free: The issue of your value is settled at the cross. On the cross, the Father said to you and me, "You are of infinite worth to me. I declare you to be worthy of my Son's blood."

Paul said, "If God is for us, who can be against us?" If Jesus died for us, then what can diminish our worth? Not rejection, not enemies, not hatred, not criticism, not abandonment, not abuse, not a spouse who leaves you or no longer loves you, not bad performances, not failures, not 'C' talks, not circumstances out of your control, or people beyond your reach. Nothing can separate you from the love of God in Christ.

The issue of your value is settled at the cross. This is the truth that you must hold on to. This is the truth that you must appropriate every time the lies threaten your security, value, and identity. This is what God has accomplished in your spirit, and what you must hold on to and work out in your soul. This is the foundation that you must build your life on. Upon this foundation you can find peace, love, acceptance, security, significance, and all you need in life.

> The issue of your value is settled at the cross. This is the truth that you must hold on to.

One day as I was wrestling through the lies that I believed, I sensed the Lord say to me, "Even if Jen left you, I would be enough for you. Even if the church failed, my love will not fail. Even if you lost all you have, I would still be with you. The issue of your value is not dependent on whether or not Jen loves you. The issue of your value is not dependent upon your performance or whether you can control the outcomes of your life. The issue of your value was settled at the cross. This is what you must build your life on. Only when you stand on this foundation can your soul be healthy."

I realized that I couldn't love Jen freely until I didn't need Jen's love to make me feel secure or valuable. If I needed Jen to love me, I always came to the relationship seeking to take something from her to make up for something missing in me, otherwise her lack of love for me made a value statement about me. Only when I received my love from God could I freely give love to Jen. We can't give what we don't have. Only on the foundation of God's love could I act in secure and mature ways with her no matter how she felt, no matter what circumstances confronted us.

This realization didn't fix everything in my soul and in our relationship. It has been a lifelong journey to continually shift to this true foundation. But I began to change the way my self-talk ran in my head. When people disagreed with me, I began to say to myself, *I want people to love me. I hope they will love me, but even if they don't love me, I'll be fine because Jesus loves me, and that's enough for me. The issue of my value was settled at the cross.* The security of that phrase enabled me to listen more and defend less, and yet still be lovingly courageous.

That phrase became a slogan that I held on to. Over the next few years, I reminded myself of this truth thousands of times. That is not an exaggeration. Every time Jen was angry with me, I returned to this slogan. Every time someone criticized me, I came back to the true foundation. Every time I felt like a little kid in the principal's office about to get yelled at, I reminded myself of the unshakable truth that the issue of my value was settled on the cross. I paused in God's presence to renew my mind. I allowed the Holy Spirit to minister the truth of the Father's love into the depths of my soul. I would take a moment, wherever I was, to pause, to listen, to access God's loving presence, to hold on to the truth. This precious pause, and intentional shifting of the foundation, became the key to transformation.

PRACTICAL STEPS TO REBUILD THE FOUNDATION

Let's end this first Soul Care Principle with some practical steps to rebuild the foundation of your life. As you go through this section, I encourage you to pray and ask the Spirit for insight, and then journal the insights that you receive.

Identify the Lies

First, identify the lies that you believe and the manifestations of those lies in your life. I can see how all three lies have affected my life, but one lie had more pull than all the others—it was the root lie. My dominant lie was the issue of my value being dependent on whether I could get certain people to love me. The manifestations of the lie included self-talk like, "I don't care what people think," imaginary conversations with people who were upset with me, a mind that was racing and hard to quiet down, and low levels of anxiety. Whenever I felt these symptoms appear, I knew I was standing on the wrong foundation, and I could not live a healthy life from there. These symptoms became like blinking lights in my soul that alerted me to the faulty foundation under my feet; they became my triggers to go to God and repair the foundation.

Take time to define the lies you believe and the manifestations of those lies. These symptoms become important clues when you are standing on the wrong foundation, and you need to shift to the true foundation.

Reposition the Issue of Your Value

Second, recognize when you are standing on the wrong foundation, and immediately reposition the issue of your value. You have to know what it feels like when you stand on the wrong foundation, and you have to intentionally choose to shift foundations. You have to hold on to the truth at the exact moment when you are being assaulted with the lie.

For example, another of the symptoms I struggled with was defensiveness and an inappropriate use of my passion in a conversation—I would power up. When someone disagreed with me, I would ramp up the passion level as I felt defensiveness rise within me. I began to recognize these feelings and behaviors as a symptom of standing on the faulty foundation, and I would take a precious time-out to reposition the true

> The more consistently you catch yourself standing on a faulty foundation and use that as an opportunity to renew your mind, the more secure the true foundation will become under your feet and the healthier your soul will be.

foundation underneath me. Sometimes I would literally take a break in the middle of a staff meeting. I'd go to the restroom and take a deep breath and remind myself once again: *I want these people to love me. They are important to me. But just because they disagree with me doesn't mean they don't love me. And even if they don't, the issue of my value is settled at the cross.*

I could feel the RPMs slowing down in my heart and peace being restored as I reminded myself of God's love. The more consistently you catch yourself standing on a faulty foundation and use that as an opportunity to renew your mind, the more secure the true foundation will become under your feet and the healthier your soul will be.

This is what it looks like to hold on to the truth so the truth can set you free.

Access the Presence of the Spirit

Third, allow the Holy Spirit to minister love to your heart. Create some space for God to reveal Himself and his love to you. This, again, is why time alone with God is so crucial to your spiritual development. Only God can change a heart; you need revelation to experience transformation. Give the Holy Spirit space to speak and reveal His love to you. Often, in the middle of conflict, I would give the Holy Spirit a moment of quiet to reassert His love for me; He would whisper the truth of His affections to my soul again, and my internal tremors would quiet down.

Romans 5:5 says, "God's love has been poured out into our hearts through the Holy Spirit, who has been given to us." Some days I need a fresh dip in the outpouring of His love in order to secure the foundation under my feet.

This was particularly true for me during those early days of our marriage crisis. After Jen and I had these conversations in which she would talk to me about the things she was upset about, I would go to my study and get alone with God. I worshiped. I could feel anxiety, the urge to defend myself, and the pull toward imaginary conversations (all of which were sure signs of the faulty foundation under my feet). But rather than acting on these things, I would remind myself that the issue of my value was settled at the cross. Then I would ask the Holy Spirit to once again reveal and pour out the love of God in my heart as Romans 5 promises.

Often I would sit before the Lord, after I quieted my soul, and listen to the still, small voice of the Holy Spirit reminding me of His love for me. This would restore my peace, subside my fears, and reposition the true foundation under my feet. Sometimes it would take me two hours to get to that place of stillness, but I could get back to the true foundation of my soul.

Often in the beginning I felt such intense anxiety that I had to worship for an hour or more before I could calm down. My mind was racing. I felt extremely anxious because in my soul I was still wrestling with the lie that my value was dependent on Jen's love. Every night I would worship until my soul calmed down, and then I would hold on to the truth that my value was settled at the cross. I would listen to the Spirit reveal His love for me.

Once I was there, I would ask, "Now, Lord, what is true from what Jen told me? What do I need to hear?" On the foundation of God's love, I could hear the truth. And secure in the love of God, I could own my part and take responsibility for my life. Painfully, and slowly, I was getting healthier because I was fighting for the right foundation by renewing my mind. I was holding on to the truth, and the truth was setting me free.

Act in Courage

To do the hard work of repairing your foundation, you must act in courage from the true foundation. Whatever you act on, you reinforce in your life. James said, "Faith by itself, if it is not accompanied by action, is dead. . . . Show me your faith without deeds, and I will show you my faith by what I do" (James 2:17, 18). You have to act on the truth in order for the truth to become a firm foundation under your feet. Just believing will not set you free, but holding on to the truth and acting on it in courage is a certain path to ultimate freedom.

> Don't wait for God to make you feel better before you act. Act on what you believe by trust and dependence on God.

Don't wait for God to make you feel better before you act. Act on what you believe by trust and dependence on God. Renew your mind and act while you are still wobbly in your faith! This is why, I suspect, Paul says we need to work out our salvation with fear and trembling (Philippians 2:12). It isn't always easy to act appropriately while we are still repairing the foundation. It takes courage.

For example, you may be a person who has the lie of performance and the lie of love at play in your soul. These two lies form in such a way that you tend to be a people pleaser. It is hard for you to have a difficult conversation with people. You avoid conflict. You run around and try to make people happy; you try to serve everyone and sometimes even enable people, hoping things will change, but they don't.

Difficult conversations are a necessary part of mature relationships. You are doing the work of repairing the foundation. You are reminding yourself that your value is settled at the cross. But in the midst of this, you will also need to act in courage for the foundation stones to set well under your feet. You will have to soak in God's love, and then go in courage to have a difficult conversation even though you still feel anxious and fearful. The more you act on the truth, the more the truth will be strengthened in your life.

This is a daily process. It is not an event. Shifting your life onto the sure foundation of God's love is going to take time, and there aren't any shortcuts.

You need to renew your mind with the truth. You have to combat the lies of your soul with the truth of God at the precise moments when the lies come knocking on your door. You have to hold on to the truth with a relentless, steely resolve that will permanently shift the foundation under your feet from a lie to the truth that your value is settled at the cross.

TWO SPECIAL CASES

Let me end this chapter and first Soul Care Principle with two special cases of an identity in need of repair. First, sometimes we have an *identity wound.* Think of your soul as a bucket. When you have an identity wound, it is like having a hole in the bottom of your bucket. No matter what gets poured into the bucket, it doesn't stick—it just leaks out the bottom.

People with an identity wound can have an encounter with God's love, but the love leaks out. People say loving and kind things to them, but nothing sticks. They have to repair the hole in the bottom of the bucket.

For example, growing up in a home in which parents are highly critical leaves a hole in a person's bucket. No matter what you did, it wasn't enough. You brought home four A's and one B on the report card, and you were criticized for the B—even if it was somewhat in jest. There was just no affirmation for the A's.

Or, you cleaned out the garage and spent hours trying to do it just right, and you were critiqued for the things that you missed, not affirmed for the hours of hard work and positive change that had been made.

> Toxic shame is a sense that you are not lovable. That something is wrong with you. To break toxic shame, you must get your eyes off yourself and onto Jesus.

Sometimes the hole is formed because you grew up in a home where you were never told that you were loved; you were never affirmed and appropriately hugged and touched. These kinds of identity wounds leave you with a feeling of toxic shame.

Toxic shame is a sense that you are not lovable. That something is wrong with you. To break toxic shame, you must get your eyes off yourself and onto Jesus.

Toxic shame, ironically, is the flip side of the coin of pride. With toxic shame, you are looking to make something of yourself, to prove your worth by what you do and what you have.

To break free from this shame, you have to repent of pride. You have to confess that you have not believed what God has told you about yourself, that you are deeply loved. It is pride to reject God's love because you feel unworthy.

When you are stuck in toxic shame, you often tell yourself, *God loves other people, just not me.* That is a proud, eyes-on-me statement. You think you know more than God. Essentially, you are calling God a liar. You must repent of your pride, take your eyes off yourself, and put your eyes on Jesus. You must catch these toxic statements you are making to yourself and break the cycle.

The second special case of identity repair is the bent will. If you grew up in a home where you were abused—physically, spiritually, emotionally, or sexually—your will gets bent. When someone has been bullied, his or her will gets bent toward the bully. They are often overpowered, so they have no choice but to yield to the stronger abuser. But after living this way for some time, the will gets badly bent, and the person feels like a victim. Your soul has to catch up to the reality of what has transpired in your spirit in Christ.

The reality is that you may have been victimized, but you are not a victim. In Christ, you are more than a conqueror. In Christ, you have what it takes to overcome. This is true in your spirit, but it surely doesn't feel that way in your soul. Your soul has to catch up to the reality of what has transpired in your spirit in Christ.

The problem is that the person with the bent will once again has their eyes focused on themselves. Try this: bend your head straight down and see how it impairs your viewpoint. With your head in this bent position, you can only see yourself. Your eyes get focused on you, your limitations, your circumstances, and your lack of resources, and you feel like a victim, defeated and overwhelmed.

> You must remind yourself that you may have been victimized, but you are not a victim—that is not your identity. That is a lie.

The key to breaking toxic shame and the bent will is to get your eyes off yourself and onto God. You must lift up your head, and you must break the victim mentality. You must remind yourself that you may have been victimized, but you are not a victim—that is not your identity. That is a lie.

At times I have had to deliver someone from demonic spirits, a person who was severely abused. Often the person will end up on the floor in a full-fledged demonic manifestation. The demon bullies them as they refuse to engage their will in the battle, and they bow to the bully. They crawl up in a fetal position on the floor and cry uncontrollably. I command the spirit to stop, and then I look at the person and say sternly but compassionately, "Look at me. You were victimized. But you are not a victim. I need you to fight with me. I need you to lift your eyes off yourself, off the demons, and onto Jesus. Look to Jesus. He isn't nervous. He has you, and He has this battle. Look to Jesus."

The person will take a deep breath, and their body will shudder as the tears stop. They will look to Jesus, and I can see their will being strengthened for the fight. I am speaking strength into their will. Many times they will literally straighten their posture as their will is strengthened, and this is what a person who has a bent will must learn to do. As long as they keep their eyes on Jesus, they will fight through to victory.

The bent will is increasingly becoming a problem for people in our day and age. People often have a weakened will, many times because of abuse, but sometimes because they have grown up in a smothering, controlling environment. They feel and act like victims; they feel like they can't do anything about their current problematic situation.

More frequently than ever before, I find myself saying to people, "You have been victimized, but you are not a victim." The problem is the feeling of victimization breeds passivity and a lack of personal responsibility. This is dramatically increasing in our society. I have to address this far more now than I did even ten years ago.

I suspect it is a cultural phenomenon resulting from at

least these three factors. First, a Darwinian world view has permeated people's belief systems. It is a deterministic, fatalistic world view. A fatalistic attitude makes people feel hopeless and helpless and leaves us with a "whatever" or "WTF" attitude; we feel that we have no control over our destiny. Many have no sense that they are empowered image bearers who were created and redeemed for Kingdom rulership and authority. Rather, they view themselves as cosmic accidents, a product of fate, and subjected to its whims.

Another factor is that we live in a culture of entitlement, which leaves us sitting by waiting for someone to hand something to us, to solve problems for us, to give us answers. Again, this weakens our steely resolve to address issues and get through them. We are left feeling like someone else is responsible to fix our problems, so we easily become too passive. This often transfers into our relationship with God, and we wait for God to sovereignly deliver us from our frailties. Rather than taking responsibility for our part of the equation of life change, we put all of it on God.

Finally, there is an increase in victimization - more people do truly seem to be victimized by things like abuse, violence, and neglect. And yet there are others who are growing up in overprotective, highly controlled environments. All of this weakens the will. Thus, the will gets bent in this cowering posture, and people submit to all of the stronger forces in their life and they play the victim. It certainly can be, and often is, rooted in shame, but ultimately the bent will is about a weakened resolve. We must address our identity in order to find freedom in Christ.

The issue of your value was settled at the cross. The love of God is a sure foundation under your feet. But you must stand on that foundation. You are not stuck in the weightiness of your past woundedness. The darkness of the past does not define the limits of your future—because Jesus has overcome.

Identity is not something that is achieved by your performance or by your control or by how people perceive you. Identity is a gift that is received from a loving Father who has adopted you because He wanted you and chooses you to be in his family.

Unless a house has a solid foundation, the house is in jeopardy. Unless we build our lives on the solid foundation of Christ's love, our souls will be a mess. It isn't enough to know the truth; we must relentlessly hold on to the truth so that the truth can set us free.

When my kids were little I noticed a strange phenomenon. After I disciplined them (nothing harsh; I am talking about giving them a timeout), I called them over to hug them. I wanted them to know that they were still loved. But my kids didn't want to come over for the hug. They would get a pout on their lips and turn their head away from me and put their hand up toward me in a "speak to the hand" gesture.

I had a friend who was a child psychologist, so I decided to pass this by her one day and gain her insight. She said, "That is a universal response of children. They don't believe that you could love them when they are naughty." I said, "Really? Are you serious?" (She was.)

As soon as I got home, I called my oldest over to me. At the time she was not yet four. She sat on my lap and I said to her, "Does Daddy love you even when you are naughty?" She shook her head, and said, "NO!" It was as if I had said something completely ridiculous. I was shocked. I looked her in the eyes and said, "Of course I do. I always love you. Do you know why I love you, even when you're naughty?" Her eyes got as big as they could, and she shook her head no and asked very sincerely and sweetly, "Why?" I said, "Just because you are my little girl. Nothing can ever change that. God made you just for me, and I will always love you, even when you're naughty. Now, life works better when you're well-behaved. But, even if you're not, I'll always love you."

That became a regular conversation in our house as our kids grew up. "Does Daddy love you when you're naughty?" And they learned to say, "Yes. Just because we are yours."

And that's right. That's how the Father feels about you. This is what your identity is rooted in. It isn't rooted in your getting it right in life. It is rooted in the Father's love for you. May you build your life on this one true foundation!

SPIRITUAL ACTION STEPS

- Spend time alone with God, and journal. Ask the Holy Spirit to reveal to you the lies that affect you. Which of these three lies discussed in the chapter impact your life the most? How do they manifest? What makes you feel most vulnerable? What image of yourself are you most attached to? What are you most proud of? What are you most defensive about? How do you use these things to fend off your feelings of vulnerability?

- Fill in the blank: The issue of my value is dependent on _____. Are there any specific memories connected to those lies? How do those lies manifest themselves in your life? What do you feel when you are standing on this faulty foundation? What do you say to yourself? What are the imaginary conversations you have in your mind? What are the symptomatic expressions of this lie in your life? How does it manifest?

- Put the lies in a sentence. Then come up with a truth slogan, or a Scripture, to replace each lie.

- Do you struggle with an identity wound or a bent will? Do you know why? How does it manifest itself in your life?

• Share your discoveries in a safe group you meet with to journey through this book.

SOUL CARE PRINCIPLE #2
REPENTANCE

I spent an hour on the phone recently with a distraught woman whose husband is in an affair. She caught him. Over the years I have had conversations like this hundreds of times. She was desperate to fix the situation, desperate to say something or to have someone do something that would change her husband and their circumstances. I would be desperate if I was in her situation, too.

My heart went out to her, as it does to anyone in such a situation. But there was one fundamental problem. He didn't want to change. She wanted him to change more than he wanted to change. And if you want someone to change more than they want to change, you are going to feel frustrated, and they are going to feel pressured, controlled, and manipulated. No one changes unless they come to a point where they are ready to repent.

When John the Baptist announced the coming of the Kingdom of God, he preached, "Repent, for the kingdom of heaven has come near" (Matthew 3:2). Jesus inaugurated his ministry shortly thereafter with the exact same words: "Repent, for the kingdom of heaven has come near" (Matthew 4:17). There is no entrance into the kingdom without repentance. There is no advancement in the kingdom without repentance.

Repentance is not a popular word or concept in society today. We value tolerance. The only problem is that we have a faulty understanding of tolerance. We act as if tolerance means everyone has a right to his or her opinion, and everyone's opinion is of equal value. But that isn't tolerance. That's insanity. That means Mother Teresa's opinion would be the same as Adolf Hitler's opinion.

Tolerance really means that everyone has a right to his or her opinion, and everyone should be treated with dignity and respect. But everyone's opinion isn't right, and everyone's opinion isn't of equal value. In a society whose number one value is a faulty understanding of tolerance, the capacity to call people to repentance without creating offense is all but lost.

In our culture today, everyone decides for themselves what is right or what is wrong, and the measuring stick for a person's morality is what they feel is right for them. No one else has a right to call that into question. That is truly a sad state, because our well-being, according to Jesus, depends on our repentance; it is essential to the healing of the soul. God has established the principles of a healthy soul, and they are inviolable. Unfortunately, even if you justify a behavior because you feel like doing it, and it seems right to you, the principles of soul health remain intact, and your soul will suffer the consequences.

SOUL ALIGNMENT

Repentance is more than just a change of behavior. Biblical repentance is about changing your mind and purpose; it is about changing the way you think. It is about bringing yourself into alignment with God. When your heart, your behavior, your belief system, or your thinking deviates from God's ways and doings, your soul gets out of alignment.

It is like having your car out of alignment. I had a car that constantly had alignment troubles. It was a good car in every other way. But when I drove the car down the road, if I took my hands off the wheel, the car would pull to the right. Sometimes the car got so far out of alignment it would pull me immediately hard to the right, toward the ditch, and I felt like I had to constantly fight to keep the car on course.

When I took the car into the shop to get it aligned, I would then leave the garage, head down a straight road, take my hands off the wheel, and the car would drive straight and true. It was like I could hear that car giving a sigh of relief. It was no longer battling with itself; it was finally back on course. But within a few months, the car would be pulling to the right again, and I would be fighting to keep it straight.

Repentance is like a soul alignment. It makes your soul breathe a sigh of relief. It is soul-refreshing to be in right alignment with God. But when you are not in alignment with God, your soul is subject to disease.

If your soul is going to get healthy, you have to be in right alignment with God, and when you are out of alignment, you must repent. You must admit when your thinking and your behaviors are different than God's ways and doings, and then you must turn from your wayward path and turn back to God. You won't get well until you are more concerned with being good than you are with looking good. Pride is the enemy of true confession and ultimate freedom. I believe it was John

Bradshaw who said, "You are only as sick as the secrets that you keep." If you are going to walk free, you must not walk in secrecy. It is a powerful thing to be open and honest. There is no healing where there is pretending.

The apostle John understood this. He wrote:

> This is the message we have heard from him and declare to you: God is light; in him there is no darkness at all. If we claim to have fellowship with him and yet walk in the darkness, we lie and do not live out the truth. But if we walk in the light, as he is in the light, we have fellowship with one another, and the blood of Jesus, his Son, purifies us from all sin. If we claim to be without sin, we deceive ourselves and the truth is not in us. If we confess our sins, he is faithful and just and will forgive us our sins and purify us from all unrighteousness. If we claim we have not sinned, we make him out to be a liar and his word is not in us (1 John 1:5-10).

God shines His light into our hearts. He reveals what is there. When our minds, hearts, and behaviors are out of alignment with Him, He shows us the truth. We have, in that moment, an opportunity to get back into alignment. We simply need to say yes to God. We need to acknowledge our sin and bring it into the light.

When I started South Shore Community Church, I raised enough money to be able to hire an associate pastor, Randy. When he came on staff, I put him in charge of the small group leaders I had been training. I had spent time with these people, mentoring them, discipling them, doing life with them. Now I was one level removed, and he was in their life more. They began coming to me and telling me how wonderful Randy was. "Randy is so loving." "Randy is so helpful." "Randy is so encouraging."

I started feeling something dark. I wanted Randy to do well, just not as well as I did. I wanted Randy to be liked, just not as liked as I was. As I started to feel this dark feeling, I brought it to the Lord. He said to me, "That's envy."

We have to walk in the light with God and others if we are going to get free. So there was only one thing to do. I walked into Randy's office and confessed. I told him I wanted him to be liked, just not as liked as I was. I wanted him to be successful, just not as successful as I was. I confessed my envy, knelt before him, and asked him to pray for me. The envy broke. Light always dispels darkness.

Jesus' blood is greater than all our sin. Jesus' love is stronger than all our waywardness. He is faithful and purifies us from our sin. He washes our hearts clean and realigns our souls with God so we can dwell in the river of God's presence and walk intimately with Him once again.

> Jesus' blood is greater than all our sin. Jesus' love is stronger than all our waywardness.

John does make a leap of logic in this text that is imperative to note. John says, "God is light; in him there is no darkness at all. . . If we walk in the light, as he is in the light, we have fellowship with one another" (1 John 1:7).

If you follow the logic of the text, it appears what John is about to say is, "if we walk in the light, as he is in the light, we have fellowship with Him." But that isn't what he says. Why does John make this switch?

If you are truly in the light with God, you will be broken and contrite, and the broken and contrite person does not desire to live in hiding from others. But if you are hiding from, or even with, others, it is because you are not genuinely broken and contrite before God. Only the proud seek to cover up and pretend to be more than they are.

Norman Grubb, in his book *Continuous Revival*, wrote, "Openness before man is the genuine proof of sincerity before God, even as righteousness before man and love to man are the genuine proofs of righteousness before God and love to God. Note also that hiding the truth about ourselves before men—pretending to be better than we really are—is the supreme sin which Jesus drove home to the Pharisees."[5]

A soul in alignment is a soul without secrets. We cannot walk free if we will not repent from sin and bring it into the light with God and others.

> A soul in alignment is a soul without secrets. We cannot walk free if we will not repent from sin and bring it into the light with God and others.

For those of you who are trying to help others on the spiritual journey, there is another important corollary here. You only have authority over that which you walk in victory. You teach what you know, but you reproduce who you are. Peter talks about some false teachers in 2 Peter 2:19. He writes, "They promise them freedom, while they themselves are slaves of depravity—for 'people are slaves to whatever has mastered them.'"

I can only help you get free from some area in your life if I am walking free in that area in my life. We only have authority over that which we walk in victory. These false teachers couldn't offer freedom that they didn't have. Freedom begins with repentance.

CULTIVATING CONTRITION

Proverbs 4:23 says, "Above all else, guard the heart, for it is the wellspring of life" (NIV). The first order of business in

---

5. Norman Grubb, *Continuous Revival* (Fort Washington: Christian Literature Crusade, 1997), p. 20.

keeping your soul rightly aligned with God is to guard the condition of your heart. A healthy soul has a contrite heart; a soul that is rightly connected to God is in a state of brokenness or humility. When our behavior or thinking gets out of alignment with God, the Holy Spirit convicts us.

Conviction

Sin threatens to harden our hearts and get us out of the river of God's presence. Conviction is designed to soften our hearts and bring us back into the river, so He pricks our conscience. Usually there is some internal disequilibrium associated with this conviction. You feel uneasy; your inner peace is disturbed; you have this sense that something is wrong and you are no longer at rest.

I learned early on in my spiritual walk with Jesus that when my inner peace was disturbed, I needed to get alone with Him and ask Him what was at the root of the disturbance. Quite often He would bring me back to a careless word that I had spoken which had offended Him and potentially hurt someone else. If I then received the light God was offering, and confessed that careless word as sin, and called the person and repented and asked for their forgiveness, I would immediately sense a return of the inner peace. I was walking in the light with God and others. If your soul is going to be rightly aligned with God, you must be vigilant about guarding the condition of your heart.

> If the Spirit convicts you, respond. But don't allow the enemy to bury you in a grave of condemnation.

When the Holy Spirit is convicting you, He is very specific. He will remind you of a specific offense—for example, a word that you spoke that hurt someone. Then when you confess that sin, and apologize to the person that you hurt, the Spirit will bring release; the peace of Christ will return. But when the enemy of your soul is condemning you, he often uses generalities that you can't confess. You may feel like you are a disappointment to God, or that you are not loving enough. But there aren't specific sins to confess, and there is no release from the guilt. If the Spirit convicts you, respond. But don't allow the enemy to bury you in a grave of condemnation.

If you fail to obey the prompting of the Spirit's conviction, God will take other steps to get you back into the light, to get your heart soft and contrite again.

The Law of the Harvest

For example, Galatians 6 speaks of the law of the harvest: "Do not be deceived: God cannot be mocked. People reap what they sow. Those who sow to please their sinful nature, from that nature will reap destruction" (v. 7, 8).

The law of the harvest states that a person reaps what they sow, and God uses the consequences of our poor choices to lead us to repentance. Sadly, sometimes we refuse to listen even to this warning. Proverbs 26:11 says, "As a dog returns to its vomit, so fools repeat their folly." It's a gross image, but think about it. Why did the dog throw up in the first place? Sometimes the dog throws up because it ate something that was like poison to its system. Rather than learning from its mistake, the dumb dog goes back and eats the regurgitated poisonous food. So it is with a fool—they don't learn from their mistakes, and they keep repeating them. Their heart is hard toward God, and they refuse to reflect upon the law of the harvest and see that their consequences have taken place to lead them to repentance. This is a gift from God, but only to the wise of heart who will reflect upon the consequences of their choices and change directions.

Discipline

If conviction and consequences do not bring you to contrition, the Lord will use discipline. Hebrews 12:7-11 says:

> Endure hardship as discipline; God is treating you as his children. For what children are not disciplined by their father? If you are not disciplined—and everyone undergoes discipline—then you are not legitimate children at all. Moreover, we have all had parents who disciplined us and we respected them for it. How much more should we submit to the Father of spirits and live! Our parents disciplined us for a little while as they thought best; but God disciplines us for our good, that we may share in his holiness. No discipline seems pleasant at the time, but painful. Later on, however, it produces a harvest of righteousness and peace for those who have been trained by it.

The discipline of the Lord is not punitive; it is restorative. He is a good Father. He disciplines us not in wrath, not capriciously or whimsically, but lovingly for our good—to make us like Jesus. It is, of course, unpleasant, even painful. But it produces the fruit of righteousness and peace if we endure discipline.

God is trying to soften your heart. When my heart is broken before God, it is as if the soil of my soul is pierced. The pierced heart is the broken and contrite heart. The pierced heart is the heart that is receptive to God, accessible to God. The pierced heart is soft, not hard, receptive not resistant, contrite not rebellious, open not closed, accessible not inaccessible. The pierced heart is like soil that has been plowed and prepared to receive the seed. If the seed is planted in hardened soil, it will not be as likely to mature and bear a harvest. It is only when the heart is pierced that the soul can be healthy. When the heart grows hard, God uses conviction and consequences and discipline to pierce the heart and bring us back into the light with Him and others. These tools are developmental; they are not designed to shame or condemn but to re-store us to right relationship with God and develop us toward maturity. You must choose to cooperate with God's work in piercing the heart. There is no freedom without honesty; there is no breakthrough without brokenness.

OWNING UP

When I reflect back on my story with Jen, I can see now that the Lord had been convicting me about some of the things that led to trouble in my marriage. He had been con-victing me about my selfishness and my proud and passion-ate opinions that left Jen feeling stomped on. But I had blown through those stop signs. I can look back now and see how the Lord was trying to get my attention with the law of the harvest. I can see how my actions were reaping consequences that I didn't desire, but I was too busy defending myself and blaming Jen. I wasn't listening; I wasn't standing in the light.

But, finally, the combination of conviction, the law of the harvest, and the discipline of a good, loving Father brought me to contrition. I finally came to the place where I was bro-ken before God and ready to listen, ready to receive, ready to change. Above all else, God longs for us to cultivate a contrite heart. We need to respond to the work of the Spirit.

It is hard to stand in the light. It is like waking up in the middle of the night and someone snapping the light on. You squint, and turn your head, and do all you can to avoid the penetrating, offensive nature of the light. But it is only in the light that you can find healing and freedom; only in the light is your soul aligned properly with God.

David Benner said, "The self that God persistently loves is not my prettied-up pretend self but my actual self—the real me. But, master of delusion that I am, I have trouble pene-trating my web of self-deceptions and knowing this real me. I continually confuse it with some ideal self that I wish I were."[6]

Imagine that: God didn't love me more when I repented and got into right alignment with Him and Jen. God loved me as much in my sin as He did in my obedience. This is so hard for us to believe. But it is biblical. Paul wrote, "Christ died for the ungodly. Very rarely will anyone die for a righteous person, though for a good person someone might possibly dare to die. But God demonstrates his own love for us in this: While we were still sinners, Christ died for us" (Romans 5:6-8). The beautiful message of the Gospel is that though you are deeply flawed, you are even more deeply loved. God invites you to come into the light.

God cannot cleanse our excuses. God cannot pardon our denials. God cannot cleanse that which we will not confess. God cannot heal that which we will not admit. There is no freedom without forgiveness, and there is no forgiveness without repentance. Hiding creates darkness, and darkness destroys the soul. You must resolve to walk in the light with God and others.

No Secrets

I have made a series of resolutions that have guided me and greatly aided my walk with God. One of the resolutions I made early in my spiritual journey was that I would die with

---

6. David G. Benner, *The Gift of Being Yourself* (Downers Grove: InterVarsity Press, 2015), p. 60.

no secrets. I would keep my confessions current with God and other dear friends.

When I was walking through the journey of inner healing in the midst of my marriage crisis, I sat down with my friend Rich Schmidt and did a total life confession. We went on a retreat together, and we told our entire life story; we were determined to have no secrets. Since then I have done a total life confession with several people. It is a liberating feeling to get up in the morning, look yourself in the mirror, and know that you have no secrets. There are no skeletons in the closet; no one is going to accuse you of something that you have not already told another. It's powerful.

I chose to share with people who are full of truth and grace, who already had demonstrated that they loved me, who would never use this information against me, and who were always rooting for me. Not everyone is worthy of this sacred trust, but everyone needs someone with whom to share their secrets for the sake of their soul's health. The bond we shared only grew deeper in the confessions we made. Even now, it is not uncommon for us to get together and for someone to update his confessions. We continue to walk in the light with God and each other. It is the only way to live.

> Only the light of God can purge, cleanse, heal, restore, and set you free. If you want transformation, you must embrace the light of God.

I want to encourage you to find a person with whom you can do a total life confession. Get everything into the light. Choose someone who is loving and truthful. Choose someone who can handle it, it won't cause them to stumble, it won't damage their faith, and your confessions won't hurt them personally.

Secrecy and darkness produce a false sense of security in

the midst of a heart full of fear, but they can never result in freedom. Only the light of God can purge, cleanse, heal, restore, and set you free. If you want transformation, you must embrace the light of God.

Sometimes people say to me, "I can't do that. I'm afraid." The enemy of our souls makes honesty terrifying and secrets appealing, but only as we walk in the light with God and others can we truly get free. I always feel empathy for them, but simply ask, "Do you want to get free?" I determined to live in the light with God and others because I was desperate to live free.

CULTIVATING GODLY SORROW

Sometimes even though we confess our sins we cannot get free. Oftentimes it is because we confess our sins to God with worldly sorrow, not Godly sorrow. There is a big difference. Paul writes in 2 Corinthians 7:10, "Godly sorrow brings repentance that leads to salvation and leaves no regret, but worldly sorrow brings death."

Worldly sorrow says: "I am sorry that I got caught. I am sorry about the consequences. I am sorry you think poorly of me." But Godly sorrow says: "I am sorry for my sin. I am sorry for the way I have hurt you and offended God." Godly sorrow flows from a pierced heart.

You have to cultivate Godly sorrow for true repentance. Here are three steps you can take to help cultivate a contrite heart that flows with Godly sorrow.

Ask God for a Contrite Heart

First, ask God for a broken and contrite heart. He has promised that He will do the heart work. Ezekiel 36:26 says, "I will give you a new heart and put a new spirit in you; I will remove from you your heart of stone and give you a heart of flesh."

Whenever I sense my heart is hardening, I claim this promise and ask God to give me a soft, contrite, broken, pierced heart once again. I often will accompany that prayer with fasting. The Lord promised us that He will give us a heart of flesh, and He revealed to us that guarding the heart is of primary importance to our spiritual well-being, so when I pray and fast for a fresh work of the Spirit in my heart, I come with complete confidence in His willingness to answer that prayer.

You have to pay attention to when your heart is growing hard. You have to know what it feels like. For example, when Jen comes to me and says, "When you said that, it hurt my feelings," and my immediate reaction is to defend myself, I know that my heart is not in a good place. But if Jen comes to me and says, "That hurt my feelings," and my immediate reaction is to tear up and say, "I'm so sorry, sweetie. Please forgive me," then I know my heart is contrite, soft, and broken before God. A soft heart produces a soft response. When my heart starts to grow hard and crusty in places, I become defensive. When I see symptomatic expressions of my heart growing hard, that is when I go to God and ask Him to soften my heart.

Stand in the Light

Second, to cultivate Godly sorrow, choose to stand in the light with God and others. Too often when God shines light into our soul, our reflex reaction is to blame, excuse, justify, rationalize, or deny our sin. This only contributes to the hardening of our hearts. Only when we fully embrace our responsibility can the hardened heart soften again.

We live in a culture of entitlement. Entitlement breeds irresponsibility. Irresponsibility results in victimization. Until we take full ownership for our life, our hearts cannot be broken, and our lives cannot be free. God calls us into the light for our benefit, not to shame us or condemn us, but to liberate us.

I know you may be reluctant to come clean with your sin and your secrets. But I cannot tell you how many times I have taught this principle about walking in the light with God and others, and someone comes up and confesses their sin to me, and they then tell me afterward that they felt like a cement block had been lifted off of their souls. I know it is scary, but there is more freedom here than you can imagine. Be brave.

Pastors, teachers, church leaders, and small group facilitators must create communities of grace where confession is expected and accepted. We must lead the way with open, honest, confessional lives. If the leaders are pretentious or judgmental, the followers will hide in secrecy. And where secrecy is encouraged by our actions, sin will flourish.

> But even though I won't speak about that struggle from the pulpit, I will share it with people who are in my inner circle—I won't let it go slinking off into the dark netherworld of secrecy.

I am not advocating that leaders use the pulpit to confess their sins as some form of public therapy. My rule of thumb for vulnerability is if it will help the people I am speaking to, I will share it. If it doesn't help the audience, if it could cause someone to stumble, if it could weaken someone's faith, I won't speak about it publicly. But even though I won't speak about that struggle from the pulpit, I will share it with people who are in my inner circle—I won't let it go slinking off into the dark netherworld of secrecy.

For example, a number of years ago I was wrestling with the question, "Does God lie?" I talk about this in my book *River Dwellers*. I was struggling with the question on an emotional level, not a theological one. I knew God didn't lie, but

I felt deceived, like Jeremiah (see Jeremiah 20). But I couldn't share this struggle from the pulpit while I was in the throes of the turmoil. That would have caused people to stumble.

Asaph was struggling with his faith in Psalm 73 because the wicked were prospering, and he didn't understand, but he wouldn't speak publicly about it while he was in the midst of his faith struggle. In Psalm 73:15 he writes, "If I had spoken out like that, I would have betrayed your children." So like Asaph, I didn't articulate my struggle publicly at that time. However, I did process with some good friends, with Jen, and with Ron Walborn, the dean of the seminary where I teach. I didn't let the struggle go underground—that is a dangerous thing to do.

When I got out and to the other side of the struggle, I shared openly about it. I did a talk about wrestling with the question, "Does God lie?" And I shared my experience in that setting openly and vulnerably from a position of victory. It helped people immensely, and that is exactly what Asaph does in Psalm 73. When he is in the struggle, he doesn't talk about it publicly lest he cause people to stumble, but when he gets to the place of victory, he writes a Psalm about it to help the rest of us through such faith struggles.

Whether you are a pastor or parishioner, a church leader or church member, you must walk in honesty if you are going to experience liberty. If you have secrets, you are carrying around baggage in the suitcase of your soul, and it is time to unload the suitcase.

Own Your Part

Third, to cultivate a contrite heart that flows with Godly sorrow, take full ownership for your part. You are the only one responsible for you. Sometimes we are reluctant to confess and fully own our sin because we have been victimized in a relationship. For example, let's say a man cheats on his wife, and the two of them come for marriage counseling. She can see his part of the relational dysfunction without any problem. But it is sometimes hard for her to see her part, because she is afraid that somehow, if she owns her part, it will let him off the hook for his adulterous affair. Nothing she has done justifies his affair, but there was clear dysfunction in the relationship before the affair happened. She must own her part, and he must own his part.

> You can never change a relationship by focusing on the other person's faults.

Owning your part doesn't validate anyone else's sin that has been committed against you. If you are in a relationship and 10 percent of the relational problem is your fault, then you need to own 100 percent of your 10 percent without any excuse! (And chances are you're responsible for more than 10 percent!) You can never change a relationship by focusing on the other person's faults. The more you try to get the other person to own their part, rather than owning your part, the more likely your heart will harden in the victimization and blame. Own 100 percent of *your part*. Fully own your sin. You are the only one responsible for you.

If you are taking full ownership for your sin, then you can't make any excuses. Sometimes we excuse ourselves by saying things like, "Well I only said that because you said this." Sometimes we excuse ourselves because a lot of time has gone by. We think, "Well, that was a long time ago. I don't need to deal with that now." Time does not cleanse our sin. Only the blood of Jesus cleanses our sins, so we have to bring our sins to Jesus. I've had the Lord bring to my memory sins that I had committed in high school—more than a decade had gone by, but I hadn't confessed it. As He convicted me, I confessed it, and felt His cleansing.

When necessary, we need to make restitution for our sin. If you stole something, return it. If you spoke words against someone that hurt them, call them and apologize and ask for forgiveness. Taking full ownership of our sin helps us keep our hearts soft and allows us to go free.

STUCK IN SHAME

Even as you cultivate Godly sorrow and work toward repentance, you may find yourself stuck and confessing a sin more than once. You may have committed it once a long time ago, but you keep confessing.

I talked to a man whose girlfriend had an abortion. More than a decade had passed, yet he told me that he confessed that sin every day of his life. It had only happened once, but he was still living under the weight of that abortion every day.

Jesus doesn't just want you to know, cognitively, that you are forgiven, He wants you to experience true release. I am convinced that Jesus not only wants to help you be forgiven so you can have right standing with God, He also wants you to experience the liberation of your forgiveness. Your spirit is free, forgiven, purged. But often your soul is still clouded with guilt, shame, and condemnation.

Jesus wants the work of the cross to permeate your soul so you can experience true freedom. He doesn't want you to have to wait until you get to Heaven to experience the benefits of the cross. You need to experience the forgiveness of Jesus, and then you can turn around and help others experience the forgiveness of Jesus.

In John 20:21-23, Jesus appeared to his disciples in the upper room and he said to them, "'Peace be with you! As the Father has sent me, I am sending you.' And with that he breathed on them and said, 'Receive the Holy Spirit. If you forgive the sins of anyone, their sins are forgiven.'"

Catholics have had no problems with this passage over the years. The priest receives a confession and absolves someone of his or her sin in the name of Father, Son, and Holy Spirit. But Protestants haven't quite known what to do with what Jesus said here.

I think the context is critical. Jesus breathed on them and they received the Holy Spirit. Then he said, "If you forgive the sins of anyone, their sins are forgiven." I think the key to experiencing the forgiveness that Jesus has purchased for you at the price of His blood is the revelatory presence of the Spirit. The Spirit must reveal to you the forgiveness of Jesus. He appropriates it, ministers it into your inner being, and you are released from your sin. There is a clear lifting of the burden, breaking of the chains, releasing of the debt, and freeing of the soul when the Spirit of God ministers the forgiveness of Jesus through revelation. The Holy Spirit takes that which has been accomplished through Christ in our spirit, and He reveals it and appropriates it to our soul.

This revelatory presence of the Spirit is the key to both receiving forgiveness that is experienced in your own soul and the key to having the authority to minister the forgiveness of Jesus to someone else.

Imagine that someone comes to me and confesses some deep, dark secret from their past. They say, "I have confessed this sin every day of my life for twenty years, and I still don't feel forgiven." I could quote Scripture, such as 1 John 1:9: "If we confess our sins, he is faithful and just and will forgive us our sins and purify us from all unrighteousness." But this person has read the Bible; they have that verse memorized! They have quoted it and prayed it over and over. The problem is that there is still no release. They need a revelation of the Spirit about this truth. My words will have no power to help them; they need the truth of God illuminated to their soul by the presence of the Holy Spirit. Shame is blocking them from receiving the release of forgiveness that is their inheritance.

REVELATION OF THE SPIRIT

How do we access the revelation of the Spirit that brings a release? There isn't any formula. There are, however, helpful principles. Bringing our sin into the light with God and others is a vital principle in helping us experience release. I know my total life confession helped conquer some shame that I was carrying in my soul.

Another key principle is to follow the Spirit's leading. Theology 101: God is smart, He knows stuff I don't know, and He likes to tell me what He knows. I don't know what will "click" and bring release to shame. I don't know how to manufacture revelation. Revelation is the work of the Spirit, so I need to rely on Him.

> Theology 101: God is smart, He knows stuff I don't know, and He likes to tell me what He knows.

If someone confesses a past sin and they say, "I've never told anyone this before," immediately I know I am dealing with shame. Or if they say to me, "I've confessed this to God hundreds of times," I know what I am dealing with is not unconfessed sin, but shame. Shame is blocking them from experiencing the release of forgiveness that Jesus offers. So I wait on the Spirit of God for wisdom. I know my words aren't going to release them. My words have no power. They need revelation. If they have been a Christian for a long time, they likely don't need me to quote the Bible to them, either. They already know it. This is not a knowledge problem. Paul said "all Scripture is God-breathed"—they need the breath of the Spirit to blow across these eternal truths so that what is known will become revelation, enabling their release to come.

There have been times when the Spirit led me to have someone write down the sin that they just confessed and literally nail it to a cross. I've seen people kneeling before a rough-hewn wooden cross with tears streaming down their cheeks as they left their sin at the foot of the cross, and the revelation of God finally came and broke their chains of shame.

There have been other times when I have been praying for someone who has confessed a secret that has bound them for years, and the Lord simply showed me a picture of his face. I could see his compassionate gaze, and I saw that there was absolutely no judgment there. I simply said to the person, "I see the face of Jesus. I am going to pray you see His face, that the Spirit of God will just show you a picture of Jesus. Tell me what you see." And with a shudder, and a revelation of the Spirit, tears spill out of a soul once again released from shame.

I had a person come to me who had committed adultery multiple times. He was deeply convicted over his sin, had long since turned from it, but he was still stuck in shame. He called me and told me what he was struggling with, and he asked if I would meet with him later that week. I told him I would, and asked him to meditate on John 8—the account of the woman who was caught in adultery. I told him to simply read the passage over and over, to picture himself as the person who was caught, and to ask the Holy Spirit to reveal the truth of Jesus to his heart.

The day before I was supposed to meet with him, he called and said, "I don't need to meet with you." I asked, "Why?" He said, "Jesus met with me, and the shame has been broken. I have been released." I said, "Jesus is better than me anyway!" I don't have any magic. I can't help someone experience release or revelation—that is the Spirit's job. But I can listen to the Spirit with them and help connect them to the Spirit so that release can come.

If you are stuck in shame, you can listen for the Spirit's revelation in your own life. If you still can't break through the shame, you can get together with another discerning believer who can graciously love you and listen for the Spirit's releasing revelation for you. God doesn't want you to carry around the shame in your soul that He has already paid for on the cross.

Years ago I was preaching on 1 John 1. I called people to walk in the light with God and others, to live a life without secrets. A woman came down front and asked me to meet with her that week. I could tell she was carrying a heavy burden. When we got together she averted her eyes, stammered, and said, "I've never told anyone this before." She was packed with shame. She told me that twenty years earlier she had an abortion, and since that day she had confessed it every day of her life. Still, she was still living under the weight of condemnation and shame.

I sensed the Spirit of God leading me to take her back to the scene. I said to her, "Do you remember the abortion clinic?" She said, "Oh, yes. I've lived there every day of my life in my mind." I said, "Close your eyes. Picture the scene. Describe it to me." She went on and described the scene in details: the sights, sounds, smells, the décor—right down to the color of the carpet. I said to her, "Jesus is always with us. He was with you that day. I am going to ask the Spirit of God to reveal to you the presence of Jesus in that scene. I want you to watch and listen; tell me what He does and what He says."

I then simply prayed, "Come, Holy Spirit. Reveal Jesus. He was there that day. Show her Jesus." She started sobbing; it went on for probably 45 minutes. I didn't console her; I didn't say, "It's OK." I just let it go. She had twenty years of grief, guilt, and shame locked up in her soul, and all of it needed to come out. The Spirit was doing a work, and I needed to let it happen. He is the Comforter, not me. Too often when we are praying with someone or ministering to someone, we shut down the work of the Spirit by patting them and telling them, "It's OK" because we are uncomfortable with the emotional display. Let the Spirit access the heart and bring release.

After she stopped crying, I asked her to tell me what had happened. This is what she described. Jesus came into the room, and He was holding her baby. He said, "It's a boy. You'll meet him when you get to Heaven. He is not angry with you, and neither am I. I have forgiven you, and so has he. Now, go free from this sin. You are released." It was powerful. Years later, I had a follow-up conversation with this woman, and she told me she has not confessed that sin since that encounter with Jesus. That's the power of revelation, and that's the work of the Comforter. Jesus told his disciples to receive the Spirit, and then to go and forgive as they had been forgiven. The Spirit holds the keys; He can reveal the forgiveness of Jesus. He can release us from our shame. We need the presence, power, and revelation of the Spirit. If you follow Jesus, the Spirit of God is in you and can bring release to your soul. And the Spirit of God can work through you to bring release to others.

> Maybe He will lead you back to the place of the sin; maybe He will lead you to picture Jesus on the cross. *Let Him lead you.*

BREAKING FREE

Even now, if you are reading these words and have sins from your past that you have confessed to God, and even to others, but you still have not felt release, take a moment to stop reading and just be alone with God. Let the Holy Spirit direct you. Maybe He will lead you back to the place of the sin; maybe He will lead you to picture Jesus on the cross. *Let Him lead you.* Ask the Spirit to reveal Jesus, and ask Him, through His revelation, to bring you release from the shame. Watch for

Jesus in any picture that comes to your mind, and listen for His whispers.

It might help to picture Jesus on the cross. He died to take up your sin. Picture yourself before Him on the cross, and take this sin—like a black spot off your soul—and give it to Jesus. Watch and listen. See what Jesus does, and listen to what He says. Let the Holy Spirit's revelation come to you. May God break you free from your shame.

Sometimes people struggle to see Jesus. I have had many people through the years say to me, "I see His feet." That is because they are looking down in shame, and I simply ask them to lift their heads, and I've seen the shame break and the revelation come. If you can't break through on your own, bring this openly to others, and have them pray with you. Also, if you are in a small group where you are practicing confession, make sure you confess everything. Partial confessions lead to partial freedom. And if you are one who is listening to a confession, compassionately ask, "Is there anything else?" People are often reluctant to come clean, but if there is a loving, gracious person receiving the confession, they will bring it all into the light.

Unconfessed sin can wreak havoc in our lives. David says in Psalm 32: "When I kept silent, my bones wasted away through my groaning all day long. For day and night your hand was heavy on me; my strength was sapped as in the heat of summer" (vv. 3, 4). He was experiencing physical, emotional, and spiritual effects from his unconfessed sin.

It is not uncommon for someone to come to me and ask for healing prayer for a physical problem. As always, when I go to pray for someone, the first thing I do is pause and listen for any whisper of the Spirit. And sometimes when I pause, I hear the Spirit say, "Ask them if they have any unconfessed sin." I ask, the person confesses something, and the physical problem goes away. The physical pain was a symptom of a spiritual

> Determine to live your life in the light with God and others. Make a steely resolve to live with no secrets.

root—unconfessed sin. I've seen the same thing with emotional pain like anxiety or depression. Of course, not all physical or emotional problems have their root in sin. But some do, and God always knows the roots and the cure.

Don't read this chapter and continue to live with secrets. Please, for the sake of your soul and your freedom, bring all of your sin into the light. Determine to live your life in the light with God and others. Make a steely resolve to live with no secrets. Have at least one other person who knows all about you.

A final word of caution: When someone is caught in a sin, they seldom are ready to change. Deep inside, they are aware that coming into the light may break trust in relationships and create all kinds of other problems. But if you are stuck in a secret sin, don't wait until you get caught. Respond to the conviction of the Spirit and come into the light with God and others. If you have been caught, then commit yourself to tell the whole truth. Don't shade anything. Darkness always produces bondage.

It's time to come home. Repent. The Father awaits your return.

SPIRITUAL ACTION STEPS

- Spend some time journaling. Is there any unconfessed sin in your life? Ask the Lord: "Search me, God, and know my heart; test me and know my anxious thoughts. See if there is any offensive way in me, and lead me in the way everlasting" (Psalm 139:23, 24).

- Are there any areas in your life where you have confessed your sin but don't feel the release of forgiveness? Have you confessed those sins to others as well?

- Where do you see worldly sorrow in your life instead of Godly sorrow?

- Are you willing to do a total life confession with another? Will you bring all of your secrets into the light so you can get free? If so, make a resolve to do so, and set a time to get together with another willing fellow sojourner.

SOUL CARE PRINCIPLE #3

OVERCOMING FAMILY SIN PATTERNS

When I was in my early thirties, after a Sunday morning service, I sat in a car with my friend Martin Sanders for two hours. I talked with Martin about my struggle with lust. I desperately wanted to be a man of God, to finish well, and to honor the name of Jesus all my days. But lust had been a battle.

I have always been faithful to Jen. There weren't any sordid tales to tell or any dark secrets. I wasn't addicted to pornography or anything like that. But I felt this pull in my soul toward lust that I couldn't get rid of. I was able to walk in victory, but the pull was still there.

Martin listened as I walked through my struggle and talked of my fear that one day I would blow up my life if I couldn't conquer this. I had learned the value of walking in the light. I was determined that I would not go underground with the struggle, but I wanted to figure out why I was struggling with this issue for so long.

The easy and quick answer people gave me was: "It's because you are a young man." That worked for me in my teens and twenties, but now that I had moved into my thirties, was I going to keep using this excuse? There was something deeper. I was on the journey of sorting out the issues of my soul at this point, and one of the areas that I began to explore, which was connected to my struggle with lust, was the power of family sin patterns.

THE POWER OF FAMILY SINS: BIBLICAL EXAMPLES

Family sin patterns have unusual pull on our souls; they are often the most stubborn sin patterns to break. Think with me about some biblical examples. Look at David's family tree and the sexual immorality that plagued it. David commits adultery with Bathsheba and has many wives and concubines. His son Amnon rapes his daughter Tamar. His son Absalom rebels against his father and sleeps with his father's concubines in public for all to see. Solomon married many foreign women, and they led his heart astray from God. This sin plagued the entire family; it even seemed to get worse as time went on.

Think about Abraham. He struggled with lying when the pressure was on. He lied that his wife was his sister because he was afraid that someone would kill him and take her—even though she was a fairly old woman! Do you think he could have had some fear in his soul underneath that lying pattern? Then Isaac doesn't even get original with lying; he just repeats the old man's lie. By the time the pattern hits Jacob, he is actually nicknamed "the deceiver." This is not a good family trend.

While we are on this patriarchal family, let's look at the effects of favoritism in this clan. Isaac is the favored child of Abraham and Sarah. He is the promised child, but poor

Ishmael gets tossed to the curb with his mom Hagar—even though it was Sarah's idea that Abraham sleep with Hagar to have a son. She runs them out of the house not long after Isaac is born.

Isaac grows up and marries Rebekah, and they have Esau and Jacob. Isaac favors Esau, and Rebekah favors Jacob. Rebekah and Jacob resort to the old family pattern of lying to swindle Esau's birthright from him, and with it the family blessing. Jacob runs away and gets married to a couple of gals, Rachel and Leah, but not without running into their trickster of a father, who pulls a fast one on "the deceiver" himself.

Jacob plays favorites too. His favorite son, of twelve, is Joseph, but all of this favoritism that has been increasing over the generations finally comes to a head. His father picks out a special robe for Joseph, to display his favoritism, and Joseph's brothers don't like it one bit. Genesis 37:3, 4 says: "Now Israel (Jacob) loved Joseph more than any of his other sons, because he had been born to him in his old age; and he made a richly ornamented robe for him. When his brothers saw that their father loved him more than any of them, they hated him and could not speak a kind word to him."

Favoritism had created enmity in the family tree; it was so strong it motivated them to sell their brother into slavery. Certainly, they overreacted, but the entire tale shows us how the sin pattern multiplied over the generations. The good news is that God redeems the journey into slavery, which is because God is so good He can redeem evil, but don't think for a minute God condoned it. Favoritism has devastating effects on a family. And it wasn't just Joseph's older brothers that it affected; it had lasting effects on Joseph too. God had to heal him from the effects of the favoritism, but we'll come back to that later.

HONORING OUR FAMILY IN VICTORY

Family sin patterns are devastating in their power and effect. People who are abused often vow never to become like their parents, but they end up being abusers themselves. Children of alcoholics swear that they will not be like their parents, and often they end up repeating the family cycle of addiction. On a tragically sad number of occasions, I have sat down with someone who has landed in the gutter of their family's sin, and with their head bowed in shame and their eyes filled with tears of regret, they have said, "I have become like my parent. I promised myself I never would." This is the pull of a pattern of family sins.

It is important for us to explore our family sin patterns because doing so can help us become self-aware and ultimately free. Self-awareness is the gateway to freedom; it does not guarantee freedom, but we cannot get there without it. In my role as a professor at Alliance Theological Seminary, I have the opportunity to work with many cultures. And often when I speak about this topic, people from cultures with a high regard for honoring their parents and elders say to me, "We can't talk about this. It would dishonor our parents and our elders."

> When Kingdom culture clashes with my American culture, or my family-of-origin culture, I must choose Kingdom culture. And it is Kingdom culture to walk in the light with God and others so we can be free.

But I reply, "The most honorable thing you can do is to break your family sin patterns. It brings your family no honor if you repeat their sinful behaviors." When Kingdom culture clashes with my American culture, or my family-of-origin culture, I must choose Kingdom culture. And it is Kingdom culture to walk in the light with God and others so we can be free. We can do this in ways that honor our elders. I love my parents and grandparents, and my extended family, and they love me. If I didn't talk about these things, if I repeated the sexual sins that have been in my family tree, how would that bring them honor? It would bring disgrace to the family name and to the name of Jesus. To conquer the pattern brings far greater honor—and we can't do so without admitting the pattern. We don't talk about our family sin patterns to blame our families or make excuses for our lives. We talk about our family sin patterns to gain victory so that we can honor our family legacy.

Family sin patterns always affect us. We can gain victory over them, but not without a fight. As I sat there talking to Martin that day, I reviewed with him some of the sexual immorality that had been part of my family tree. I knew the background because I had talked to my grandmother openly about it. I used to go visit her regularly, and she would tell me stories. She was keeper of the family legends, and as she got older, she wanted to tell them. I wanted to get free, and I talked with her openly about these topics.

I said, "Gram, I want to walk free and honor God, but sexual purity has been hard for our family. I think it would help me if you told me some of the story. I love our family, and the most honoring thing I could do is to break some of these patterns that have plagued our family tree."

She loved me and wanted me to honor God, so she shared the stories. I found out there was a lot of sexual immorality in the family tree. There was adultery, we had family members who were sexually assaulted, and there was even one old man in our family who groped some of his granddaughters and his daughter-in-law. It was a sad tale.

As I asked questions and listened, I discovered sexual sin pervaded our family tree for four generations, as far back as I could trace it. Not all of the sexual sin was committed by my blood relatives; many times it was people who married into our family. But there was a long history of sexual immorality, and it could not be ignored.

It was a terrible story to listen to, but that story was part of the background to my own struggle, and if I didn't understand it, I may never have been able to battle it appropriately. Jesus once told a parable that said if one doesn't know the strength of his enemy, he would be foolhardy to do battle (Luke 14:31). As I discovered the long history of this sin pattern, I knew I needed to prepare for battle, because this enemy was entrenched. Sometimes we see our family sin and we rebel against it in an effort to overcome it. But there is no victory in rebellion. In a spiritual kingdom there can be no victory through rebellion, only in submission to the king. The kingdom of God is a spiritual kingdom that can only be advanced in submission to the king—not in rebellion. Rebellion only leads to different forms of bondage.

> There is no victory in rebellion. In a spiritual kingdom there can be no victory through rebellion, only in submission to the king.

For example, I know people who grew up in a home with an alcoholic parent, and they determined that they would never drink because of the horrible pain of their upbringing. True to their word, they never drank, but they had all sorts of other compulsive, addictive behaviors. They may have struggled with workaholism, or addictions to pornography, or co-dependent relationships—but they had not overcome their family sin pattern through their rebellion.

We have to recognize our vulnerability in these areas of our life; this is an essential first step to gaining the victory. If we refuse to examine these areas in our family tree, they will still have their unusual pull over us, and we will not be prepared for the battle that ensues.

Family sin patterns often work in tandem with the other areas of soul care: lies, wounds, bitterness, fears, and demonic issues. For example, a whole family can struggle with the lie that their individual value is dependent on performance. Families also have similar wound patterns. It is not uncommon to see a family with generations of physical abuse in their relationships. The father abused the mother, they had a daughter, and the daughter grows up to marry an abuser. These are common family sin patterns that get repeated.

Families often get stuck in bitterness. Anger gets passed from generation to generation. Families are afflicted by the same fears. I mentioned that Abraham had some fear underneath the pattern of lying; that fear was passed from generation to generation. We must become aware of these areas before we can overcome them.

OVERCOMING FAMILY SIN PATTERNS

One of the reasons is simply because they have been modeled for us, and they were modeled for our parents before us, and their parents before them.

Why are these areas so hard to overcome? One of the reasons is simply because they have been modeled for us, and they were modeled for our parents before us, and their parents before them. These behaviors have often been modeled and reinforced for many generations. They are entrenched.

Sometimes these areas have demonically reinforced power. Deuteronomy talks about blessings and curses, and it says that when a clan repeats a sin from generation to generation, it becomes a curse. This is a pattern of behavior that has demonically reinforced strength applied to it. In the chapter dealing with demonic issues, we will talk about curses and breaking their strength.

How do you overcome these behaviors? How do you break through these family sin patterns and their unusual strength in your life? There are several principles that can help you.

Admit the Family Sin Patterns

First, it starts with self-awareness. You have to fully admit the behavioral pattern in your family and its effects on you. You cannot heal that which you will not admit. You have to bring these patterns into the light.

Families tend to guard secrets. There is a sick sense of family loyalty that can keep a person in bondage. For example, some may say, "We don't talk about the things that happen in the family." But when abuse is happening, and the abusers use this sort of shaming technique to keep the children from talking about it, it is a means of twisted control. In honoring the secret, we give strength to the bondage.

> You cannot heal that which you will not admit. You have to bring these patterns into the light.

If honoring a family member means honoring a family secret and family sin pattern, then in honoring the family, the person is making a choice to dishonor God. It also keeps us from finding freedom, and it enables our family members to remain in their sin. So you must begin by admitting it. You have to be ruthlessly honest with yourself in order to find freedom.

I have talked to many people who tell me their story, and it is obvious to me that they were physically abused, but they have never admitted this to themselves. They can't get freedom until they admit the truth. There is no victory in darkness.

It is often easier to see the flaws in others, in your parents, in your siblings, before it is to see the flaws in yourself. Let me illustrate. My dad had a quick temper when I was growing up. This was before he had come to faith, and my dad has changed a lot over the years. But when I was a child, he had a short fuse. I didn't like being yelled at, so I decided I wasn't going to be angry. It wasn't a conscious decision; it was just the way I processed my childhood.

Later in life, when I got upset with Jen, I would never say anything, or yell at her, or demean her, or belittle her. I just became silent. She often said to me, "Are you angry with me?" I said, "No, I'm not angry. I'm just disappointed." Or "I'm just upset." I had more euphemisms for anger than anyone I knew because I couldn't admit my anger. But this is the key: I hadn't overcome anger by denying its existence. I just channeled my anger in a different direction. Rather than yelling, I walled up and became silent. I gave Jen the silent treatment, and she knew I was angry and she felt the effects of my anger, but I couldn't overcome anger until I admitted it.

One day after I had one of these conversations with Jen where I denied my anger, I went to my study to be alone with God. The Lord spoke to me: "Not only are you angry about this issue. You are an angry man. It's time to deal with it."

When you get a prompting like that, you have to decide if you want to get free. If you want to be free, then you must choose to live in the light with God and others. I went downstairs to Jen and told her exactly what God had told me, and I gave her permission to call me on my anger anytime I reverted back to the silent treatment.

It took about two weeks. We were driving to New York, and as we drove along I was like a stone wall. She said, rather coyly, "Are you angry at me?" I said, "Yes! Yes, I am." She asked, "Why?" I said, "I have no idea." And I didn't; I had denied anger so long I didn't know why I was, but I knew I must be because I was silent. I could feel the emotional walls that I put up when I was angry. I was just starting to get in touch with some of the symptoms of my anger; I wasn't close to the disease yet. I said, "If you let me drive quietly for a while, I'll go inside and process and figure it out. Then we can talk."

We drove in silence for two hours as I processed, but after two hours I said, "I've got it. I said most of my anger is because I had a selfish goal, and you didn't do what I wanted. That's on me, and that's 75 percent of it. But the way you rejected my request was hurtful to me." I owned my part, she owned her part, and I was beginning to learn how to deal with my anger in a healthy way. That one victory didn't eliminate the entire struggle, by any means, but I was growing in self-awareness and starting to go through the gateway to victory.

Take the necessary time to reflect on your own family. What are some of the patterns that you see? How have those sin patterns affected you? Embrace the truth; it is the only path to freedom.

Don't Compromise

As you work to overcome family sin patterns, you have to be careful not to compromise. Because the undertow of these patterns is so strong, you have to be careful not to get sucked out to sea by the pull of these sins.

I was once swimming in the ocean at Cape Hatteras, North Carolina, and there was a riptide. At the time, I did not understand about riptides, or how to break them. I was with a group of friends, and we were out riding waves. We had been out there all day, and I was tired. I decided I'd ride one more wave. We were out over our heads, and were treading water waiting for the next wave to come. But I got too tired and decided to swim back. I swam for a little while, looked up, and realized I was farther from the shore than when I had started. I put my head down and swam harder but made no progress. I started to panic. I was caught in a riptide. I won't leave you in suspense: I got through it, and back to shore, but when I got to shore I just collapsed on the beach in utter exhaustion. The riptide effect of these sin patterns is so strong that it can pull you out to sea. Even after you have apparently overcome one of these areas, if you start to dabble around the edges again, you may find yourself lost at sea.

You have to create a zero tolerance policy for these difficult areas of your life. In the Christian life, there are some gray areas. Paul talks to the church at Corinth about food sacrificed to idols (1 Corinthians 8). They lived in a culture in which, often, the meat that they purchased in the marketplace had been sacrificed to an idol before going to market. So some people didn't eat meat purchased from the market because they weren't sure if that meat had been offered to an idol.

Paul could eat food that he purchased at a market without it bothering his conscience. But he understood that this was a questionable thing to many. And Paul tells the Corinthians that in the matter of questionable things they should use their knowledge but limit it by love. One person may be able to eat food purchased in the market, another might not because their conscience will bother them. But a person who has freedom should not use that freedom to cause another to stumble (1 Corinthians 8:9).

I think one of the principles in this passage is that there are some things that are permissible for other Christians that are off limits for you. There are some areas of our lives that are questionable areas for us but may be perfectly legal and acceptable for others.

For example, if you have a long history of alcoholism in your family, and you know that you have an addictive personality type, it would be unwise for you to drink. These susceptible areas are places in your life where you cannot afford to compromise. A compromise in these areas could lead to greater consequences. You need to set greater restrictions on yourself in these areas for the sake of your freedom.

It's like a fence. Imagine you live on a busy street with small children. You are fearful that your children may get hurt playing near the street, so you put up a fence. The fence is there to protect your children. It actually gives them more freedom to play—without concern—in the yard. It is the same way with these family sins: you may need to put up some fences in your life that will give you more freedom.

Take a few moments right now and examine your life. Look at your family patterns. Where do you have vulnerabilities in family sins that need more protective measures? Where can you use a no-compromise policy? How can you set up a few safe fences that ultimately give you more freedom?

Get Help

As you seek to break family sin patterns, it's important to get help. Use all the human resources available to you to break through. Sadly, because these areas are often reinforced with shame and secrecy, people are frequently reluctant to reach out for the help they so desperately need.

I reached out to Martin that day in the car because I was more concerned with break-

It often helps to work through these areas with a wise spiritual guide, to radically repent, be completely honest, and pray through the strongholds that confront you.

110

through than I was with reputation or image. It often helps to work through these areas with a wise spiritual guide, to radically repent, be completely honest, and pray through the strongholds that confront you. That day Martin listened, prayed, and offered support and advice. Over the years, he continued to be an invaluable resource as I battled to stay pure.

As part of my plan to access all the human resources I could, I also developed some gracious prayer partners who I determined to have a no-pretending policy with since I was seeking to gain victory. In the early days, I determined that if I were struggling with lust, I would send my friend Rich an email. We would pray for each other. I would keep my confessions current; there would be no hiding. I also made a covenant with him and Jen that if I even had synergy with another woman, I would tell them. I wouldn't wait until I was struggling with an emotional attachment or lust; I would let them know if I was even in danger of *developing* an attachment. If I was looking forward to being with someone because I enjoyed their company, yet never had an unwholesome thought about them, I would still let them know that I had synergy with this woman, and I would solicit their prayers.

I know some people would say to me, "That's over the top." Maybe for someone else, but it wasn't for me. I know the havoc sexual sin had wreaked on my family, and I know the pull it had in my soul. I wasn't going to play around the edges of this one.

If I have to fight a giant, I know this: I won't go it alone! Family sin patterns are giants that threaten your freedom. Get all the help you can. Don't let your pride cripple you and allow the giants to take over the land.

Deal Severely with Your Sin Patterns

Jesus said in Matthew 5:27-30:

You have heard that it was said, "Do not commit

111

adultery." But I tell you that anyone who looks at a woman lustfully has already committed adultery with her in his heart. If your right eye causes you to sin, gouge it out and throw it away. It is better for you to lose one part of your body than for your whole body to be thrown into hell. And if your right hand causes you to sin, cut it off and throw it away. It is better for you to lose one part of your body than for your whole body to go into hell.

Obviously, Jesus was using hyperbole. He didn't expect us to literally cut out an eye when we struggle with lust. This was Jesus' point: We need to deal radically with sin before it deals radically with us.

This is especially true when it comes to breaking free from generationally reinforced patterns of behavior. What does this look like practically? Here's one example. When Jen and I got married I said to her, "I don't want to have cable TV. I've struggled with lust. This has been a family pattern. [Though I didn't know then how deep it ran, I knew it was there.] And I don't want to fall prey to it. Would you be willing to live without cable TV?"

> If you are battling for your soul, it is better to admit your weakness and take a radical step that helps you fight for freedom than act like you're strong and end up caught in the riptide of your family's sin.

She was willing, and for a long time we didn't have a TV at all, and for most of our marriage we didn't have cable. I knew if it was in the house I would be tempted to look at things on TV that were not beneficial to my soul and would cause me to lust. I wanted to be man of God.

I know religious people who would say, "Well, just don't

do that." Great advice, and I appreciate it. But if you are battling for your soul, it is better to admit your weakness and take a radical step that helps you fight for freedom than act like you're strong and end up caught in the riptide of your family's sin.

Now we have a TV and we have cable, but I didn't watch it for so long that it has no appeal to me at all. I travel quite a bit and spend a lot of nights in hotel rooms. Over the last few years I've turned on the TV in a hotel room one or two times—to catch a baseball playoff game. Dealing severely with the sin pattern was one of the important steps I took toward victory.

Reflect on your own life. Which family sin patterns have enough pull on your soul that they demand you deal with them severely? What severe steps can you take to deal with this sin pattern?

Practice Spiritual Disciplines

Another tool to help you overcome family sin patterns is practicing spiritual disciplines that counteract your family sin. Engaging in certain disciplines will help you counteract certain sin patterns more effectively. For example, if you are struggling with an addictive behavior, whether your addiction is drugs, alcohol, food, or lust, you may try fasting.

> Engaging in certain disciplines will help you counteract certain sin patterns more effectively.

Addictions have a couple of things in common: they are rooted in shame, and they are narcissistic. Because addictions are focused on self-gratification, practicing a spiritual discipline that focuses on self-denial counteracts the behavior. You may want to go on a longer fast, for a couple of weeks, to break through, and then add fasting to your regular spiritual practices. Of course there is also spiritual power in fasting, but just using a discipline that counteracts your self-gratifying tendencies has power to help you overcome.

You may also want to consider deeds done in secret. Again, there is no gratification there. If you give someone a secret gift, and you don't tell anyone about it, I mean absolutely no one, there is no gratification in it from people's approval, or from looking good. You have done the deed out of the sheer desire to do a good deed. All acts of self-denial help break the pattern of self-gratification.

Let's say you wrestle with co-dependency or people pleasing. Try engaging in solitude and silence. Listen for the whispers of the Spirit, for the Father's voice of love in your time of silence. His affirmation will break your need for people's approval. If you don't know how to hear God's voice, I wrote a chapter on this in my book River Dwellers, and it provides some very practical help. Being alone will keep you from trying to please others. And in the Father's approval, you will discover freedom.

If your family is proud and pretentious, engage in a total life confession, and update your confessions regularly. Stop defending yourself when someone points out your wrongdoing. Get alone with God, listen, and honestly reflect over what has been said. Then take every opportunity you can to apologize and admit when you are wrong. A confessional lifestyle will begin to break down the walls of pride that have been strengthened throughout the generations.

You may also want to engage in secret acts of kindness—again, there is no credit there to be had, so the acts of secrecy are for you and God alone to notice.

Think about your own family sin patterns and your struggle with them. What spiritual disciplines could help you counteract them? If you aren't sure, you may want to ask the Spirit for direction. You may also want to read a book on spiritual disciplines. I recommend Richard Foster's *Celebration of Discipline.*

Meditate on Scripture

Consider meditating on Scriptures that focus on the virtue you want to construct in your life. Focus on the virtue that is opposite of the vice you are battling against. Meditation moves truth from your head to your heart. It embeds the truth of God's Word into your heart as a core value, and out of the overflow of the heart we speak and act (Matthew 12:34; Matthew 15:18, 19; Luke 6:45).

> Meditation moves truth from your head to your heart. It embeds the truth of God's Word into your heart as a core value, and out of the overflow of the heart we speak and act .

I often don't notice things. I can walk right through a room in our house where things are out of place and not even notice the mess. I have also had to battle selfish tendencies. This is a bad combination for marriage. Jen feels most loved when I notice and when I help. I am good at speaking words of affirmation to her and expressing my heart to her, but she needs me to notice and serve.

Lust feeds self-centeredness; it is all about self. We objectify people and use them for our own selfish gratification. I eventually realized that my own selfishness and family sin pattern contributed to my marriage problems. To help overcome, I began to meditate on Philippians 2:3, 4. Paul writes, "Do nothing out of selfish ambition or vain conceit, but in humility consider others better than yourselves. Each of you should look not only to your own interests, but also to the interests of others."

I wrote the verses down. I memorized them. For one season of my life, I meditated on them every morning and as I went through the day. I noticed that I began to drive differently—I was less aggressive and more gracious. Jen noticed, too. I was more helpful around the house, and she said to me one day, "What happened to you? You're more helpful." I told her I had been meditating on this verse. Just meditating on the virtue I wanted to build into my life helped me break free from some of the selfishness in my soul.

What virtues do you need to build into your life, given your family sins? What Scriptures can you begin to meditate on and pray into your life?

JOSEPH: BREAKING FREE FROM FAVORITISM

Let me end this chapter by returning to Joseph. Joseph was greatly affected by the family sin of favoritism. It wasn't just that his brothers hated him. He developed an attitude of pride, and he struggled with comparing himself with others. This is typical of someone who has experienced favoritism in his or her upbringing. They are competitive and comparative; they are always seeking to establish their pecking order, fearful that their place in life may be lost.

In the beginning of the story, it says that Joseph "brought a bad report" about his brothers (Genesis 37:2). I don't see any indication that his brothers were lazy good-for-nothings. He brought a bad report about them because his father's favoritism had created a comparative battle between him and his brothers. The only way Joseph could stay on top was by being better than others. So he tore them down to keep his position as the favorite and to reassure himself that he was actually better than them.

That's the way favoritism works. You don't feel secure in your favored post; you have to fight to keep it. Favoritism creates animosity between siblings, jealousy in the ranks, division between family members, pride, and toxic shame.

Joseph had two dreams; they were dreams about his prophetic destiny. But in both dreams, his brothers bowed down to him. In his pride, he unwisely reported the dreams to his brothers—to tweak them a bit, no doubt. They were more than a little tweaked. I think it is fair to say they overreacted, and they sold him into slavery.

I have often wondered why God gave this brash, proud, 17-year-old insecure kid these dreams. He obviously couldn't handle them emotionally. I think the answer is that before God meets you in your damaged places, and breaks you free from your dysfunction, He often gives you a picture of what you can become. The prophetic picture can steady you in the breaking, healing, and rebuilding process that is to come so that you can reach your potential.

Joseph ended up in Potiphar's house, and the Lord was with him and gave him success (Genesis 39). The favor of God was on him. Joseph wasn't in slavery because God was angry with him over his pride; this wasn't punishment. Yes, he was a brash, proud, unwise young man, but God loved him—even as he was. This experience was about shaping; it wasn't about condemning.

Ironically, what God used to heal the favoritism of Joseph's family dysfunction was the favor of the Father. Favoritism negatively shaped Joseph and made him proud, but God's favor would humble him, and in his humility, Joseph would discover both healing and security. God wasn't trying to knock him down a peg; God was restoring a man who had been damaged by a family system rooted in generations of favoritism.

God healed Joseph's soul with His unmerited favor—not favor because of Joseph's birth position, or from being the son of Jacob's favored wife; it was not favor based on what Joseph did or what he had. It is a revelation of the unmerited favor of God that cures the proud and heals the soul.

Potiphar noticed the hand of God upon Joseph and promoted him to a leadership position. Sadly, Potiphar wasn't the only one who noticed. His wife noticed too. Joseph was a good-looking young man, one who had confidence because of the favoritism that had been bestowed on him, and he knew how to dress well! This woman tried to seduce him, and Joseph ended up in prison because he was falsely accused.

> It is a revelation of the unmerited favor of God that cures the proud and heals the soul.

Notice what happened. In the beginning of the story, the author told us that Jacob robed Joseph in an ornamental robe, and Joseph brought a bad report about his brothers. But, now, while fleeing from Potiphar's wife, she grabbed his robe and Joseph is disrobed; she created a bad report about him! God turned the tables on the young man.

Again, this wasn't punitive; rather, it was developmental. In order to restore him, God had to break down the damage of the family sin pattern. He had to strip Joseph of his pride and self-reliance. Joseph would not have the character needed to achieve his destiny with integrity unless he dealt with the bondage of his family sins.

Joseph went to prison, but once again, he found the favor of God there. Genesis 39:20, 21 reads, "But while Joseph was there in prison, the Lord was with him; he showed him kindness and granted him favor in the eyes of the prison warden." Again, Joseph was promoted to a leadership position.

Joseph started to learn an important lesson. He was not favored because he was better than others. He was not favored because of what he did or what he had or what he wore or even because of what his father thought of him. He was favored because God was with him; it was the unmerited favor of God, the grace of God, that was curing the sin pattern of favoritism in his soul. God must meet us in our unbroken, unsurrendered soul-damaged places before He can take us to our greatest kingdom potential.

While Joseph was in prison, two of the king's men who were imprisoned had dreams: the cupbearer and the baker. This, of course, must have reminded Joseph of his dreams. They were upset because no one was there to interpret their dreams, but Joseph offered to interpret them. I love this, because it reveals to us that Joseph was not hardened, nor had he grown skeptical in spite of his hardship. He was still holding on to his dreams. The favor of God was received in his soul, and it kept his heart soft.

Joseph interpreted the men's dreams and asked the cupbearer, who was restored as Joseph predicted, to remember him when he returned to power. But the man forgot! Two years later, Pharaoh had a dream that disturbed him, and the cupbearer suddenly remembered Joseph.

The story continues: "So Pharaoh sent for Joseph, and he was quickly brought from the dungeon. When he had shaved and changed his clothes, he came before Pharaoh. Pharaoh said to Joseph, 'I had a dream, and no one can interpret it. But I have heard it said of you that when you hear a dream you can interpret it.' 'I cannot do it,' Joseph replied to Pharaoh, 'but God will give Pharaoh the answer he desires'" (Genesis 41:14-16).

Notice the pattern: Jacob robed Joseph with an ornamental robe at the beginning of the story, and Joseph gave a bad report about his brothers. Potiphar's wife disrobed Joseph, and she gave a bad report about him in the middle of the story. And now, at the end, Joseph is re-robed, and a good report is shared about him. All of these years in slavery, in prison, all these years of being forgotten, all these years under God's favor, accomplished something in Joseph's heart that no one noticed. No one but God.

The unbroken man became broken. The man who gained his sense of worth because of his superiority became humble. The man who based his identity in comparison and favoritism was now a man who had an identity rooted in the unmerited favor of God. His soul had been deeply healed, and now he was ready for the destiny God had carved out for him from the beginning.

The person whose security is rooted in being better than another is never secure, lest a better person come along. But the person whose security is rooted in God's grace is secure, because God's grace is an unending source. The favor of God rendered a change in Joseph's heart, and when Pharaoh complimented his capacity to interpret dreams, Joseph replied, "I cannot do it, but God will." No longer proud, no longer self-reliant, this humble, secure man was ready. Joseph was now promoted, and the dream was fulfilled.

No matter how dark your family dysfunction, no matter how strong the riptide of your sin patterns, God can set you free. There is no soul in bondage beyond God's redemptive reach; there is no sin damage beyond God's reparative presence. God wants to meet you in your unbroken, unsurrendered soul-damaged places—and in doing so He can take you to your greatest kingdom potential.

SPIRITUAL ACTION STEPS

- What are the sin patterns in your family? You may want to take time to do a genogram. This is a family tree diagram that displays your family sin history so you can see patterns and grow in self-awareness. At various sites online, you can find help to create a genogram.

- How do those family sin patterns manifest themselves in your life? Be honest.

- What actions do you need to take to overcome them? What gracious prayer partners can help you? What spiritual disciplines would be most important to you? What Scriptures do you need to meditate on?

SOUL CARE PRINCIPLE #4

FORGIVENESS

When I graduated from seminary, I became the assistant pastor of a church in New England. I had only been there about a month when the secretary came to me and asked, "Do you know John Smith?" I said, "No. I don't think I've met him." She said, "I saw him at breakfast this morning, and he told me you were in an affair." I said, "John *who*?" I didn't even know John, but now I wanted to! I told the secretary, "I've never slept with anyone but my wife. Who is this guy?"

A couple of weeks went by, and someone else came to me and asked, "Do you know John Smith?" "No," I responded, "but I'm starting to know him. Why?" They said, "I was talking to him the other day, and he said you stole money from the church." I explained that I didn't even have access to the finances.

A couple of more weeks passed. I still hadn't met John, but

more people came and reported to me that he was spreading lies about me. I was livid.

A little while later, the district superintendent called me. "Do you know John Smith?" I said, "Not really, but I've heard a lot about him!" He said, "Well, he called the district office and told me that you are in an affair and you have stolen money from the church. I know it isn't true, but I just called to tell you to watch your back. For whatever reason, this guy is out to get you. And you aren't the first pastor he has come after." I thanked him for the warning.

I tried to set up a meeting with John so I could confront him according to Matthew 18. I also tried to take it to the leadership of the church, but they didn't want to address it with him. John wasn't willing to meet with me, and he never repented. Each Sunday morning he would come by and shake my hand with a big phony smile and say, "Nice to see you today, pastor." I wanted to stick my foot out and trip him!

What do you do when people have deeply hurt you? What if they won't own it, and they won't repent? The answer is as clear in Scripture as it is uncomfortable: you forgive them.

THE MARK OF THE FATHER

Jesus said, "You have heard that it was said, 'Love your neighbor and hate your enemy.' But I tell you, love your enemies and pray for those who persecute you, that you may be children of your Father in heaven" (Matthew 5:43-45).

In Matthew 6, Jesus taught us to pray: "Forgive us our debts, as we also have forgiven our debtors" (v. 12). He went on to say, "For if you forgive others when they sin against you, your heavenly Father will also forgive you. But if you do not forgive others their sins, your Father will not forgive your sins" (Matthew 6:14, 15).

We don't get any credit, according to Jesus, for loving our

friends—even the pagans do that. But when we love our enemies, we are marked by the Father's love. The single greatest indicator that we have been infected with divine love is our capacity to love our enemies. It is the mark of the Father on our lives.

Ephesians 4:26, 27 says, "'In your anger do not sin.' Do not let the sun go down while you are still angry, and do not give the devil a foothold." The Greek word for foothold is topos: an inhabited place. Paul was warning us to deal with our anger quickly lest Satan get the upper hand in our souls. If we don't take the high ground and forgive, Satan will take up ground in our souls.

> The single greatest indicator that we have been infected with divine love is our capacity to love our enemies. It is the mark of the Father on our lives.

Harboring unforgiveness is like putting up a welcome sign in our souls for the enemy to come in and wreak havoc, and he never rejects such an invitation. Paul wasn't saying it is a sin to be angry. He was reminding us that when we are angry, we are more likely to sin. Our anger can lead us out of the river of God's presence and into some very dark places, so we need to be careful. We need to deal with our anger quickly so we don't develop any bitter roots.

Paul went on to say, "Be kind and compassionate to one another, forgiving each other, just as in Christ God forgave you" (Ephesians 4:32). Forgiving others is vital to our spiritual well-being. Jesus spoke about it often because we often get hurt in relationships. We get offended at home by our spouse, children, parents, and siblings; we get hurt in the workplace by coworkers, customers, and bosses. We get annoyed with inconsiderate friends and rude neighbors. Life in a fallen world is fraught with opportunities for conflict.

Our Part and God's Part

In Luke 17, Jesus had one of His many dialogues with His disciples over offenses. Luke 17:1-3: "Jesus said to his disciples: 'Things that cause people to stumble are bound to come, but woe to anyone through whom they come. It would be better for you to be thrown into the sea with a millstone tied around your neck than for you to cause one of these little ones to stumble. So watch yourselves.'" Jesus was simply stating the obvious. People sin, and others suffer the ill effects. We sin, and others are left in the backwash of our bad decisions. Sin has consequences on relationships. Sin is bad, but sinning in such a way that it causes others to sin is worse.

Jesus warned us to be careful not to influence others down the path of sin; we must watch ourselves. But His teaching leads Him to make a jump in logic, because He anticipates his disciples' response. He immediately turns the conversation from when we sin and its affect on others to when they sin and how that affects us. In both cases, Jesus keeps the focus on our responsibility, because it is the only thing we can control.

In Luke 17:3, 4, Jesus goes on to say, "If a brother or sister sins against you, rebuke them; and if they repent, forgive them. Even if they sin against you seven times in a day and seven times come back to you saying 'I repent,' you must forgive them."

Jesus says we must forgive when people sin against us, even if they are repeat offenders. This is getting tough for the disciples to swallow. So they raise a flag. In the next verse, the apostles said to the Lord, "Increase our faith!" Jesus replied, "If you have faith as small as a mustard seed, you can say to this mulberry tree, 'Be uprooted and planted in the sea,' and it will obey you" (v. 6).

The apostles were saying to Jesus, "We can't do this! This is too hard! You have to increase our faith." They were trying to shift responsibility for this away from themselves and onto

> The smallest amount of faith in the God of the impossible is more than sufficient to do all God requires of you.

God! One of the trickiest parts of walking with Jesus is sorting out our part from God's part. And sometimes when following Jesus feels really hard, we want to shift our responsibility onto God's plate; that's why the disciples say, "Increase our faith!"

Jesus' response is thought-provoking. He tells them if they will have faith only as large as one of the smallest-known seeds, they can uproot a tree and throw it into the sea. The smallest amount of faith in the God of the impossible is more than sufficient to do all God requires of you. But forgiveness isn't about faith. So what is it about?

Jesus finished the conversation with a parable:

> Suppose one of you has a servant plowing or looking after the sheep. Will he say to the servant when he comes in from the field, "Come along now and sit down to eat?" Won't he rather say, "Prepare my supper, get yourself ready and wait on me while I eat and drink; after that you may eat and drink"? Will he thank the servant because he did what he was told to do? So you also, when you have done everything you were told to do, should say, "We are unworthy servants; we have only done our duty" (Luke 17:7-10).

Forgiveness is a matter of obedience, not a matter of more faith. Forgiveness is *your* responsibility and choice, not God's responsibility. Forgiveness is the duty of a faithful follower made possible by the grace he or she has received. You have to choose to forgive. You have to resolve to release people from your debt. You have to determine not to get even, not to hold onto a grudge. It is a duty of the servant of a cross-bearing Savior.

WHY SHOULD WE FORGIVE?

Some may object and say, "But if you knew what was done to me, you would never ask me to forgive. Why should I forgive this person after what they did to me?" Let me provide some motivations on why you should forgive before we explore how to forgive.

Forgive Because You Are Forgiven

First, you ought to forgive others because God has forgiven you. This is where the discussion begins and ends. In another conversation Jesus has with His disciples about this painfully difficult subject of forgiveness, Peter asked the Lord, "How many times shall I forgive someone who sins against me? Up to seven times?" (Matthew 18:21).

It seemed a pretty generous offer from Peter! Seven was the perfect number, and the rule of thumb for the day was to forgive someone three times, so he was doubling that and adding one. I think Peter felt pretty good about this one, magnanimous even! But Jesus quickly puts out any good feelings with a mind-numbing answer: "I tell you, not seven times, but seventy-seven times" (Matthew 18:22). Some translations say seven times seventy, but listen, whether the number Jesus said was seventy-seven or four hundred and ninety, I think His point is clear: quit counting!

To seal the deal on this teaching, Jesus tells another story:

> Therefore, the kingdom of heaven is like a king who wanted to settle accounts with his servants. As he began the settlement, a man who owed him ten thousand bags of gold was brought to him. Since he was not able to pay, the master ordered that he and his wife and his children and all that he had be sold to repay the debt (Matthew 18:23-25).

This is a parable of what the kingdom of God is like. This

is what kingdom people are like, because this is what the King is like, and if you follow the King, you behave like the King.

The story involves a guy who owed a debt that was about twenty years' worth of his salary. Now, think about your salary, or household income, multiply it by twenty, and picture yourself with that kind of consumer debt. The only way you could get to that level of debt would be unchecked reckless behavior. That's the context.

The master told him to sell off his possessions and his family to pay off the debt; it was time to settle accounts. This was a common practice in the Roman Empire. The first century practice of slavery was not racial in nature, it was economic.

This man had no recourse. There was no one who could help him manage this debt. There was no way he could come up with the money on his own. He had no chance to get himself out of the predicament that he found himself in by no one's fault but his own.

So he threw himself upon the mercy of the master. "The servant fell on his knees before him. 'Be patient with me,' he begged, 'and I will pay back everything.' The servant's master took pity on him, canceled the debt and let him go" (Matthew 18:26, 27).

Pause here. The master canceled a debt worth twenty years' wages because of a plea for mercy. What does this tell you about the master? The guy wasn't even asking for the cancelation! He was asking for some time with the promise that he would pay it back—but the master knew that no amount of time would allow this man to pay back this recklessly accumulated debt. So in his enormous magnanimity, the master cut the chains of debt from this man's soul and set him free. The debt was canceled: he was not sold into slavery, and his family was spared from the consequences of his irresponsible behavior. Though the debt had a price tag on it, if he could never afford to pay it back, it became a priceless gesture of release. The only appropriate response would be sheer, giddy joy and abounding gratitude—a lifelong debt of love.

But that's where the story takes a dark turn. Jesus continues the account.

> But when that servant went out, he found one of his fellow servants who owed him a hundred silver coins. He grabbed him and began to choke him. "Pay back what you owe me!" he demanded. His fellow servant fell to his knees and begged him, "Be patient with me, and I will pay you back." But he refused. Instead, he went off and had the man thrown into prison until he could pay the debt. When the other servants saw what had happened, they were greatly distressed and went and told their master everything that had happened. (Matthew 18:28-31)

This servant, who mercifully escaped being sold along with his family into slavery because of his reckless behavior, met another servant who owed him one hundred days' wages. Take your salary and multiply it by .274, and that's how much someone would owe you, if they made the same amount as you. It's a large amount of money. If you made $100,000 last year, the person would owe you $27,400. I would want that money back, too, if I had lent it out.

The man's fellow servant pleaded with the very same words that he himself had used earlier with the master: "Be patient with me, and I will pay you back." The only difference is this time the begging man actually *could* pay it back. It would take time. It would require sacrifice and hard work, but it was possible to pay off this debt. If he made $100,000 and owed $27,400, it would be similar to paying back a car loan. But the servant who just narrowly escaped lifelong bondage had no pity on his fellow servant. Even when the fellow servant fell to his knees and used the same words that he himself had spoken to the master, his conscience was not pricked, his heart was not moved, and he shook the guy down for his debt. The mercy of his master had not provoked him to become a merciful man; he threw his fellow servant into prison. It is a dark and incomprehensible scene that Jesus paints. But it gets worse, because a group of servants went and told the master what just transpired.

> Then the master called the servant in. "You wicked servant," he said. "I canceled all that debt of yours because you begged me to. Shouldn't you have had mercy on your fellow servant just as I had on you?" In anger his master handed him over to the jailers to be tortured, until he should pay back all he owed (Matthew 18:32-34).

It is a sobering parable.

The key question lingers in every soul touched by the grace of God: Shouldn't you have mercy on your fellow servant just as He has had on you? The whole point of the parable is simply this: It is utterly absurd for us to hold someone in our debt in light of the remarkable forgiveness God has offered us. He has canceled a lifetime of sin against us, for the sake of His merciful name, at the cost of His precious blood. Who are we to hold a grudge? When the mercy of the Master does not move you to become a merciful person, there is something dreadfully wrong with your soul. There is a disconnect between your head and your heart. You have truths in your head that have not permeated your heart; you have doctrines you espouse that have not been experientially transformational.

> It is utterly absurd for us to hold someone in our debt in light of the remarkable forgiveness God has offered us.

I sometimes wish that Jesus had left things unsaid. I wish He had ended the parable there, as if that wouldn't be weighty enough. But He doesn't. He goes on to make one final probe into our souls with these words: "This is how my heavenly Father will treat each of you unless you forgive a brother or sister from your heart" (Matthew 18:35). Ouch. We will be turned over to the torturers if we refuse to forgive. That leads me to my next motivating reason to release others.

Forgive So Satan Won't Get Ground

You ought to forgive because bitterness gives Satan a foothold in your life. It gives him a topos—ground, an inhabited place (Ephesians 4:26, 27). You are turned over to the jailer to be tortured.

I think the concepts that Paul and Jesus speak about are very similar. When you hold someone in your debt, the enemy gets a stronghold in your life. The stronghold of the enemy gives him access to your soul, and he torments you; he tortures you. Sometimes the bitterness that is there leads to depression. Depression is often (not always) in part a result of unprocessed anger turned inward. Sometimes the soul pain that is underneath the bitter root leads you to turn to some comfort sin pattern. You attempt to numb the pain with drinking or eating or prescription drugs or TV or pornography.

Then the enemy torments you further by shaming you for your choices. It's a vicious cycle—he tempts you to be bitter, you accept, and he torments you with the effects of bitterness. Then he tempts you to act out in some way that brings comfort to the pain in your soul that your bitterness has buried. You accept again, and he batters you with condemnation because you have sinned. You have been given over to the torturer, and he is working you over.

Until you forgive, you remain in his grip. There is no other doorway that leads out of this prison—other than to forgive as you have been forgiven.

Forgive Because Bitterness Is Corrosive

Finally, you ought to forgive because bitterness is a poison to your soul. There is an old proverbial statement that says, "Bitterness rots the soul." Someone once said, "Resentment is like drinking poison and waiting for the other person to die." The only person who dies is the person who consumes the poison. So you must forgive for your *own* sake. You must forgive for the sake of God, who has had mercy on you and is worthy of your obedience. You must forgive for the sake of your freedom and your fullness in Christ. You must forgive so you don't give the tormenter any access to your life.

Unforgiveness isn't just self-destructive; it also is corrosive to community. Hebrews 12:15 says, "See to it that no one falls short of the grace of God and that no bitter root grows up to cause trouble and defile many." Bitterness causes us to leak. We malign others, gossip against them, and spill anger. It doesn't just hurt our soul, it becomes an infectious disease in the community of believers. In the end, we cause others to stumble, which Jesus warned against. We must process our anger and forgive.

HOW DO YOU FORGIVE?

There are some very practical steps you can take in forgiving others. These are steps I have taken and they have proven effective in my journey. They are not simply theoretical concepts; I have trudged down these steps often and can testify that this is a tried and true path to freedom. I pray that they will help you, as they have helped me and countless others who have come through Soul Care classes and conferences.

Remember God's Grace

Start with remembering God's grace to you. When you are hurt, and struggling with unforgiveness, when you find yourself having imaginary conversations with the person who hurt you and rehearsing the offense in your mind, then it's time to remember God's grace.

The unmerciful servant failed to take this step. He rehearsed his fellow servant's offense, and his own losses, but he failed to remember the master's grace to him. You can't rehearse your hurt and remember God's grace at the same time.

To help me remember God's mercy, I often listen to worship music that centers on the grace of God. I sing the songs. I let them soak over me. I meditate on Scriptures that boldly proclaim the merciful heart of the Father. I may read over the accounts of Jesus' death on the cross for me and contemplate the price that Jesus paid for my ransom. I may return to this parable in Matthew 18 of the unmerciful servant or perhaps read the passage in Luke 17:1-10. I set my heart on the grace of God.

Sometimes I get out my journal, and I begin to write down all the sins I have committed that God has forgiven, and I recall God's mercy with a grateful heart. Usually by the time I get to the second page, I'm feeling more gracious. Set your heart on the grace of God.

Pray Blessings

Second, pray blessings on those who have sinned against you. In Luke 6:27, 28, Jesus said, "But to you who are listening I say: Love your enemies, do good to those who hate you, bless those who curse you, pray for those who mistreat you."

I began the chapter with the story of the man who spoke lies about me behind me back. One day I was seething over what this man had done; I had just heard from the district superintendent, and I was angry. I was talking with God about it, and I heard the whisper of the Spirit. He prompted me to read this verse from Luke 6. I knew the verse, but I didn't want to read it.

I said, "Lord, I don't want to read that verse. How about some of the Psalms— those imprecatory psalms of David, where David prays for you to get his enemies— how about we read those?" He was unmoved and unrelenting; He is a merciful Master—not just to me, but to my enemies as well.

I went on. "Lord, I know that verse. I know what you said, but you didn't really mean that stuff." As soon as I said that, I thought about what Jesus said about his enemies on the cross: "Father forgive them, they know not what they do."

I said, "OK, Lord, you meant it. But you don't really expect me to pray blessings on this man, do you?" I knew the answer deep within my soul: He absolutely did. He meant every word of it. So I relented. I said, "Lord, OK. I'll pray blessings—but not for him, I'll do it to obey you, because I love you. But you need to know, I don't mean a word of it. I'm willing to mean it, but I can't change my heart. I can obey, so I'll obey."

And with that, I started praying blessings. They didn't sound very sincere, but I did the best I could in the moment. I prayed, "Lord, I pray you would bless John. I pray his wife would like him, if that is even possible. I pray his kids wouldn't turn out to be like him, somehow!" I went on praying blessings like that, and I continued to do it every day. Day in and day out, I kept praying.

I would see him in church on Sunday, and he would smile and say, "It's so good to see you." But I knew he was still speaking lies about me. I kept praying blessings on him. Over time, my prayers started sounding more sincere: "Lord, I pray that he would know your love. He would know your peace. I pray that you would help him to repent so he doesn't have to live with this bitterness in his soul."

One day he came past me at the front door on a Sunday morning, shook my hand, and said, "It's so good to see you" with his fake smile. I shook his hand and said, "It's good to see you"—and I meant it. I felt love surging from deep within my spirit—and I knew it was God. It wasn't me; it was Christ in me loving through me. It was a miracle.

That was the day I learned an invaluable lesson: If you do what God asks you to do, He will do what you cannot do—He will change your heart. Often we wait for God to change us before we obey. We pray, "God you need to change my heart so I can obey." That's like the disciples saying, "Increase our faith." But that's not the way it works. God calls us to obey Him, even when our hearts are not yet in alignment with Him. And as we step out in faith, with our eyes on Him in trust, we find God does a deep work in the heart.

When I pray blessings on those who sin against me, I simply pray for them all the good things I want in my life. I want to know God's love and peace and joy, so I pray that for them. I want my family to experience God's favor, so I pray that for them.

Your spirit has already been changed; it has already been perfected. When you keep your eyes on Jesus and step out in faith to obey Him, the work that has been accomplished in your spirit gets actuated in your soul. Bless those who curse you. Keep blessing them so God can work the change deep within you.

See Yourself Like Your Offender

A third way to extend forgiveness is to see yourself more *like* than *unlike* your offender. I love the wisdom of the writer of Ecclesiastes when he says, "Do not pay attention to every word people say, or you may hear your servant cursing you—for you know in your heart that many times you yourself have cursed others" (Ecclesiastes 7:21, 22). It is as if he is saying, "Don't take yourself so seriously, and quit getting so upset

> If you do what God asks you to do, He will do what you cannot do—He will change your heart.

with what others say and do against you. You know you've done the same thing."

When I have been really hurt by someone else's words or actions, I try to put myself in their shoes and I try to think, "If I grew up in their home, and had their life, I could have been like them, and I could do this same thing that they are doing." It doesn't excuse them—or me—from our bad behavior; it simply helps soften my heart and prepares me to forgive.

See yourself more like them. It will help you access forgiveness.

Offer Forgiveness at the Level of Offense

Fourth, offer forgiveness to the level of the offense. Early in my relationship with Jen, she brought up a hurt from our dating years. It wasn't the first time we had discussed it; this had come up several times before. I said, "Sweetie, we talked about this, and I asked your forgiveness, and you forgave me." She said, "I know." I said, "Why do we keep going back to it?" Jen said, "I don't know."

Then one night we talked about it again. She actually yelled at me, which may have been the only time in our marriage she shouted at me. This time when she talked about her hurt, I understood. It pierced my heart, and I got on my knees and asked her to forgive me with tears. She forgave me, and it was the last time we ever discussed the issue.

The problem was that I kept offering her a cup worth of apology, but she had a five-gallon offense. (I am indebted to Roger Barrier for this word picture.) We couldn't get through the issue until I offered her a five-gallon apology, and she offered me five gallons of forgiveness.

Learning how to listen is vitally important if you are going to forgive to the level of the offense. Often people practice what I call "content listening." Content listening is when your spouse says to you, "I need you to help more around the house." And you respond by repeating back the content in your own words: "So, you would feel more supported if I helped more around the house." We are simply making sure we understand each other with the content of what is being conveyed.

But there is a much deeper level of listening. It is what I call "emotional listening." Now, I am not just listening to the content of what you are communicating, I am also listening to the emotional tone and weight behind your words. I am picking up on the intent.

I couldn't offer Jen a five-gallon apology when I was only content listening because I didn't know there was a five-gallon hurt. I needed to hear her at a deeper level. I had to understand how deeply she was hurt. I needed to hear her heart.

Sometimes we are too quick to apologize, and it keeps us from listening at deeper levels. Don't misunderstand me: I am not saying we should be slow to apologize and quick to defend. Not at all. I am saying that sometimes we apologize quickly because we feel uncomfortable with the light that is being offered to our soul.

Imagine someone comes to you and says, "When you said this, I felt hurt." You might say, "I'm so sorry. I'm so sorry." They are a nice person; they've been trained in Christian niceness, so they say, "It's OK. I forgive you." But you are offering a cup worth of apology, and they are offering a cup worth of forgiveness.

The problem is there is a five-gallon offense, and the quick apology has led to a pseudo reconciliation. It would be better if we took time to listen to each other on a deeper level, if we gave people space to share their heart and their hurt. It would be better to ask, "Help me understand how that made you feel. Is there anything else you want to say?"

Only when we have come to feel the pain of our offense

can we offer an appropriate apology that suits the level of hurt the person is carrying.

Choose Forgiveness

Forgiveness is an act of the will that we must choose. Forgiveness is a gift offered by the offended party. It is never deserved or earned. Therefore, you can forgive someone unilaterally; they don't need to apologize. This is a gift from God—otherwise you would be bound to bitterness by someone's unwillingness to own their part and repent. Thankfully, this is not true; you can forgive someone if they never apologize. You can forgive someone even if they have died and can never apologize.

> Forgiveness is a gift granted by the offended party. Trust is earned. And while forgiveness is unilateral, reconciliation is bilateral; it requires that both parties fully participate.

However, there is a difference between forgiveness and trust. Forgiveness is a gift granted by the offended party. Trust is earned. And while forgiveness is unilateral, reconciliation is bilateral; it requires that both parties fully participate.

In order for reconciliation to occur, the offended party must fully forgive to the level of the offense: if there is a five-gallon offense, there must be five gallons of forgiveness. And the offender must fully repent to the level of the offense: he or she must offer a five-gallon apology. Only then can trust can be re-established and the relationship reconciled. When someone is unwilling to repent, you can still fully forgive them, but the relationship will be shallow at best.

Forgiveness is a choice to release the person from your debt.

Resolve not to nurse a grudge or rehearse the offense. I try to monitor my self-talk and what is flowing through my mind. If I find myself having an imaginary conversation with someone who has hurt me, or if I am thinking about the incident, I use these as triggers to remind me that I need to bless the person. As soon as I catch my thinking drifting down these paths, I re-affirm my decision to forgive them and release them from my debt, and I start praying blessings on the person. The enemy is pretty reluctant to continually bring up the hurt if it inspires me to pray a blessing on my enemy! You must choose to offer the gift of forgiveness.

Process Through Forgiveness

Forgiveness can feel like a process. At times it is like an onion, and it comes off in layers. It can be a little disheartening to someone who thinks they have worked through forgiveness only to feel resentment rise again. But don't be discouraged. Keep affirming the decision you have made, and keep praying blessings on the person who has sinned against you. Keep working through the process of forgiveness.

Sometimes forgiveness feels like a process because you are not aware how deep the hurt goes. You are offering a cup of forgiveness, but there is a lot more hurt down in your soul. You have to keep processing through until you have fully forgiven.

Sometimes forgiveness feels like a process because you are in a relationship with someone who keeps hurting you and they aren't repenting or offering an apology that is commensurate with the offense.

You need to clearly establish appropriate boundaries. There is a difference between a shield and a boundary. A shield is something I pick up to protect myself. I can pick up defensiveness, anger, withdrawal, or silence as a shield, and I can use that shield to keep the offender away from me and protect myself. It neither protects my dignity nor the dignity of the other person.

But a boundary is used to preserve both my dignity and the other person's dignity. When I put up a healthy boundary, I don't stoop to the level of someone else's dysfunction, and I call the other person to live at a higher level too, and this preserves the dignity for both of us.

For example, let's say someone meets with me at the office and they are angry with me about something. Imagine they start yelling at me and calling me names (which has happened to me before). I simply say to the person, "I want to hear what you have to say. But you have to treat me with dignity and respect. That's how I treat you. If you can reframe what you are trying to say without calling me names, and yelling at me, I would be happy to listen. If not, I'm going to ask you to leave."

I am actually putting up a healthy boundary that preserves their dignity as well as mine. I am happy to listen to them if they treat me with respect, and I am calling them to live at a higher, more mature level.

We need boundaries when people are attacking us. But shields are actually dangerous. The problem with shields is they are indiscriminate. They not only block out the person who is trying to hurt us, they block out God from trying to heal us. We need to lay down our defensive shields that are attempts at self-protection and establish healthy boundaries that arise from a desire to preserve the dignity of people for whom Christ died.

Healthy boundaries come from a healthy identity. When you know that you are deeply loved by God, you don't allow people to run over you, but neither do you seek to control others. You treat others with dignity and respect, and you require them to treat you with dignity and respect as well.

Think of boundaries as a fence. When our boundaries are violated, either we jump over into someone else's yard and try to take responsibility for their life, or we allow them to jump into our yard to take responsibility for ours. In order to have healthy boundaries, we need a clearly differentiated self. We need to know who we are, what our responsibility is, and what other people's responsibility is. I am the only one responsible for me. Too often people struggle with co-dependency, and they are trying to take responsibility for someone else's life. A classic example is when someone is an addict; the spouse often tries to take responsibility for the other person's sobriety. They are jumping fences. Stay in your own yard and take responsibility for your own life.

Establishing healthy boundaries is part of the process of learning to forgive. Otherwise you end up getting hurt over and over again in the same direction because people keep jumping over your boundary fences.

Remember That God Is Redemptive

When you are working to forgive others, it always helps to remember that God is redemptive. Paul reminds us that God can use anything that comes into our lives to make us more like Jesus (Romans 8:28, 29). He can redeem even the hurts we suffer at the hands of our enemies and use that pain to make us more like Jesus. This is always hopeful to me.

When I am hurt, I pick up this promise, and then I pray that God will redeem this circumstance in my life to make me more like Jesus. Again, this tends to soften my heart; it gives purpose to the event in my life. It doesn't excuse the person's offense, but it does give me hope and purpose in the midst of the hardship.

Invite the Holy Spirit to come and heal the wounds that have resulted from the hands of your enemies. (We will discuss this more later.) As God heals your wounds, and you experience His love and redeeming work, it makes extending forgiveness to others easier.

One day I was struggling because some people wrote negative things about me online. I was feeling hurt, angry, and struggling with rehearsing the offense. But I brought it to the Lord and I prayed blessings. The Lord led me to me to this passage from Jesus' Sermon on the Mount: "Blessed are you when people insult you, persecute you and falsely say all kinds of evil against you because of me. Rejoice and be glad, because great is your reward in heaven, for in the same way they persecuted the prophets who were before you."

As I read that passage, it was like I saw what it said for the first time. I am blessed when people insult me for what I do for Jesus. I am blessed because they have increased my reward in Heaven ("great is your reward in Heaven"). They actually help my cause! My eternal reward is getting better because of these folks. I owe them a debt of gratitude. And not only that, but they elevate me to the status of the prophets ("for in the same way they persecuted the prophets who were before you"). The Spirit changed my attitude about these sorts of attacks against me that day. I looked at what was written against me with a whole new attitude. The Lord would take it and redeem it, not just in the here and now, but for all eternity. No wonder you can rejoice and be glad when people attack you.

Grieve Your Hurts and Losses

In order to get through the process of forgiveness, it helps to grieve the hurts and losses you have suffered. Many people only associate grieving with death. But grief is about loss. You need to grieve over your losses in life: loss of relationship, loss of a dream, loss of reputation, loss of opportunity, loss of innocence, loss of love, and loss of a loved one. If you grieve your losses, you keep your heart from filling with darkness. Sometimes your affections are withered by the space pain occupies in your soul, and you cannot recapture your affections until you grieve your losses. And without grieving our losses, it is incredibly hard to work through forgiveness. Unprocessed hurts produce bitter roots.

Your expectations and your disappointments are tied together. The more you get hurt, the more your disappointments will rise. But as your disappointments rise, your expectations fall. It's like they are on an old-fashioned teeter-totter. When the one side goes up, the other side goes down. Unless you grieve your disappointments, you can't recover your expectations. Often what keeps you from grieving your disappointments is a bitter root. You have to address the bitter root and then grieve the disappointment in order to break free.

The problem is that your passions are tied to your expectations and hopes. And when your disappointments rise, and your expectations fall, your passions get displaced. You still have passion within you. But it no longer runs to the places of your former expectations, hope, and dreams. The result is that you end up with newer, unhealthy passions. You no longer have passion running toward your healthy hopes, dreams, and expectations. Instead, those displaced passions have been stopped up in bitterness and anger. Oftentimes we run toward unholy passions to numb the pain, hurt, disappointment, and bitterness that have accumulated in the basement of our soul. Again, the healthy choice is to grieve your disappointments so you can dislodge those displaced passions of bitterness and recover your healthy passions for your God-given dreams.

Your unhealthy passions may run toward bitterness and judgment and envy against others. Your unhealthy passions may run toward spending money and living the good life, settling for the pleasures of this life. Or your unhealthy passions could run to illicit pleasures that help numb your soul, like sexual sins. You must process your disappointments in order to reignite your expectations and once again channel your passions to the healthy places.

Praying the psalms can be extremely helpful in processing grief. Real life enemies who caused him heartache often chased David. Many of his psalms involve processing these dark emotions of hurt, betrayal, grief, loss, and pain, and so praying those psalms can help you process your own losses.

You must process your pain and grief for your soul to be healthy. If you trap these emotions inside, the problem isn't just that you have negative emotions like anger, your positive emotions start to close down on you as well—you feel less joy, less love, less peace. You may also start to engage in comfort sins to help you cope with the internal pain you are not acknowledging.

Whether you acknowledge it or not, the pain is there, and your soul cries out for relief. Think of your soul like a suitcase. If your suitcase is packed with a bunch of T-shirts and sweatshirts labeled *pain, hurt, disappointment, grief,* and the like, then there is no room in the suitcase for T-shirts and sweatshirts like *joy, love, peace* and *fullness of God.* You have to unpack the suitcase before you can create room for the freedom and fullness of God. Too often you have a suitcase that is three-fourths filled with soul sludge, and there remains so very little room for the fullness of God. If the suitcase of your soul is filled with hurt and anger, there is no room for joy and peace. You have to grieve and forgive to open up space in the suitcase of your soul.

The temptation for comfort in the midst of such soul pain can be overwhelming. I was speaking at a conference one day and a woman came up to me. It was late at night and she was the last person in the prayer line. Her opening line was forthright, if not shocking: "I hate everybody."

She was a neatly dressed elderly woman who had been attending church her entire life. She went on to elaborate: "I hate my husband. I hate my children. I hate my pastor." At this I stepped back a bit, just in case. But she continued, "And I am drinking in secret. No one knows." The bitterness and the hurt filled her soul. She needed something to comfort her pain-soaked soul, so she drank.

Sadly, too often in the church we just focus on behaviors. We say, "Stop that. Don't do that. Do this." So often, the issue is not the issue. And religious talk that focused on behaviors could not help this woman. The issues she battled with were in her soul.

There was only one question to ask that could help her. I simply asked, "Why don't you tell me about your pain?" She went on and spoke of the losses in her life, the hurts, the heartaches, and the pains. She had suffered a lifetime of loss and hurt, and she just kept picking herself up and doing the right thing, trudging along like a good soldier, because that's what she thought she was supposed to do. All of this pain got stuffed inside. Her heart could take no more.

I said, "Are you ready to let Jesus access your heart and your pain?" She nodded, and I prayed, "Lord Jesus, come. And drain the pain that is locked inside her heart."

The presence of God came and touched the untouchable core of pain that had been buried in her soul. She started sobbing. She wept for more than thirty minutes, tears that were long overdue. It was the beginning of a journey toward forgiveness and healing. But it had to begin with grief. She had to unpack the suitcase to make room for God. She had to grieve and forgive in order to get free and experience the fullness of God.

You have to acknowledge your pain in the presence of God so you can access his healing love. Fenelon said, "Soon time will give way to eternity and our suffering will be over. Soon God will wipe away our tears with His own hand."[7] We grieve

---

7. Francois Fenelon, *Let Go* (New Kensington: Whitaker House, 1973), p. 39.

with hope in a compassionate God who heals the broken-hearted.

CHOOSING TO FORGIVE

When I was in my mid-twenties, I went to a John Maxwell conference. He said, "I will die with no enemies. There are people who don't like me, but the feeling is not mutual." That day I made a conscious choice. Deep in my soul I made a steely resolve that I will die with no enemies. Therefore, I have decided to bless everyone who curses me. I have determined to hold no grudges, nurse no wounds, nurture no disappointments, and hang on to no resentments. I will process my anger and pain at all costs, and I will forgive my enemies. That decision has saved my life countless hours of internal anguish and torment.

> We grieve with hope in a compassionate God who heals the brokenhearted.

There are people who do not like me, but the feeling is not mutual. John Maxwell said that day that the only reason people didn't like him—or don't like you, or me—is because they lack discernment. I love that line. I've taken it as my own and added to it. I say, "The only reason people don't like me is because they lack discernment . . . because my Father likes me and He has perfect discernment."

Sadly, many times people do not choose to forgive. They come to this brink of decision and walk away with bitterness lining the walls of their soul. They simply refuse to let go. There is no freedom there. If you hold on to bitterness, your soul will be diseased. Corrie ten Boom said, "Forgiveness is the key which unlocks the door of resentment and the hand-cuffs of bitterness."[8]

You have to consciously choose to forgive those who sin against you. Denying your hurt and anger will not lead you to freedom and forgiveness. You have to consciously walk through these steps of forgiving those who sin against you. You have to decide to forgive, give up control, and let go of resentment. You have to let the person off the hook—and entrust them and yourself to God.

SPIRITUAL ACTION STEPS

- Quiet your heart before the Lord. Ask the Holy Spirit to bring up the names of anyone you need to forgive. As the names come up, write them down. Even if you think a person is someone you have already forgiven, write that name down. Don't filter.

- Consciously choose to release these people from your debt. Walk through the steps of forgiveness listed in the chapter.

- Commit to praying blessings on each one until you sense you are free from resentment.

- Commit yourself to die with no enemies, and resolve to love your enemies, forgive those who sin against you, and bless those who curse you.

---

8. Corrie ten Boom, *Tramp for the Lord* (London: Hodder & Stoughton, 1975), p. 182.

SOUL CARE PRINCIPLE #5

HEALING WOUNDS

Have you ever had an infected splinter? If you had a splinter in your thumb that was infected and I just accidentally bumped against your thumb, you would have a disproportional reaction to the impact. Even if I just barely touched your thumb, you would jump out of your skin because of the infection.

We all have splinters in our soul that get infected. Have you ever had someone say to you, "You are overreacting" or "Why are you getting so upset about this?" Or "You're blowing this out of proportion"? Chances are, they were right.

When you have past wounds that get infected in your soul, and someone bumps against them, you have a disproportional reaction. These are like infected splinters in the soul.

We all have some baggage from our past. It is just part of growing up on a sin-stained fallen planet. But some people are carrying around more hurts, hits, wounds, and dings than others. Not everyone is hurt equally or in the same way.

When I meet with people who are looking for help, the first thing I do is ask them to tell me their story. I've listened to thousands of stories from all over the world, all different cultures, and all different circumstances. Everyone is carrying around some hurts, some emotional bumps and bruises. Unless these wounds are healed, they can negatively influence our reactions, our decisions, our behaviors, and our relationships, and they are limitations to our lives. Sadly, sometimes these hurts are protected behind a fortress of defense mechanisms that keep us from accessing them. The fortress is not a healing refuge. The walls must come down, and we must let Jesus into our painful places, for He alone is the Healer.

GOD REDEEMS YOUR PAIN

The good news is that Jesus died on the cross, not only to take up our sins, but also to heal our wounds. He wants to make us whole. One of the most famous Old Testament prophecies about Jesus is found in Isaiah 53. The passage predicts Jesus' atoning work on the cross, but that work includes more than just forgiving our sins. Redemption involves making us whole.

Isaiah 53:4, 5 says, "Surely he took up our pain and bore our suffering, yet we considered him punished by God, stricken by him, and afflicted. But he was pierced for our transgressions, he was crushed for our iniquities; the punishment that brought us peace was on him, and by his wounds we are healed."

Jesus took up our pain on the cross. That Hebrew word for pain is used throughout the psalms, and it refers at varying times to physical pain, emotional pain, and spiritual pain. Jesus took up our sins and all the painful effects of sin on the cross. He bore our suffering—yes, He died in our place and suffered on our behalf because of our sin, so that we could be justified before God. But He also bore the suffering that sin causes. He took up your pain on the cross.

The punishment that Jesus suffered on the cross on our behalf brought us peace—and that certainly includes peace with God because we are forgiven. But the Hebrew word for peace is *shalom*, which also includes a sense of wholeness or well-being. Jesus' death gave us access to healing and wholeness, a deep internal peace of the soul. It is because of His wounding that we are healed.

> There are few things that mature us as much as a trusting response to a redeeming God in a time of suffering.

God can redeem the pain of our lives to make us more like Jesus. As I look back on my life, I can say I have learned more from failure than success; I've grown more in pain than in prosperity. There are few things that mature us as much as a trusting response to a redeeming God in a time of suffering.

In Romans 8:28, 29 Paul writes, "And we know that in all things God works for the good of those who love him, who have been called according to his purpose. For those God foreknew he also predestined to be conformed to the image of his Son." God can take everything, even the most tragic and painful things in our lives, to make us more like Jesus.

This doesn't mean God ordained these evil things to happen in our life. God isn't evil, and He has no evil to give. He doesn't cause people or ordain people to suffer evil like rape, molestation, or physical abuse. But God is so good that He can redeem even these horrible evil things.

James 1:5 adds to this: "If any of you lacks wisdom, you should ask God, who gives generously to all without finding fault, and it will be given to you." We often quote this verse when we are faced with a big life decision. We may be about to get married or change careers, and as we seek God's direction, we quote James 1:5.

We can quote this verse in those times of decision-making and trust God to give us wisdom, but that isn't the context of this verse. The context is: "whenever you face trials of many kinds" (James 1:2). James is saying when we are going through hardship, difficulty, and trials, and we don't know how God can redeem those to make us more like Jesus, ask Him. He will give us wisdom. He will show us how He can redeem these circumstances to mature us.

It is important for us to believe that God can redeem the pain in our life. Not that God sent it, but that God can redeem it. He turns the arrows of the enemy meant to destroy us into the scalpels of the Great Physician meant to heal us. It gives us hope in every circumstance.

> He turns the arrows of the enemy meant to destroy us into the scalpels of the Great Physician meant to heal us.

It is equally important not to associate God with the evil things that are done to us. We don't want to blame God for evil; God is good. I've heard people say, "God brought this abuse into my life for a reason." God didn't bring abuse into their life; some person perpetrated an evil act against them.

But God can redeem it.

Beyond Forgiveness

In the healing process, we will need to forgive the person who has wounded us, but even after we have forgiven, the wound itself often still needs healing. Imagine someone hits you with a baseball bat. You need to forgive the person who hit you, but there is a physical wound that still needs healing even after you forgive. More than that, there is a soul wound too, and it also needs healing, even after you have forgiven, and sometimes long after the physical effects of the wound have healed.

Let's say that your father or mother abandoned you when you were little. As a toddler you were too young to have truly processed an event like that. You didn't have the emotional development to grieve such a major loss; you simply coped and survived. But as you got older, you realized you were carrying around some soul baggage because of the abandonment you suffered. Somewhere along the way it occurred to you that you missed out on having this parent's influence in your life, like many of your friends had. You missed out on the emotional support; you were left with a love deprivation and abandonment wound.

The loss also has left you with a lot of anger toward this parent who left a void in your life. It cost you deeply, and you have to grieve that pain and loss and forgive the offense to the level of pain you have suffered. But even after grieving the loss of this parent in your life, and forgiving them for abandoning you, you will likely still suffer from the lasting effects of abandonment. Possibly every time you go through a hardship in life you feel as though God has abandoned you, and you pull away from Him, even rebel against Him. It may be that you don't trust men or women in your life, or you have bought into the lie that no one is safe; no one can be trusted. Not only do you need to forgive, you also need the abandonment wound to be healed to make your soul healthy and whole. Jesus heals.

Not all wounds affect all people in the same way. Some events may leave one person deeply wounded, and another person may process it differently and have only a slight soul bruise. We have to be very careful not to live in denial. But we are all wired differently, and we all process life through

PROCESSING YOUR PAST

I love my children dearly, and I think I am a reasonably good dad. But I am not perfect, not even close. As my children get older and get married and have children of their own, they are going to have to process their life if they want to drop some of the baggage that they carry around and become healthier people. I want them to do that because I love them and want their best.

I grew up in a reasonably healthy home with loving parents, but like me, they weren't perfect. When Jen and I got jammed up in marriage problems in those early years, I knew I needed to process my life. I was carrying around some inner wounds, and outer baggage, that affected my relationship with Jen adversely. She was carrying around inner wounds and outer baggage from her upbringing that played into our relationship as well. It was time for those childhood issues to be addressed.

Paul said, "When I was a child, I talked like a child, I thought like a child, I reasoned like a child. When I became a man, I put the ways of childhood behind me" (1 Corinthians 13:11). Sooner or later we have to take responsibility for the baggage we carry, and we have to process it, and then we can receive healing. You only become a grown-up when you take responsibility for your life and choose to put the ways of your childhood behind you. That means you must face your past, and you must process the events of your past that have contributed to your present broken ways. You must find healing, and you must change, or your soul will not be healthy. You don't look into your past to blame your parents but to take responsibility for your baggage so you can get free.

As I mentioned previously, my father had a temper when I was growing up. My brother wasn't affected by this in the same way I was. I also had separation anxiety, and I was more susceptible to being adversely affected by anger. It made me more anxious in conflict, and this shaped the way I handled conflict. I viewed conflict as a bad thing, one to be avoided. I stuffed anger because I was sensitive to it. If Jen got angry, it triggered my angst, and I would shut down. But the way I processed the events of my childhood affected the way Jen and I handled conflict in our relationship.

I had to discover why I was avoiding difficult conversations, and why I was stuffing anger, so that I could break free from these childish ways. Too often as adults we continue to deal with conflict the way we learned to deal with it as children. But we need to deal with our past, heal our wounds, and put our childish ways behind us.

Processing with Others

It is often helpful to talk to family members when you are seeking to heal your past hurts and wounds. When I was processing my own life story, I called my brother because I wanted his perspective. He lived in Texas, and I was in Massachusetts, so I had to do it by phone.

I said, "Can you give me the afternoon? I want to spend an afternoon with you on the phone and process our childhood." He just laughed. My brother is a pretty private guy, and this wasn't a typical conversation for us. But he was willing, in spite of the initial awkwardness of the moment.

We spent several hours on the phone talking through our growing-up years. We talked about our relationship, our experiences, our parents, our extended family, our friends, our schooling years, and our sports teams. It was a meaningful conversation and incredibly illuminating. We had grown up in the same home, with the same parents, the same extended family, and a lot of the same friends, but the way we processed our experiences was very different. It was an important conversation on my way toward healing.

My brother wasn't the only family member I talked with. Every family has a keeper of the family legends. It is the person others confide in, and this person keeps the family secrets; they archive the family stories. If you want to know more about your family, your past, and your family sin patterns, you have to talk to the keeper of the family legends.

So I went to talk to my grandmother because she was that person. As I mentioned earlier, I talked to her about sexual sin in our family tree, but that wasn't the only thing we talked about. We talked about the family heritage—the good things our family passed from generation to generation, as well as the dark side that was part of our story. I was not interested in uncovering my family secrets to harm anyone or to bring shame on the family. Just the opposite. I wanted to be a man of God, but I was struggling, as I said earlier, with lust and anger, and I wanted to overcome. I needed to know as much as I could about the battle I was waging.

I went to my grandmother and asked her to be honest with me. I told her I wanted to finish well. I wanted to honor God and the family. I told her how much I loved her and our family, but I needed to know more to know how to overcome. She shared openly.

The more I understood the story, the more I understood the struggles. The more I understood the story, the more my life made sense. My grandmother was a fearful woman, and over time I started to see how fear was affecting my relationships. Part of the reason I was shutting down my anger was the fear I had in my soul. We talked about fear and anxiety. I had to break through my internal hurts that led to my external baggage before I could be free to be the man I wanted to be.

In the doctoral program where I teach at Alliance

Theological Seminary, we have the students do a family voyage assignment. We ask them to interview members of their family to get the story, to discover the family blessings, to uncover the secrets, and ultimately to help them to break through and mature. It is a scary assignment, but every year we hear stories of healing and breakthrough that come from the self-discovery and honest conversations that take place. Often the families talk about things they have never talked about before; they connect in deeper ways than they ever have. Healing often results in these families. I didn't have anyone to guide me through with an assignment like this when I was on my own journey. I just knew I had some internal damage and external baggage that affected my marriage, my life, my ministry, and my walk with God, and I was desperate to get well. So I started asking questions and having some of these difficult conversations; it was healing for me and others.

One day I was having a conversation with my paternal grandmother. This conversation occurred years after I had been through my own inner healing journey; this was just a few years before my grandmother died. I was asking her questions about her past, about her story and her upbringing. On this occasion, I wasn't asking for my sake; I wanted to get to know her more, so I asked about her story.

She made a comment about her stepfather and referred to him as a "bad man." I didn't let it slip by. She had said it before, and I knew there was more to the story than had come out. I took her by the hand and said, "Nana, I've heard you say that before—that he was a bad man. Why do you say that?" She repeated, "He was just a bad man." I pressed in a little more: "Did he hurt you?" She told me that he molested her and her sisters. She had never told anyone, and she was nearing 90 years old. For nearly eight decades she had held this secret and lived with the internal pain and shame. That day I held her hand and she cried, and I cried, and I loved her with the love of Christ. And in the end, I helped her spiritually, and walked her through the process of forgiving. That conversation was a gift to her, as well as to me. These conversations are difficult, but when they are done honorably, they can be healing.

Everybody carries internal pain and external baggage that affects their relationships, their walk with God, and their well-being. It's part of being born in a sin-stained world, but there is hope. We need to process this baggage and allow Jesus to heal this pain so our soul can be healthy. It doesn't matter how good your family was, there is always some baggage.

I have one staff member who has thanked me for being there for her kids in times of crisis and helping them sort out some of the baggage of their past. I just laugh and say, "Payback is coming. I have four kids." Don't be afraid to face your past. It is necessary to find healing in the soul and put the baggage down once and for all.

HEALING THE SOUL

How do we access Jesus' healing power in our soul? Isaiah makes it clear that Jesus died on the cross and took up our pain, as well as our sin, and that His wounds are what heal us. There is healing in the cross for our soul. How are we healed? Let me lay out the big principles, and then I'll illustrate them.

Big principle #1: God isn't trying to fix us; He wants a relationship with us. There isn't a formula for healing. Often we want Him to fix us because we are in pain. Many times the reason we enter the healing journey is because we are in crisis. We want to feel better, so we come to God in desperation, and we beg and cajole Him to fix us. We want to alleviate the symptoms and pain. But God isn't interested in fixing us; He wants a relationship with us. The truth is if He fixed us, some of us would walk away from any meaningful and dependent relationship with Him because the urgency would be gone. It is in relationship that we find healing. Keep this front and center.

Sadly, sometimes we only seek God long enough to feel better; then, once we feel better, we stop seeking. We don't drain the tank of all the hurt and pain that is there because we don't press in and press through. We are more interested in comfort than we are in wholeness. We are more interested in what God can do to make us feel better than we are interested in God Himself. It is of paramount importance that we set the right goal in our spiritual journey. Our goal should not be to feel better; our goal should be to know and be like Jesus. As we get to know and become more like Him, our souls will be healthier, and that will bring its own rewards.

Big principle #2: Theology 101—God is smart, and He knows stuff we don't know, and He likes to tell us. He knows what needs to be healed, and He knows how to heal it. We have to trust Him. We have to listen to Him. This trusting, listening interaction is an essential part of relationship. He knows what we need.

If you were physically abused growing up, you will likely have many memories of abuse. You will remember specific events that occurred, times when you were abused, and rooms where those painful events took place. To find healing from the trauma of abuse, you don't have to go back to every single event of your past and relive it. But you may have to go back and face a few of those key memories to find freedom and healing from the effects of the trauma. God knows; you can trust Him. You will have to go back and call it what it was— abuse—or you will not get free from its effects. God knows what memories need to be revisited, and He knows how to bring healing to those memories and the internal wounds beneath them.

You can approach this healing on your own, but sometimes it is beneficial to have others who are sensitive to the Spirit's leadings pray with you, friends who are familiar with healing prayer. When I pray with people, the most important thing I do is listen. I listen to the person, and I listen for the Spirit's whispers. I never launch into prayer; I wait and listen for God to lead.

Big principle #3: Tell me your story. I don't do pastoral counseling anymore. Now I mostly teach in larger settings and equip people in the ministry of soul care. But most of the time when people come for help, they come with a presenting problem. They are struggling with something, which is why they have come—they are struggling with anxiety or depression or they may have marriage problems or an addiction they are battling against.

Presenting problems are usually symptoms. They are not the disease. So the first thing I always do is ask them to tell me their story. If I can listen to their story, I can usually understand why they do what they do, and how they came to where they are. I can connect the dots between their story line and their present problems, their hurts, and the lies they believe. People have an intuitive sense about the important components of their story. It's uncanny. Unless they are lying intentionally, or they have repressed memories, the vast majority of time they will tell the key events that have shaped their lives. I listen carefully to their story, and I am also listening to the Spirit of God for insights, wisdom, and revelation.

Tom came to me one day because he wasn't feeling many emotions. He was shut down. He could access anger, but that was about it. He wasn't abusive; he was a good man. But he knew something was blocking him from accessing a wider spectrum of emotion, and he knew it was robbing him of the fullness he could have in life.

So he came for help with this as the presenting problem. I asked him to tell me his story. As Tom did, the most important element involved his mother's tragic death when he was a preteen. She died in a drowning accident right in front of him and his brother. They tried to rescue her, but they were little, and they couldn't. Sadly, his father's response left him feeling blamed.

Now, if I were going to go back and pray for healing over any event in Tom's life, this would have been the event. It was, by far, the most painful, tragic event of his life, and it stood out above everything else in his story.

But I have learned not to jump to conclusions. God is smart, and He knows stuff I don't know. So rather than just assuming that God wanted to address this tragedy in Tom's life, I listened to the Holy Spirit. I said, "Tom, the Holy Spirit knows the key to unlock your emotions. I am just going to ask Him to bring any memory to your mind that He needs to address to unlock your emotions." I prayed that simple prayer, and then I waited. I explained to Tom that several memories may flit through his mind, but that one would likely stand out as compared to the others, and when he got to that memory, he should let me know. It only took a few seconds.

He said, "I've got it." I said, "What is it?" He said, "The day my father died." Now this surprised me. He hadn't even mentioned his father's death when he told his story. I asked him to tell me about it. His dad had died several years before our meeting. He lived down the road from Tom, and Tom went over to check on him one day. His dad was lying dead on the living room floor; he had died of a heart attack.

Tom said he walked over to his dad and punched him in the chest and yelled, "You son of a _____ !" And all of a sudden the Holy Spirit turned on the lights for me. That was the day he started to shut down his emotions. That was the day he gave up hope that he could have his relationship with his father restored, or that he could ever know his dad's approval. We prayed over that event. Jesus' presence was palpable, tears flowed, and God began to unlock Tom's emotions once again.

Big principle #4: Only God heals the soul. There is healing in the presence of God. If you tell me your story, I can have compassion for you. I can speak words of kindness and love to you, but I can't heal your soul from the inner wounds you have suffered. I can't heal your internal hurts or free you from your external baggage. Only God can heal the soul.

The longer I do ministry, the more I realize that I have nothing. Jesus said it: "Apart from me you can do nothing" (John 15:5). People come to me all the time because I have been involved in soul care ministry for years. They come desperate, hoping for breakthrough, and they want me to pray for them. I say the same thing all the time, and it isn't modesty: "I have nothing. Only God can heal the soul." And I mean it. I have no delusions about this. I don't have any magic. I can't fix a broken heart. My goal is simply to put a person with soul wounds in the presence of the Healer. I look to Jesus, and you must look to Jesus too. If you look to me or anyone else, you'll be disappointed. Only Jesus can heal. Look to Jesus.

> They come desperate, hoping for breakthrough, and they want me to pray for them. I say the same thing all the time, and it isn't modesty: "I have nothing. Only God can heal the soul."

The Healing Presence

One of the ways the Spirit brings healing is for the person to become aware of the presence of Jesus in a hurtful memory.

162

Jesus is always with us, even if we can't see Him or aren't aware of Him. We need to become attentive to Him.

Years ago I was in Ecuador doing a Soul Care conference for leaders. The people were extremely receptive, but there was one man sitting in the back left corner of the room who sat there with his arms folded the entire time I spoke. He did not look happy, and he was a big man; frankly, he was a little scary-looking. I kept teaching, and I would look at all the friendly Ecuadorians who were listening attentively, and I would feel encouraged. Then I would peek over into the corner, and the man was still sitting there, scowling with his arms folded, so I would go back to preaching to the friendly Ecuadorians.

I taught all day on Saturday, and his disposition never changed. I finished speaking and people came forward for prayer. I stood in line for three hours praying for people that afternoon. People confessed sins, encountered God, and experienced healing. Tears flowed, the presence of God was palpable—and that man sat there in the corner with his arms folded the entire time.

Finally, I was praying for the last person in line, and this man stood up and started coming down the aisle toward me. I checked to see if there was a back exit just in case! When he got to me, he put his hands on my shoulders and leaned his forehead within inches of my forehead and whispered, "From the moment you started speaking, I have had such a pain in my chest that I thought I was going to have a heart attack." I thought, *Oh, I'm sorry. My bad. That was pain on your face!* My own soul care issues had affected my view of this man—they are the lens through which we view life.

Instantly, two words came to my mind: Father abuse. I said to him, "You were abused by your father." He nodded. Another impression immediately flowed and I said, "You have a specific memory right now of a time when you were tortured by your father." He was crying. He told a terrible story of hor-rific torment. Again, the Spirit gave me direction and I said, "Jesus was there with you that day. I'm going to pray that you can see Him in that memory."

The memory was vivid, imprinted on his imagination by the terror he had suffered. He saw Jesus pick his father up with one hand and push him out of the room they were in. Then Jesus shut the door and picked up the small child that was being tormented, and He held him in His arms and rocked him back and forth and spoke words of tender love over him. The man wept for forty minutes, uncontrollably, as the loving presence of Jesus ministered to his inner wound.

The next day I was scheduled to preach at their church service, and this man came running up to me before the ser-vice. His face was so changed that I barely recognized him. He was speaking rapid Spanish, and I don't know Spanish, so I waved down my translator.

This was the story that emerged: the man was excited because he brought a friend with him. It was a sick woman, and he told her that I would pray for her and she would be healed. (No pressure!) But it got worse. I looked over, and the woman was in a wheelchair. I thought, *You have got to be kidding me! I don't do wheelchairs! I do inner healing on a good day!*

But, of course, God thinks He is so funny! That morning I was scheduled to preach on divine healing, and we were going to anoint the sick and pray for healing. It was a divine setup! I said to the man, "Let me preach, and then I'll pray for people who come forward for prayer. You wait to the side. And then

I'll come over to you at the end, and I'll linger in prayer with you and your friend."

He eagerly agreed, fully anticipating a miracle; I wasn't so sure. I preached. We prayed for some sick people. And then I made my way over to the woman in the wheelchair. As I was walking toward her, I heard the Spirit of God whisper to me, "The woman who touched the hem of my garment."

I got my translator and give him some instructions for the woman. I wanted to know if she was a believer. I asked him to read James 5 and check if her confessions were current. And then I asked if she knew the story of the woman who touched the hem of Jesus' garment. She was a believer, she updated her confessions, and she knew the story.

I told her to picture herself as the woman in the story, and to reach out and take Jesus by the hem of the garment. I asked her to close her eyes and just picture herself holding Jesus' hem and then to wait on Jesus and watch what Jesus did and listen to what He said. That was all I had, and I waited with her. I have nothing. So I just kept my eyes on Jesus. Only Jesus heals—whether body or soul. Only Jesus heals.

After waiting a little while, I asked her what was happening; she said Jesus had stopped. I thought, *Well, of course he stopped, you grabbed the hem of his garment.* She said, "He turned around, and he's touching my legs." This is good. My faith started building a bit, and I prayed for divine heat; often when God heals someone they feel heat. I wasn't praying out loud; I was praying this silently, and suddenly she said something in Spanish. I asked for the interpretation and the translator said, "She said she is sweating. She feels like her legs are on fire." I said, "Tell her this is good! This is good!" Now I was feeling more faith, and I prayed, "Mas fuego! Mas fuego!" I don't know much Spanish, but I had that one covered!

About twenty minutes later, the woman said that the fire was all gone, and the only pain she had left in her legs was

When you encounter the manifest presence of Jesus in miraculous power, it increases your faith for the next miracle.

where she had received a pain-killer shot earlier that week. She then proceeded to stand up and walk for the first time in three years; she walked across the platform to give testimony that Jesus heals. Now that is a good day in the Kingdom!

I did not have the faith to believe that woman would be healed, but that big Ecuadorian man who had encountered Jesus' healing presence did. When you encounter the manifest presence of Jesus in miraculous power, it increases your faith for the next miracle. You may be one encounter away from the miracle for which you long.

HEALING MEMORIES: SANCTIFYING THE IMAGINATION

Sometimes people are troubled by this use of the imagination. Some have even attacked it, fearful that something bad will happen. To me, this is sad; religion always instills fear. If you are seeking Jesus, and centered on Jesus, you don't have to be afraid. He isn't nervous.

God gave us our mind and our imagination. He has told us to renew our mind. Our minds have been damaged by some of the tragic events which we have locked away in our memories, and God can renew our mind by revealing Jesus' presence in these past events and healing our memories by involving our imaginations.

Acts 2:17, 18 says, "In the last days, God says, I will pour out my Spirit on all people. Your sons and daughters will prophesy, your young men will see visions, your old men will dream dreams. Even on my servants, both men and women, I will pour out my Spirit in those days, and they will prophesy."

This prophetic word of Joel, which Peter quotes on the day of Pentecost, indicates that in the last days, which biblically began with the resurrection of Jesus and remain until He returns, the people of God will experience God's speaking to them through prophetic words. These prophetic words include prophetic images—dreams and visions. God gives His people prophetic images to meet them, encounter them, speak to them, and renew their minds. God sanctifies our imaginations with His prophetic pictures. This is part of the way He heals the soul with His presence and His voice. Keep your eyes on Jesus, trust the Holy Spirit, and believe what the Scripture promised in Acts 2. He can give you a prophetic picture that can heal a past memory.

Paul tells us that when a prophetic word comes, there is a manifestation of the Lord's presence: "Now to each one the manifestation of the Spirit is given for the common good" (1 Corinthians 12:7). Paul then lists through various revelatory gifts that fall under the umbrella of the prophetic. These gifts are revelatory in nature—they reveal something about God. When one of these revelatory gifts is demonstrated there is a manifestation of God's presence. That is why God sometimes gives people a picture of a past memory infused with Jesus' presence; as His presence is manifest, healing occurs.

Leanne Payne was a Wheaton College graduate, a high church charismatic, who was a leader in the inner healing movement. She said that the language of the heart is symbol. Words often do not heal the heart. God gave us our imaginations, and He gives us prophetic pictures, dreams, and visions that bring healing to our damaged souls, which have been afflicted with painful memories. We have soul bruises from past events and memories, but Jesus was present at the time of our wounding, and often a revelation of His presence, a picture of His presence, accompanied by His voice, can allow the healing to flow to our souls.

Again, I want to caution, this isn't a formula. Sometimes I sense the Holy Spirit leading me to go back into a past memory, to pray for people to see Jesus, and to ask them to watch and listen. But there isn't any magic to this method. The key is the presence of Jesus. Jesus heals, not the method.

Blocks to Healing Memories

Sometimes you will try to access the presence of Jesus in a memory, but you may run into a block that requires discernment. Again, you can do this on your own, but you may need the help of some people who are discerning and sensitive to the Spirit. If you are trying on your own, and can't get through a block, get some other discerning people to pray with you.

Some people can't see Jesus in a memory because they are wrestling with introspection. Introspection is a disease of the soul in which your eyes are focused on yourself. It is often connected to toxic shame. Even when you are listening for the Spirit of God to speak to you, you will question what you receive. "Is that God? Is that me? I'm not sure. How can I tell?" With introspection, you talk yourself out of faith. Introspection ultimately is rooted in pride; it is a self-focus. You need to repent of pride, lift your eyes off of self and up to Jesus, and let the Spirit speak as you walk in faith to accept what He brings.

> With introspection, you talk yourself out of faith. Introspection ultimately is rooted in pride; it is a self-focus.

Sometimes the block can be demonic. I've prayed for people who were trying to access a memory, and they will say to me, "All I can see and feel is darkness." I've had to deal with the demonic block (which we will talk about later) before I could help them access the healing presence of Jesus.

Sometimes the person I am praying with says, "I can't see Jesus." I pause and discern the block with the help of the Spirit. I'll ask questions to help. Sometimes they can see the memory in their mind, but they can't see Jesus, even though they can feel Him. And sometimes when they can feel Him near, they can hear Him speak, so I may have them listen. There are many times when they say to me, "I can't see His face." And after I ask them a question or two, I discover that they can only see His feet. That is because they are looking down. This is an indicator of shame.

One day I was praying for someone who said to me, "I can't see Jesus' face. I can only see His feet." I simply lifted their chin as their eyes remained closed, and they started weeping. They saw Jesus as soon as I lifted their chin, and they told me after that they could see His eyes, which were the most compassionate eyes they had ever seen; that is why they wept. It broke their shame and healed this memory of their past sexual abuse. We have to rely on the Holy Spirit. We have to listen to His voice; this is theology 101. We have to access His presence—only Jesus heals.

Following the Spirit's Leadings

There are times the Lord takes a person back to the memory to bring healing, and other times He brings healing through meditation on Scripture. Some people are fearful of meditating on Scripture, frightened that they will open their mind to something dark. But this kind of fear is *already* opened to something dark, and closed to God.

Meditation is a biblical concept. And as we already saw in Acts 2, the Spirit gives us pictures, dreams, and visions. Sometimes the Holy Spirit will have us meditate on a passage of Scripture, and He will use that passage to bring us revelation of Jesus' presence that can heal. We are one Holy Spirit breath away from a God encounter that can heal our souls every time we pick up that holy Word of God.

I had a man come to me one day who was struggling with homosexual fantasy. He was married, and he wanted to get free. He asked if I would meet with him to pray for him. I told him I would, but I also asked him to meditate on John 8, the story about the woman caught in adultery, before we got together. I encouraged him to read the passage over several times, and to picture the scene. Fully immerse himself in it: see the sights, hear the sounds, smell the smells. And then simply to picture himself in the place of that woman, allowing the Spirit to reveal to him the truths that the passage taught.

He called me back the day before we were supposed to meet and said, "I don't need to get together tomorrow. I met with Jesus today." He experienced revelation and the healing presence of Jesus in that meditation on Scripture. I have nothing. Jesus is the healer. When someone comes to me for help, my goal is never to meet with the person; my goal is to get the person to meet with Jesus. There is hope in that meeting!

> When someone comes to me for help, my goal is never to meet with the person; my goal is to get the person to meet with Jesus. There is hope in that meeting!

As you seek Jesus' healing presence, be open to the prompting of the Spirit. Pay attention to the whispers and pictures that the Spirit may bring. There are times I have been praying for someone and have seen the face of Jesus. I could see tears of compassion in His eyes. I simply said to the person I was praying with, "I see the face of Jesus. I'm going to pray now that the Spirit will reveal to you what I see." I didn't tell them what I saw. They cried and said, "He's crying for me. Tears of compassion." Only God. There are times I have seen Jesus on the cross, and I sensed God wanted the person to bring their pain to Jesus and lay it down before Him at the cross. God knows stuff we don't know. Trust Him. Let Him lead.

REDEMPTIVE SUFFERING

Sometimes healing can be significantly advanced through an encounter. But sometimes God brings healing over time. We need to be open to that. We all want God to heal us instantly, but much healing takes place over time. It is a process.

I had to learn to come to Jesus and practice redemptive suffering. I went through a season in ministry, which I describe in my book *Pathways to the King*, in which I was severely attacked. I had people do radio shows against me and write blogs against me; someone even developed an imaginary Facebook persona so they could write against me. It was a dark season. I felt betrayal, and I was being cursed. I was embarrassed to go to the grocery store in my own town because I had heard people speaking against me so often.

I was riding my bike one day in the middle of this season of attack, and I was listening to worship music. As I rode, I noticed that tears were streaming down my face. I was surprised. I said, "Lord, what is that?" He said, "It's grief. I'm pulling grief out of your soul."

I went home to be alone with God, and I sat in His presence with a sense of the loss, the hurt, and the grief, but I also sensed His presence, His love, and His peace. It was like I had two streams running within my soul. There was a stream of grievous pain and a stream of His loving presence. I sat silent before God, aware of both streams, for about twenty minutes. I did it every day for months, and every day tears would flow, and I experienced the reality of both streams.

But over time I noticed that the flow of the stream of grief was slowing down, and eventually that stream dried up, and the tears dried up with it. God healed my heart over time in His presence. As I sat alone with Him in silence, it was like He was drawing grief out of my soul like a poison—until it was finally drained. This is redemptive suffering. Sometimes God heals in an encounter, and sometimes over time, but at all times He heals through His presence. He can give you access to His presence through an encounter, through a prophetic word or image, through healing prayer, through silence and solitude, through the Word, or through a myriad of other pathways. He can do it all at once, or He can do it over time. We must seek Him. He is the Healer.

Some of you have been through much trauma in your life. You need to access the healing presence of Jesus. Ask the Holy Spirit to give you wisdom. He may lead you back to the memories and reveal His presence there. Welcome Him. Watch and listen. Only God heals. Trust Him. When God meets you in powerful ways, write it down. Journal it—record it so you can remember it and reflect upon it with the help of the Spirit, so you can learn all you can from it. You may also need to spend time alone with Him in silence, accessing His healing presence through redemptive suffering.

We are often so desperate for God to fix us; we want it now, and we want it quickly and painlessly. But sometimes God doesn't come in power and make everything better, and we wonder why. There are some things that the power of God cannot do, that only the tenderness of God can do. There are some lessons and character traits that cannot be learned or developed in a moment, but only learned over time and developed in a process. Welcome the process, trust the sovereign leading of God, and seek the Healer for his presence.

A HEALING STORY

Let me close this chapter with a story. As I came to realize that I had some internal hurts and external baggage that were adversely affecting my relationships, my ministry, and my walk with God, I knew I needed help. I didn't know what to do next to break through. One day I stood in my office full of books, and I prayed, "Lord, I need your help. I don't know what to do. Can you lead me to a passage or a book that can help me find this breakthrough? I know I need to change. I know I have some internal stuff that needs to be addressed. I just don't know how."

As I prayed that prayer, I sensed the Holy Spirit lead me to a book by Leanne Payne. I have bought a lot of books at Christian Book Distributors warehouse sales; I would pick them up for a couple of dollars, and I bought hundreds of books at a time to build my library. Many of them I had never looked at closely. They simply sat on my shelves, and this book was one of those.

But as I sensed the Lord lead me to that book, I picked it up and started reading right away. I read through all of Payne's books in a month, and I decided to go to one of her conferences. It was a soul healing conference. I told my staff they had to join me. They mildly protested, but I was the boss, and they were all working through their stuff with me as we were on this journey together. So we went.

I didn't realize it at the time, but Leanne Payne had a significant ministry to homosexual men. The conference largely consisted of homosexual men, a lot of women, and some pastors who were coming for training in healing the soul. My associate pastor leaned over to me in the middle of the first worship set and said, "This is not our crowd." We were used to hanging out at Willow Creek Leadership Summits, and that is a very different crowd. I laughed and said, "I know. Shut up.

You need healing, and so do I." He nodded and laughed.

One of the first sessions was about separation anxiety. If someone had come to me six months earlier and talked to me about separation anxiety, I would have dismissed it as a bunch of psychobabble. But desperation is the platform to breakthrough. Desperation has a way of breaking arrogance and opening the mind and heart to new revelation. I was in a different place.

> Desperation is the platform to breakthrough. Desperation has a way of breaking arrogance and opening the mind and heart to new revelation.

On top of that, from the moment this person started speaking, I experienced such anxiety that I felt like I was having a heart attack. I had never experienced anything like it. As soon as the talk was over, I nearly ran down front for prayer; I was knocking over little old ladies to get down there for prayer! I talked to the speaker and said, "Listen, I've got this thing. I need you to pray for me." He said, "Well, it's Monday. Friday we are going to have a prayer time. That ought to address it. If it doesn't, come see me then."

I thought to myself, *Are you kidding me?* We want to be fixed right away; God wants a relationship. All week long, every time I walked into that auditorium, I felt anxiety, and every time I stepped out, the anxiety subsided. Literally, I stood in the doorframe one day and stepped in, and stepped out, stepped in, and stepped out, over and over again. Every time I felt anxiety inside, but not outside, the sanctuary. I said, "OK, God, you have my attention. I came because I knew I had issues. I need you."

That Wednesday, Payne gave a talk on fear. I'm not a terribly fearful person, so I took notes because I thought this would be helpful for some of the people in my life. Jen struggled with fear quite a bit; people in the church were fearful. My grandmother was fearful. But this wasn't one of my issues.

Leanne finished her talk, and then she led us into an experience. She said, "Now, I want to lead you through the garden of your fears. Picture a garden.⁹" At this point in my life, I very seldom got prophetic images. When God spoke to me, it was mostly through whispers, or I just knew something; God had revealed it to my spirit. Also, I am not very artsy. I thought, *This is dumb. But, Lord, I know I need help, so I'm going to picture a garden. I'm going to go with the first thing that comes into my mind.*

A garden image came to mind. It was a rock garden. There were flowers in my garden. There were rocks in my garden. There was a big tree in the center of my garden. That was my garden, and I was going with it.

She said, "Now, walk through the garden of your fears. Pick out the weeds. Those are your fears. Name them as you pluck them out."

I looked around in my garden, and there was not a weed in sight. There were flowers, there were rocks, and there was a big tree in the center of my garden. But there was not a weed to be found.

I thought, *I knew this lady was a fruit loop. This is ridiculous.*

Just then she said, "Some of you don't have any weeds in your garden. You don't have any little fears. You just have a big tree in the center of your garden. That's because you just have one big, root fear. It is so big you can't pull it out. You need Jesus."

---

9. For further reading, see Leanne Payne, *The Healing Presence* (Grand Rapids: Baker Books, 1995).

As soon as she said it, Jesus walked into my garden and pulled up my tree by the roots. And I knew it was the fear of not being loved. My whole life made sense to me. Now I understood why, when people said, "I need to talk to you," I felt like a little kid at the principal's office about to get yelled at. Now I understood why, when Jen disagreed with me, I felt threatened that somehow she didn't love me, and I powered up. Now I knew why I struggled with such anxiety over her not loving me anymore, and why I was obsessing with imaginary conversations in the marriage struggle we were going through. It all started coming together.

Friday came. It was the day for the prayer time. I said to my staff, "I need to be alone." They were experiencing revelations all week long as well, and they needed to be alone just as badly as I did. We all went to our separate corners. The speakers led us through a guided prayer. They took us through many different possible life events, from the time someone is little to the time someone is grown up. They took us through infancy, through the toddler years and preschool, grade school, junior high, high school, all the way into adulthood. They said things like, "Some of you were born, and your mother died during childbirth. . . . Your father abandoned some of you when you were a toddler. . . . Some of you were physically abused when you were in grade school."

Some of the things they called out were prophetic words of knowledge, and some of the things they called out were just life circumstances that many people experience. But nothing was landing on me, nothing was a revelatory aha! moment. Nothing was the breakthrough I was desperately seeking.

Until one of the leaders called out, "Some of you were born a boy, and your mother wanted a girl." Now, I knew this. I was the second child born in my family, and my brother is almost 15 months older than me. They already had a boy, and they wanted a girl. Who cares? It wasn't like they dressed me up as a little girl or anything. But this time when they said it, I had a picture of myself being a little infant, and it was like I could feel all the pain of being rejected for being a boy. This was the root of the separation anxiety. As I grew up I didn't feel rejected by my parents, but I did feel the symptoms of separation anxiety, though I didn't know it at the time.

This was why when I was a kid I used to get nervous before bedtime on a school night. I would feel anxiety. I thought it was the normal experience of every kid. I didn't realize it was separation anxiety; it was my normal. This was my root of my fear of not being loved. I felt some primal grief that had been packed inside starting to break free. I felt the anxiety that I felt all week long stirring within me and starting to cut free from the walls of my soul.

They finished the prayer time and said, "Some of you need to go get a hug from a man or from a woman. They aren't going to pray for you. They are just going to give you a hug and a blessing." I went to this lady; I don't know her name. I never introduced myself, but she is on my list when I get to Heaven; I will find her and thank her. I collapsed in her arms and sobbed like I have never sobbed before. Heaving, gasping, wracking cries. I cried for forty-five minutes nonstop as the grief that had been trapped in my soul came crashing out.

It wasn't anybody's fault; it was the way I had experienced it as a baby, but now God was redeeming it. The entire time I sobbed, this woman spoke a prophetic word over me. She said it over and over. "Precious child, you are loved by God. Precious child, you are loved by God. Precious child, you are loved by God." She had no way of knowing it was a childhood wound, no way of knowing it was the root fear of not being loved—but God knew. And the entire time as she spoke this over me and I sobbed, I could feel the pain and grief drain from my soul, and I could feel the love of God fill me up.

I came home and told my wife this story; Jen can be a bit

of a skeptic. She said, "I don't believe it." I said, "I don't blame you. I probably wouldn't believe it either if it hadn't happened to me." It was way outside of our experiential and theological boxes. But after a few months, she came to me and said, "You remember that story you told me that happened to you at Leanne Payne? I believe it." I asked, "Why?" She said, "You're different." And I was. I had less anxiety, less anger, less fear, more of the peace and love of God in my soul. I stopped biting my fingernails. I had experienced physical pain in my body all my life. This seems inexplicable—but that day the pain left. Jesus, the Healer, had met me and unpacked some of the suitcase of my soul, and created more room for the presence of God within.

This is the power of healing the soul. Jesus died not just to forgive you. Jesus died and rose to heal your soul and set you free! Jesus is the healer. There are things in your life that only He can heal. You may have a difficult and painful past; you may feel like it is impossible to get healthy and whole, but there is hope. Jesus is the Healer. He can heal your soul and set you free!

SPIRITUAL ACTION STEPS

- Experience: recall a major wound, and ask the Holy Spirit how He wants to address this wound. Maybe He would have you invite Jesus to come. Watch and listen. Enter His presence. Follow His leading.

- What are some of the major wounds in your life? Ask the Holy Spirit to show you any areas that may need healing. Let Him surface memories to mind. Some of the memories may surprise you. Don't dismiss them.

- Take the time over the next days and weeks to allow the Holy Spirit to surface any other memories that need his healing touch. Invite the presence of God in, and listen to the promptings of the Spirit. You may want to work through some of these memories with some discerning friends who are sensitive to the Spirit.

- Find a fellow believer who is willing to pursue healing with you. Pray for one another. Talk less, pray less. Listen more. Allow the Spirit to direct your prayer time. Jesus is the healer. We have nothing.

- You may want to read the chapter in my book *River Dwellers* about hearing God's voice before you gather to pray with another believer. Bring people to Jesus as the Spirit shows you how. Humbly test the whispers of the Spirit.

SOUL CARE PRINCIPLE #6

OVERCOMING FEARS

I am not a terribly fearful person. After I planted South Shore Community Church and we had success, I received a lot of phone calls from church planters in our area. A new church planter would come in town, and say, "I am planting a church in the area, and I heard about the success of South Shore. Church planting in New England is hard, and there aren't that many success stories. Can I take you out to lunch and ask you some questions?"

I always said yes. They would ask me a bunch of questions about methodology and vision and strategy, but inevitably this question came up: "How did you overcome your fear of failure?"

About the sixth or seventh time this happened, I came home and said to Jen, "Were you ever afraid that the church plant would fail?" She said, "Yeah, sure. But I didn't worry about it. I figured God would take care of us and we would find another way to make money."

Then she paused and smiled at me and said, "Failure never occurred to you, did it?" It hadn't. The possibility of failure had never crossed my mind. The previous dozen church plants in our denomination in New England all had failed, but failure never crossed my mind.

I had two gifted seminary friends who had gone out and planted a church in another region that was more friendly to church plantings, and they had significant financial backing and a core group, and they had failed—but failure for South Shore never crossed my mind. Fear was never a big part of my life. I was never afraid of heights, or flying, or taking risks, or failure. There were not many fears in my life.

But there was this one big tree in my garden of fears. No weeds. Just one big tree. The problem was I didn't even know it was there.

> People say what you don't know won't hurt you. But when it comes to the soul, they are dead wrong. What you don't know about your soul is already killing you.

People say what you don't know won't hurt you. But when it comes to the soul, they are dead wrong. What you don't know about your soul is already killing you. Fear was creating chaos in my soul and relationships, but I didn't know it existed until after that Leanne Payne conference.

THE IMPACT OF FEAR

The problem was I wasn't self-aware enough to recognize fear. I could feel the effects of fear, but they were just symptoms, and I didn't know that they were connected to fear. They were the leaves, not the root. For example, I sometimes felt anger. But sometimes anger was just fear manifesting itself, trying to reassert a sense of power in the face of weakness, a sense of control in the face of insecurity or instability.

Fear is a vulnerable emotion. Anger is powerful. When we feel fear, we have an adrenaline rush kick in. This is our fight-or-flight syndrome. It gives us a sense of power. I am not one to run away from a problem, so I would take that adrenaline and hunker down and get ready to fight. So, to me, it didn't feel like fear.

I felt power. I felt anger sometimes. I could feel my mind kick into overdrive with the adrenaline rush; my mind was quickened, sharpened, racing sometimes—but I didn't recognize that there was fear underneath. I had low levels of anxiety, but I wouldn't have called it that. I had grown up with separation anxiety; those were just normal feelings for me. There were times I obsessed with imaginary conversations because of conflict, but I didn't associate those with fear. In my mind, I was just practicing, getting ready for the real conversation. But these were just symptomatic expressions, and underneath it was fear diseasing my soul. Sadly, I didn't know it.

Many men, in particular, don't recognize fear. They also opt for power, control, and anger. They become defensive, aggressive, take-action-type people. But if you don't name what lurks in the dark shadows of your soul, it will master you.

Whether we see fear in our hearts or not, God does. He knows it is a primary motivating factor in the lives of His people. This is why the single most common command in Scripture is, "Do not be afraid" or "Fear not! For I am with you." If God makes this the single most common command to His people, how big of a problem do you think fear must be in our spiritual journey? It is a fundamental spiritual development problem. Yet I don't know if I had ever heard a single sermon on fear in all my years of church life. And the less we recognize fear and its impact on our lives, the more of a problem it will become. In our fear we often sin. We fail to follow God. There are countless Biblical examples that demonstrate the consequence of fear.

BIBLICAL EXAMPLES OF THE IMPACT OF FEAR

The Israelites failed to enter the Promised Land because of fear (see Numbers 13). They sent spies into the land, and the spies came back and gave a good report of the land, but also a scary report of the giants who lived there. Ten spies gave the scary report. Two spies confirmed the giants, but kept their eyes on God and His promises, and they urged the people to obey God and take the land. But fear caused the people to tremble, lose their nerve, and disobey God. It cost an entire generation of people their entrance into their divine destiny and their inheritance. It is a tragic example of the power of fear to derail our lives.

Think about King Saul. He was a man chosen by God to be the first king of Israel. A man with large stature who people naturally looked up to, but a man who cowered in the face of his own fears.

Saul faced a huge test when the Philistines gathered to battle with the Israelites. Samuel the prophet called Saul to wait for his arrival, and Samuel would then make a sacrifice to prepare the way for a victorious battle with the Philistines. But the Philistines gathered. Saul had three thousand men. The Philistines had three thousand *chariots*. These were overwhelming odds.

1 Samuel 13:6-8 says, "When the Israelites saw that their situation was critical and that their army was hard pressed, they hid in caves and thickets, among the rocks, and in pits

and cisterns. . . . Saul remained at Gilgal, and all the troops with him were quaking with fear. He waited seven days, the time set by Samuel; but Samuel did not come to Gilgal, and Saul's men began to scatter."

It's easy to look at this situation and judge Saul. But these were real people, and those were real odds they were up against. He was a good enough leader to combat the fear within him and rally his fearful troops for seven days, but on the seventh day, when he and the troops saw that Samuel had still not arrived, the troops started pulling out of town. And Saul buckled under the increasing weight of fear in his own heart.

> But sometimes we act in fear rather than wait on God in faith. Sometimes we rely on ourselves, our gifts, and our ingenuity rather than rely on God and his deliverance.

I wonder if he even knew it was fear. I wonder if he didn't just say, "I have to act. I'm a leader. I can't sit back and do nothing. This is what leaders do. They take bold, decisive actions." But sometimes we act in fear rather than wait on God in faith. Sometimes we rely on ourselves, our gifts, and our ingenuity rather than rely on God and his deliverance, and we forfeit our future. And if we can't identify it as fear, we will surely act on it, no matter what we call it. Saul did. Samuel arrived right after the sacrifice was illegally and fearfully made. This was the moment where Saul lost his kingdom, all because his heart bowed to fear.

Another biblical example can be drawn from Ahaz, the king of Judah, who faced terrifying circumstances when two enemies aligned against him. Isaiah 7:2: "Now the house of David was told, 'Aram has allied itself with Ephraim'; so the hearts of Ahaz and his people were shaken, as the trees of the forest are shaken by the wind."

The Lord knows the people of God make more mistakes during times of fear than any other time. So he sent Ahaz a prophetic word to support, strengthen, and encourage him: "Be careful, keep calm and don't be afraid. Do not lose heart" (Isaiah 7:4). Fear causes us to lose heart; losing heart results in cowardly actions of disobedience. God then graciously offered to the fearful king the opportunity to ask for a sign to encourage his trembling heart. Ahaz refused, but God gave him the sign anyway. "The virgin will conceive and give birth to a son, and will call him Immanuel" (7:14).

This sign had dual fulfillment. It was fulfilled in Isaiah's day when his own wife had a child and, of course, it was fulfilled with the coming of the Messiah—Jesus, God with us. The word to Ahaz, and the word to us through Jesus' coming, is that when our circumstances seem greater than our God, we have to choose to trust Him because God is with us. The ultimate proof that we can trust Him is that God has sent His Son, Immanuel. God is with us.

The number one question in the heart of people for God is, "Do you love me?" And the number one question in the heart of God for people is, "Will you trust me? I have proven my love through my Son, now will you trust me? No matter how sticky your circumstances, no matter how overwhelming your fear, will you trust the God of the cross?" This is the question God asks us.

How often do we fail to take kingdom risks because of fear? How frequently do we miss out on our prophetic destiny because we play it safe due to underlying fears? How many opportunities of eternal consequence do we pass up because fear makes us timid? How many kingdom ministries remain unfulfilled and eternal destinies remain unaltered because we fail to confront our fears? We must recognize and overcome our fear or forfeit our preferred future.

THE REMEDY TO FEAR

We can either act on fear or we can act on faith, but we cannot act on both. We can feel afraid and act on faith, but we can't act on both. We must choose. The Israelites chose to act on fear, and that generation lost the right to enter the Promised Land. Saul chose to act on fear, and he lost the kingdom. God has given us all a sign that we can trust Him—Jesus came, and God is with us. We can trust Him. But we must recognize our fear and overcome it.

David had an unusually wise understanding of the things of the soul. He made the connection between fear and disobedience, fear and soul disasters, fear and lost destinies. He probably learned this lesson by watching Saul lose his kingdom over fear. The lesson was reinforced when he had to confront Goliath, even though warriors much older and more experienced backed down in fear. David knew that if fear lurked in his heart unattended, it could cost him immeasurably, so he prayed about it. Wrestle with that: When fear lurks in your heart unattended, it is bound to cost you immeasurably. In Psalm 139:23, 24 David wrote, "Search me, O God, and know my heart; *test me and know my anxious thoughts.* See if there is any offensive way in me, and lead me in the way everlasting" (emphasis mine). David prayed that God would test him to see if he had any anxious thoughts lurking in the shadows of his soul, because he knew that these anxious thoughts could be seeds of rebellion if they were not addressed. Utter wisdom. It is often our anxious, fearful thoughts that precede our sin. If we can catch these, we can prevent many soul disasters.

> We can either act on fear or we can act on faith, but we cannot act on both.

The Peace of Heaven

God does not want us to live with our fears and be overcome by them. He has promised us peace. John 14:27: "Peace I leave with you; my peace I give you. I do not give to you as the world gives. Do not let your hearts be troubled and do not be afraid."

Jesus has a peace that is tied to Heaven. It is a peace that flows from the throne room of God. It is a peace that is not altered by circumstances or threatened by the enemy of our souls. Today Jesus sits on His throne in Heaven, and He is at perfect peace. No matter what confronts you in life, no matter how many difficulties surround you, Jesus is not wringing His hands in Heaven, saying, "Oh my, what am I going to do about that?" He isn't nervous. He is at perfect peace. And He can impart his perfect peace to us.

This doesn't mean that everything is going to work out in life. This peace is not dependent on temporary circumstances; it is linked to an eternal kingdom. There are sick people we pray for who are going to die. There are marriages we pray for that are going to break up. There are children we pray for who are going to continue to rebel. But nothing can separate us from God's love for all eternity (Romans 8), and while everything may not turn out the way we want, the love of God is enough to sustain us and grant us peace. "There is no fear in love. But perfect love drives out fear" (1 John 4:18). The perfect love of Jesus is enough no matter what confronts us. And as we learn to soak in the revelation of the perfect love of God, fear is broken, and the peace of Heaven rests in the deep places of our souls. Jesus has peace to offer you that transcends your reality and trumps your circumstances.

When I went through my marriage crisis, it tapped into my root fear: the fear of not being loved. The person I loved the most in this world no longer loved me. My heart trembled, and I was afraid. I didn't know that's what it was, but all the symptoms were there. My mind raced; I had countless imaginary conversations and real conversations to try to fix the marriage and control the outcomes. Jen often felt smothered because I was obsessed with fixing it; I was driven by fear. I struggled to find peace of mind and heart, and anxiety filled my soul. It would often take me two hours of worship after a conversation with Jen before I could find peace.

It was in this season in my life, in the midst of my greatest angst, that I discovered that Jesus' love really is enough. I knew it in theory; I believed it cognitively before this crisis. But it was only in this deep soul-shattering pain that I came to know the love of God down in the basement of my soul. Someplace in the midst of this battle, and through the revelation of the Spirit, I came to realize that I wanted Jen to love me, and life was better when Jen loved me. But even if Jen never loved me again, even if she left me, I was going to be OK, because Jesus loved me, and this was enough for me. That realization was transforming. I was learning to stand on the true foundation: that the issue of my value was settled at the cross. And the love of God was beginning to drive out fear, and peace was starting to fill my soul.

Fear often threatens the foundation of our value. In our fear we often seek to prove our worth, to control outcomes, to manipulate and control others. When we act on these things because of our fears, we actually strengthen the stronghold of the faulty foundation and lies in our lives. Ultimately, to conquer our fears, we have to surrender our fears to God and trust Him. He is with us. He is for us. He loves us. And that is enough for us. We must believe that and act on it. We must experience that reality through revelation. We must act on faith, and not on fear, or we will end up on the wrong foundation.

Believing God is redemptive, again, is critically important, because faith does not guarantee that everything will work out the way we want it to. Faith trusts God regardless of how things work out, because we aren't only trusting God to control our circumstances; rather, we are building a trusting, loving relationship with God as our Savior and Redeemer in a fallen world. Until we shift from trusting good results to trusting God in bad results, we don't really trust God at all. We trust the King and his unshakable kingdom; we believe that He can overcome our past, He is enough for our present, and He has secured our eternal future.

The complicated thing about the soul is that all of these various soul care principles are connected. The more self-aware we become, the more we can connect the dots between these principles and how they affect our lives. Connecting the dots between these various soul care issues is essential for going deeper and becoming freer. Our fears, for example, are often connected to our wounds. When a situation in our present reminds us of a wound from our past, we feel afraid, and we are tempted to act on our fear. Often when people cannot break through a pattern of behavior or a soul issue, it is because they do not understand all the deep roots of the problem and they cannot surrender their way through the issue.

For me, the fear of not being loved tempted me to act in power in the midst of conflict. I would resort to using forceful opinions to cover up the vulnerabilities I felt. Again, I didn't feel afraid: I felt the effects of the adrenaline rush, and I acted on the power of the adrenaline to protect myself. But this reinforced the faulty foundation that I was standing on—that my value was determined by whether I could get certain people to love me.

I told myself that wasn't true. I said to myself, "I don't care what people think." But that was bluster, and you can't trick your soul. The imaginary conversations I had in my head, and the racing thoughts that went on in my mind, were proof that I was standing on a faulty foundation.

Fears also often drive us to reach for comforting sin patterns; fear is discomforting, and unprocessed wounds are painful, so we engage in a sin that brings us a measure of relief and comfort, whether it is fantasy or an addictive behavior.

The lies we believe, the fears we have, the wounds we have suffered, the bitter roots we hold on to, and our sin and family sin patterns all weave together to strengthen our bondage. But as we begin to bring these things into the light, we begin to untie the weaving. As we welcome the light, and give God more access to our heart, we find healing and freedom.

IDENTIFYING YOUR FEARS

Self-awareness is the gateway to freedom. It does not guarantee it, but you can't get there without it. If you are going to get free from your fears, you must begin by identifying your fears.

Fear Indicators

Perhaps you, like me, do not realize that you even have fear. You may have told yourself that you aren't afraid. In order to identify your fears, start by recognizing some of the physiological fear responses. Recognize when the adrenaline gets kicked into your body. You may feel the need to escape (flight), or the need to become aggressive (fight). Your flight may be fantasy, withdrawal, shutting down, turning inward, passive aggressive behavior, or physically withdrawing. Your fight may be defensiveness, anger, ramping up the intensity of a conversation, attacking others, and/or controlling behaviors. When fear strikes and your adrenaline kicks in, you also may feel your heart rate quicken and your mind sharpen or start racing, and you may find yourself looking for answers and solutions.

People often reach for emotional shields as well. These shields are defensive tactics to protect ourselves in our vulnerable state, and no emotion makes us feel quite as vulnerable as fear. We pick up shields of anger, power, control, manipulation, defensiveness, withdrawal, and silence, just to name a few.

Remember though, the problem with shields is they are indiscriminate— they not only block out the person who is hurting us, they also block out God from healing us. In order for us to get to the roots, we must lay down our shields.

> The problem with shields is they are indiscriminate— they not only block out the person who is hurting us, they also block out God from healing us. In order for us to get to the roots, we must lay down our shields.

Identifying Your Root Fears

As you begin to recognize what fear feels like, it helps to identify your root fears. What is your dominant fear or most significant fears? Name them. You cannot overcome that which you will not admit. Ask the Holy Spirit for guidance and revelation. Prayerfully spend time in self-reflection and journaling. Talk to people who know you well; look at your family members and their behaviors.

I did all of these things as I was coming into the light about the issues of my soul. Look back over the other soul care principles—your wounds, your family sin patterns, the lies that affect your identity, and more . . . all of these things impact your fears.

Pay attention to the circumstances of your life. God often brings us face to face with our greatest fears—not to shame us or condemn us, but to help us overcome. Think about Saul. What was Saul's root fear? We find some clues in the text.

When Samuel first told Saul he was to be the king, Saul said, "But am I not a Benjamite, from the smallest tribe of Israel, and is not my clan the least of all the clans of the tribe of Benjamin?" (1 Samuel 9:21). It looks like humility, but I think there is fear sneaking around in the shadows of his soul. He demonstrates no humility later on in his life; what appears to be humility here is actually fear. It is timidity. He comes from the smallest tribe and the least, or most insignificant, clan. Saul is wrestling deeply with a fear of inadequacy, of insignificance.

Later on, when Samuel tells the Israelites that Saul is the man chosen to be king, he is found hiding among the baggage (1 Samuel 10:22)! Fear. Hiding is a fear-based action; people with humility still act in courage because they trust God. But Saul has a fear of inadequacy, a fear that he does not have what it takes; it is undoubtedly tied to an identity wound. It is this fear that drives him to act when he should wait. It is this fear that causes him to hide from Goliath when he should act as king. It is this fear that drives him to throw spears at David because he is threatened. He never identifies his fears, and that which he didn't know was already killing his soul.

Saul should have reflected on his reactions to these various circumstances. God chose him and anointed him king, but he wrestled with inferior feelings. This would have been a good time for Saul to pause and ask, "What is underneath that?"

When Samuel proclaimed Saul's kingship, Saul hid. This was another opportunity to probe a little deeper, to prayerfully reflect on why he hid. He never identified the identity wounds, the family sin patterns, or the fears, and in the end, his lack of self-awareness cost him and the nation.

As leaders, our actions always have consequences for others. It takes a healthy leader to lead a healthy group. We cannot afford to ignore the issues of the soul. You cannot inspire people to act in faith if you have not processed the fears in your own soul. The number one job of a spiritual leader is to discern the mind of Christ. The number two job of a spiritual leader is to inspire faith in the hearts of the people so they will have the courage to obey God wherever He leads. The leader who cannot process his or her fear cannot inspire people to take the hill of their prophetic, God-given destiny. It is a treacherous thing for a leader to ignore his or her fear.

> It is a treacherous thing for a leader to ignore his or her fear.

In my own life, God brought me face to face with my fear of not being loved. Jen didn't love me, and given my history, that may have been the only thing that could have caused me to grapple with the deep issues of my soul. If it weren't for that compelling incident that struck my core fear and my root issues, I may not have confronted the dark places in my soul. God knew. God always knows. But we have to embrace the light He offers, no matter how unpleasant or fearful it may seem. There is never freedom in darkness or hiding.

These soul-shaping crisis opportunities lead us to surrender and discover the healing grace of God—if only we embrace them and allow God to redeem them. They also lead us to deeper faith, an active faith and trust, when we choose to act on faith and not on fear.

Manifestations of Fear

Pay attention to how your fears manifest in your life. When your fears get tapped, how do they show up? What do they look like? Feel like?

We often mask our fears, and they may express themselves in ways that don't look like fear. Once you identify how your fears manifest themselves, these become your indicating clues to go to God. There are often warning signs available to us when our fears are activated.

Think about Saul, for example. One of his reflex reactions to fear was to hide. He hid in the baggage. He hid in the caves in the face of battle. If he was self-aware, his desire to take flight was an early warning sign that he was about to act on fear. It would have given him notice that he needed to get back on the foundation of God's love, and then he could have acted courageously. Other times, Saul was threatened, and he went on the offensive. He threw spears at David; he became paranoid, impulsive, and aggressive. He chased David into the desert, even though David never did anything to threaten Saul's kingdom. If Saul had become self-aware, he could have seen this fight-or-flight reflex as a symptomatic expression of his fear. This could have prevented him from making disastrous decisions.

One of my symptomatic expressions of fear is anxiety. As a kid suffering from separation anxiety, I didn't even realize what I was feeling was anxiety. The butterflies I felt in new social situations, or when going to school each day, were just normative to me. I thought it was my personality. But after the Leanne Payne conference, I became keenly aware of anxiety in my life. It is one of the most important symptoms that I experience, and it often leads me to God. I have learned to embrace it as an early warning sign; it is a gift to me that moves me to seek God.

If someone says, "I am angry with you, and I need to meet with you," that may cause my anxiety meter to spike. I'll feel an adrenaline rush. I may respond calmly, but inside I may have a little adrenaline kick, and my anxiety will rise. I will feel it in my chest, a feeling of tightness, or a lack of peace in my inner being. And if I act on that adrenaline rush, on that anxiety, I will probably have imaginary conversations. "Why is this person upset? What did I do? I don't remember saying anything to upset them. Well, there was that one thing. But, if they got upset at that . . . I didn't mean anything by it. They are just thin-skinned."

This self-talk only reinforces the lie that my value is dependent on whether or not I can get this person to like me. It only causes me more angst. Instead, when I feel the anxiety, I know I need to go to Jesus. I have learned to change the tape that plays in my mind. I say to myself, *I love this person. I want this person to like me. But even if they don't like me, it's OK, because Jesus likes me and that is enough for me. I will go and listen and respond without defensiveness; I will own whatever I can, because God surely loves me. The issue of my value is settled at the cross.* I will take a moment to get on that secure foundation, and then I will act on faith, not on fear. But it was anxiety that drove me to Jesus. It has become a gift to me that helps me realize when I am on the false foundation, and a trigger to get me back to my true foundation.

OVERCOMING FEAR

In Philippians 4:4-7, Paul offers wise and helpful words about overcoming fear: "Rejoice in the Lord always. I will say it again: Rejoice! Let your gentleness be evident to all. The Lord is near. Do not be anxious about anything, but in everything, by prayer and petition, with thanksgiving, present your requests to God. And the peace of God, which transcends all understanding, will guard your hearts and your minds in Christ Jesus." This passage leads us to some specific action steps that I have found helpful.

First, begin with worship. Paul says, "Rejoice in the Lord always. I will say it again: Rejoice!" There are only two times to worship: When we feel like it, and when we don't. And when we don't feel like it is the time we need it most.

Worship will get our eyes off our fearful circumstances and onto God. Worship accesses the presence of God (Psalm 100).

God is not afraid. Jesus isn't nervous. Each night after Jen and I had those conflict conversations in the early days, I was a mess. Fears were raging, and I would go upstairs to my study and spend one to two hours in worship. It often took me that long in order to finally calm down inside. Worship became a critical necessity in my journey to overcome my deepest fear. Worship helped me access God's presence, hear God's voice, and solidify the foundation of God's love. It was in these long nightly sessions of worship that I discovered God's love was enough for me no matter what the future held.

Second, choose a gentle response. Paul says, "Let your gentleness be evident to all" (Philippians 4:5). This is a word that has to do with submission, with yielding. Paul is inviting us to slow down, surrender, and be gentle. Often when we are fearful, we act in impulsive, angry, defensive, controlling, self-protecting, and damaging ways. We love quoting Psalm 46:10: "Be still, and know that I am God." But the context of the Psalm is vital to understanding this verse. Verse 1 sets that context: "God is our refuge and strength, an ever-present help in trouble. Therefore we will not fear." It is a time of trouble the psalmist finds himself in. His fight-or-flight reflex has kicked in. Everything within him is sped up; the RPMs of his soul are red-lining, and in this context God says, "Be still." The psalmist is choosing to slow down in a sped-up environment. This is what Paul is calling us to do. It is a counter-intuitive response in a time of crisis, but a healthy soul response to a crisis. Ultimately, it will help prevent you from acting on fear, and rather move you to act on faith.

Third, remember the Lord's presence, and fix your eyes on Jesus. "The Lord is near. Do not be anxious." It is Immanuel that gives us the sign that all is well. God is with us. God is for us. God can be trusted. Fix your eyes on Jesus. Cultivate His presence. Soak in His presence. This is why I worshiped at the end of our conflict conversations—His presence was what I needed. His presence is healing, calming, and identity-solid-ifying.

Most life change occurs alone with God. We can fix our eyes on Jesus or we can fix our eyes on our problems, but we can't fix our eyes on both. The mind struggles with what I call "mind drift." This means that your mind naturally drifts toward your greatest pressing problems. I think this a testimony to the power of fear. If you are driving down the road on a sunny day, and you are listening to your favorite music in the background, and you just let your mind drift, your mind will drift to your greatest pressing problem. If you have a marriage problem weighing on you, your mind will drift to that spot. If you have financial struggles, your mind will drift there. You will find yourself thinking about solutions, worrying about worst-case scenarios, and having imaginary conversations. Your mind will drift.

> Most life change occurs alone with God. We can fix our eyes on Jesus or we can fix our eyes on our problems, but we can't fix our eyes on both.

Peace is a by-product of fixing your mind on Jesus. He is at perfect peace in his throne room today; if you can get your eyes on Immanuel, God's presence can impart peace to your souls.

Fourth, overcoming your fears will involve redemptive suffering. When you are cultivating the presence of Jesus, when you intentionally go to Him in your time of trouble, let Him comfort you. You will be tempted during these times to go to a sin pattern that brings you comfort—like lust, fantasy, eating, or drinking. Go to Jesus instead. Feel the pain, and let His love, His presence, and His victory bring you comfort.

This is redemptive suffering: He heals us when we embrace

the suffering and don't seek to numb it out. I often practice ten-minute retreats. When anxiety gets triggered within me, I will spend ten minutes alone with God in silence just fixing my loving attention on Jesus. The anxiety doesn't always go away immediately, but I face the anxiety in His presence.

Fifth, overcoming your fears will involve surrender. So much of our battle with fear comes down to this question: Will you trust God? You have to choose to believe that God is with us, for us, and trustworthy. It is a choice.

> So much of our battle with fear comes down to this question: Will you trust God? You have to choose to believe that God is with us, for us, and trustworthy. It is a choice.

I do not always understand why things happen, but I know I can trust Him because of the cross. He is Immanuel. He did not leave us in our time of trouble. He entered into our suffering, and He suffered for us, and He suffers with us, so we can trust the God of the cross.

Too often we ask the wrong question in times of difficulty. We ask the question why. I find it counterproductive; it leaves my soul with mistrust, and God has never promised to answer that question. I have learned instead to ask the question, "How? How can you redeem this?" God has promised to answer that question (Romans 8:28-39; James 1:1-5). I ask how, and I surrender to the shaping hand of God. I choose to cooperate with the life-change process. Peace is often a by-product of a fully surrendered heart. It is the simplicity of trust, and the sweetness of surrender, that leads us to peace in the inmost place.

Sixth, overcoming your fears always involves action. In faith, you need to act in the opposite direction of your fear.

Courage is not the absence of fear; courage is doing what is right in the face of fear. You may be fearful of rejection, and you may therefore be terrified of conflict, but you don't get a pass. Being a follower of Jesus means you have to deal with conflict in a God-honoring way. And avoiding it doesn't honor God. So feel the fear, and go to Jesus with it. Solidify the issue of your value under your feet, but if you are still afraid af-

> Courage is not the absence of fear; courage is doing what is right in the face of fear.

ter all of your spiritual actions, you still need to act in courage. The final victories of overcoming our root issues often are not administered until we act in courage.

Years ago I was driving to the monastery for a time of spiritual retreat. I had been through a very busy season and had just finished teaching Soul Care at the doctoral level for ten days. Teaching Soul Care is draining on me; it is the most taxing aspect of the ministry in which I engage.

I was looking forward to this time of spiritual refreshing at the monastery. I frequent the monastery often, and the place has become a refuge for me. But this time, when I drove onto the campus, I felt anxiety strike my soul. I have felt anxiety before. But this was different. This was a different level of intensity, and I wasn't able to quickly process through it like normal, but I tried everything I could.

I got my bags out of my car, went straight to my room, and hit my knees. I said, "Lord, what is this?" But God was silent. I pressed in, "Lord, have I sinned?" Sometimes when I feel anxiety, that lack of peace in my inner being—it is because of conviction. But I heard the Spirit whisper that sin was not the issue.

I said, "Do I have too much on my plate? Is it stress?" I

sensed the Spirit saying no. I said, "Do you want to tell me what it is?" Nothing. Just silence. I did all that I knew how to do. I worshiped. I surrendered. I sat in silence. I prayed over all of the things that were possibly troubling my soul. I prayed through. But the anxiety continued roaring within me.

I had a few things that I had hoped to accomplish on this trip. I quickly scrapped my agenda, and for the next two days I spent time with God. But no matter what I did, no matter what spiritual activities I engaged in, there was no break-through. I had never experienced anxiety for days on end like this; before this, it would come and go, though I could always find relief. But not this time.

On the third day I got up and said, "Lord, I have lived for years now cultivating a sense of your peace and your presence. I can't live with this. You have to help me. Show me what this is, and what to do."

I sensed the Lord say to me, "Go into the chapel and sit in silence." So I went in and sat. I waited for 45 minutes. Finally, the Lord spoke softly and quietly within my inner being: "Psalm 23."

Of course, I know the psalm. I read it. "The Lord is my shepherd; I shall not want. He makes me lie down in green pastures. He leads me beside still waters [literally, waters at rest]. He restores my soul" (Psalm 23:1-3, ESV). That was as far as I got. That last phrase, "He restores my soul," caught in my spirit. I sensed the breath of God blowing across it. I wait-ed; I lingered with those first few verses. And after another twenty minutes, the Lord spoke.

He said, "My presence is manifest in many forms. There is my healing presence, my loving presence, my filling presence, my empowering presence. You need to access my restorative presence. You have been on the front lines of battle for a long time, fighting for renewal. You have suffered many hits to your soul, and you must access my restorative presence. My restorative presence can only be accessed through silence and stillness."

So for the next three months, I spent ten to twenty minutes, at least once, and sometimes multiple times, each day in silence before God. I didn't say anything. I didn't pray anything. I just fixed my attention on Jesus. When my mind wandered, I brought it back. Over time, the anxiety began to wane. Every day I woke up with it, and it stayed with me all day long, but as I waited on the Lord in silence to access His restorative presence, I could feel it losing its grip.

After some time it wasn't as strong; a little more time and it became intermittent. At the end of three months, it was gone completely. God restores. God heals. God overcomes.

There is a peace that passes understanding; it is the peace of Heaven. It is stronger still than all your fears, stronger still than all our angst. Fear not. He is with you.

SPIRITUAL ACTION STEPS

- What are your root fears? How do they manifest themselves?

- How are your fears affecting your relationship with God?

- How are your fears connected to the lies you believe? What are the wounds beneath those fears? Take time to pray for healing.

- What are the courageous actions you need to take to overcome your fears?

- Bring your fears to Jesus. Let Him speak and minister to you.

SOUL CARE PRINCIPLE #7
DELIVERANCE

I was on a pay phone at seminary, back around 1990, talking with Jen, my future wife. There was a young guy pacing back and forth in front of the phone, so I figured he was waiting to use it. (For those of you who don't remember, there were no cell phones in those days.) I hung up and offered this young man the phone, but he said, "Actually, I was waiting to talk to you." I didn't know him, and I had never met him, but we sat down to talk.

We weren't into the conversation more than five minutes when a thought occurred to me that had never come to me before: *This guy has demons.*

I grew up going to church, but we never talked about demons. By that point in my life, I had read the Bible from cover to cover about ten times, so I knew the Bible talked about demons. Jesus did deliverance; the disciples did deliverance.

I heard missionaries talk about demons, but those were in animistic cultures. This was the civilized world. My Western worldview had messed up my biblical worldview. But this guy, I was sure, had demons.

He was talking about hearing voices. The voices were blasphemous and telling him to do homicidal things. And the whole time I talked to him, he would periodically manifest with growling and shaking. It wasn't an act, and it didn't seem like mental illness. It sounded a lot like the demonic stuff I had read about in Scripture and had heard about from missionaries.

> Your next level with God lies beyond the boundaries of your current experience. The only way to get there is to risk more than you are comfortable with.

What do you do with a situation like this? Your next level with God lies beyond the boundaries of your current experience. The only way to get there is to risk more than you are comfortable with. So I plunged in and took a risk.

I said, "Have you ever considered that maybe, perhaps, your problem could be spiritual in nature?" He said to me, "Do you think I have demons?" I said, "Yes. I do." He told me, "John Ellenberger told me I had demons, but I didn't believe him."

Dr. John Ellenberger was one of my professors in seminary and is one of my heroes. John and his wife Helen served in Papua, a province of Indonesia, as missionaries. They were part of a team that had seen a tribe of people come to Christ who had worshiped demonic spirits that visibly appeared to the people. They had been involved in countless numbers of deliverances.

I said to the young man, "If John Ellenberger says you have a demon, then you have a demon. And I have never in my life thought that someone had a demon, until I had this conversation with you. If you are willing, I'll talk to John, and we can set up an appointment for you to have a deliverance." He agreed.

I went to see John the next day. I said, "John, I met a friend of yours," and I told him the young man's name. John took off his glasses, looked up to the ceiling, and sighed. "That is the worst case of demons I have ever seen," he told me. So the first time I ever spotted a demonic spirit was the worst case the man with the most experience I knew had ever seen. If this topic is foreign to you, and you lack discernment about these things, I am telling you this story to give you hope!

Sadly, we didn't get the man free; he was unwilling to repent of some things, and he left without getting freedom. But the experience shifted my worldview.

I graduated and took a position as an assistant pastor in a church in New England right out of seminary. I was there for less than a month when a woman came into my office looking for help. Her presenting symptoms included panic attacks, depression, and suicidal thoughts. I asked her to tell me her story, and it included some voodoo in her past. As I listened, I realized that some of what she was wrestling with was demonic.

I said, "Have you ever considered that some of these problems could be spiritual in nature?" She said, "Do you think I have demons?" I said, "Yes." She said, "So do I. I practiced voodoo." I said, "Would you like to get free?" She said, "Well, that's why I came."

I nodded and went in to see the senior pastor. He had been in ministry for more than three decades. I told him about the situation and he said, "I've never done deliverance." I said, "Me neither." He replied, "Well, if you lead, I'll pray."

Remember what I said about your next level with God? I was 25 years old, but it was time to jump in over my head. God helped, and we got her free.

I cast six spirits out, but there was a seventh spirit that I couldn't get to leave. I didn't know what to do. I waited on the Lord and He said, "This is a shared spirit." I said, "What's that?" He said, "It is shared with another person."

I had been trying to send it to the pit, but it wouldn't go because it had a right to go to this other person. He said, "Tell it to go where I send it." I said, "Go where Jesus sends you." The Spirit left, and she was free. Five minutes later her mother, who was a voodoo practitioner, called and said, "Is my daughter there?"

I was beginning to get a glimpse of the unseen world.

CHANGING WORLD

We live in a time of an epoch era shift. We are seeing a seismic worldview change in our lifetimes. Let me illustrate it with a cartoon. *Scooby Doo* is one of the longest-running TV shows in television history. It started back in the late 1960s when I was a kid.

The show presented a worldview. Every episode was the same: There was a ghost. The gang of teenage sleuths and their scared but reliable dog, Scooby Doo, would chase the ghost, and by the end of the show they would unmask the ghost and reveal that it was just some villain doing dirty deeds dressed up as a ghost. But the show was presenting a modern worldview, and it communicated this message: Behind every apparent supernatural phenomenon is a natural explanation. The supernatural world does not really interact with the natural world.

Somewhere in the mid-1990s I was visiting a friend who had a son. While we were in the kitchen I heard *Scooby Doo* playing in the other room. I took my cup of coffee and sat down with the boy on the floor to catch a little Scooby. There was a ghost—then again, there was always a ghost; this was Scooby Doo! But this time at the end of the cartoon, the ghost was still a ghost. I said to myself, "Ruh, Ro." (You Scooby Doo fans understand that line!)

Someone had just changed the worldview of a new generation of *Scooby Doo* fans. We are now teaching a new generation that behind an apparent supernatural phenomenon is an actual supernatural being. Welcome to the new postmodern world. This isn't a bad thing; in fact, this worldview is more in line with the Biblical worldview on this one issue. There is a supernatural sphere with supernatural beings, and they do interact with our world.

> There is a supernatural sphere with supernatural beings, and they do interact with our world.

However, the postmodern world also unplugged truth. Postmodernism doesn't say that there is no truth, but that if there is truth, it isn't really knowable for certain. We now have a generation that believes in supernatural beings, but also that there are no absolutes. Therefore, experimentation with the supernatural is perfectly legal because all spirits are accessible, and in some way they are looked at as equal. This has led to much more supernatural experimentation in our current generation. And with more experimentation comes more demonization and more bondage.

The church must recover a supernatural worldview and the authority to set the captives free. I think churches that don't move in power in the near future are going to become largely irrelevant to nearly everyone but the Pharisees. There is more bondage, and the church must learn how, once again, to set the captives free.

In the town where I live, we have two full-time mediums.

One of the mediums has her own reality TV show and has written a book! She is very popular. She has given people I know spot-on prophetic words, giving them very specific insights from their past. She told one woman I know that she had been in the hospital, that she had cancer, that she had a baby while she was in the hospital, that the cancer was in remission, and the baby was fine. The medium had never met the woman, but it was all true.

I asked a doctor in my church to set up a lunch with the medium since he knew her. I simply asked her to tell me her story. She came from a Catholic background, but obviously was syncretistic in her beliefs and practices. Her story included many supernatural experiences, and about halfway through her story, she paused and said, "What do you really think of this?"

I said to her, "I'll tell you in a minute, but can I say something else to you first?" She nodded. I continued, "From the moment you sat down, I could feel the Father's affections for you." She started to cry, deeply touched by the Father's love and my compassion for her. Many Christians had condemned her. She is not the enemy. The enemy dupes her, but she is not the enemy.

After she finished her story, I went on to tell her that the Bible says there are good spirits and there are bad spirits, and that some of the spirits she was talking to were bad spirits. She said, "Is that why my kids have nightmares and see things in their room?" I said, "Yes." I'd love to tell you that she was converted, but she wasn't. However, she felt loved, and we had a respectful conversation that didn't skirt the truth.

BIBLICAL WORLDVIEW:
THE KINGDOM OF GOD

Dealing with dark spirits, spiritual warfare, and deliverance has always been in the biblical worldview. Jesus did deliverance. It was a major part of kingdom ministry.

The central message of Jesus is about the kingdom of God. The kingdom of God is the reversal of everything that went wrong when sin entered the world. It is the restoration of everything back to the way God intended it to be. So when Jesus came, He saved the lost, healed the sick, cast out demons, helped the poor, overcame injustice, and set the captives free. This is because broken relationships, sickness, death, spiritual bondage (demonization), poverty, and oppression were not part of God's creation. They were effects of the fall.

These diabolical issues will not be part of Heaven. Therefore, our central role as Christ followers is to advance his kingdom. Making disciples involves the work of Jesus. We ought to do the things Jesus did: Make disciples, save the lost, cast out demons, heal the sick, and set the captives free. That's the work of the church.

Some problems are physical problems, and they need a physical solution or a miracle. Some problems are emotional problems, and the person may need a counselor or inner healing or some medication or a combination of those things. Some problems are spiritual problems, and no amount of counseling or medication will help the person find freedom. They need deliverance.

This was Jesus' perspective, and He wasn't some country bumpkin with a backwater worldview. He is the King of an eternal kingdom who saw into spiritual realities with perfect vision.

The disciples also did deliverance. Jesus gave them authority in Matthew 10 and sent them out to heal the sick, cast out demons, and preach the good news. John called the church to test for spirits (1 John 4:1). Jesus taught his disciples to make disciples of all nations, "teaching them to obey everything I have commanded you"—and that included engaging in spiritual warfare and casting out demons. This is part of the work of the church, but we have neglected our duty, and the world has suffered.

CHRISTIANS AND DEMONIC INFLUENCE

One of the big questions debated in some church circles is whether Christians can have demons. We know, certainly, that demons can influence Christians. We are told by Jesus to pray, "Lead us not into temptation, but deliver us from the evil one." So demonic forces can influence our thinking and tempt us. The question is to what degree can they influence us?

I do not use the word "demon possession." That implies ownership, and Christians cannot be owned—we have been created by God and bought for a price by the blood of Christ. We belong to God; the ownership issue is settled. So I don't think "possession" is an accurate translation. I prefer to use the word "demonization," which describes demonic influence.

I do believe that Christians can be afflicted with various degrees of demonization, and I think in some cases the only way to get them free is through deliverance or a power encounter. Therefore, in short, I do believe Christians can have indwelling demons and need deliverance. Before you dismiss this out of hand, let's examine the Scriptures and . . . not just what we were taught, or what we assumed. Here are some things to consider:

First, Jesus does the vast majority of his deliverance ministry in the gospels with Jews first and God-fearing Gentiles second. Remember there were no "Christians" yet. There were only covenant people and non-covenant people. There were Jews and there were Gentiles. Jesus does most of his deliverance with Jews, and with some God-fearing Gentiles.

Second, John tells us to "test the spirits" (1 John 4:1), and he says this to the church. He isn't telling them to test the spirits in their pagan neighbors; he is writing a letter to the church, for the church.

Third, Paul also calls the church, in 1 Corinthians, to test the spirits. This instruction is given in the context of a church service and the various spiritual manifestations that are occurring. Remember, Corinth was a pagan society, and the people in that city were syncretistic and worshiped a great many spiritual beings, which were demonic spirits. Paul knew that some of the manifestations that were taking place in their services were not of God and needed to be tested.

In 1 Corinthians 12:3 he wrote, "I want you to know that no one who is speaking by the Spirit of God says, 'Jesus be cursed,' and no one can say, 'Jesus is Lord,' except by the Holy Spirit." In my book *River Dwellers,* I talk about manifestations I have seen that are sometimes of God, other times human, and other times demonic. I have seen the exact same manifestation from all three sources. We have to discern.

Fourth, if demons were cast out upon conversion, then Jesus and his disciples never would have needed to do deliverance; they would have only converted people. But discipleship is a process of shifting people from the cultures, beliefs, and practices of this world to the cultures, beliefs, and practices of the kingdom of God. Theologically, once you put your faith in Christ, you are made perfect. Your spirit is perfected in Christ. However, the actual working out of your salvation in your beliefs and behaviors takes time. While the work of Christ is sufficient to cover all your sins, and to overcome the power of your sin, you still struggle with sin after you choose to follow Jesus.

This isn't because the work of Christ is incomplete. This is because you are working out your salvation; you are shifting from worldly culture to Kingdom culture. You are becoming in practice who you have already become in identity. Your spirit is made perfect, but your soul is still sometimes messy.

You need to work out what has been perfected in Christ in your spirit into your soul. For example, your spirit has been made perfect in love, but your soul still struggles to feel love some days because you are still a work in progress; you are still shifting cultures. And sometimes your soul still has places that can be under demonic influence and control, just as it can be infected by sin. If this is the case, you must experience deliverance in order to be freed from the control of these demonic spirits that take root in your soul.

> Our eternal salvation is secured in a moment; our sanctification (the working out of our salvation) takes one day longer than a lifetime.

The process of shifting cultures takes time, and so does our freedom from demonic influence, strongholds, and even demonization. Our eternal salvation is secured in a moment; our sanctification (the working out of our salvation) takes one day longer than a lifetime. When you meet Him face to face, you shall be like Him, but in the meantime, you are still on a journey of cleaning up the mess in your soul.

Fifth, I have heard some people argue that darkness cannot dwell with light. They often quote 2 Corinthians 6:14: "Do not be yoked together with unbelievers. For what do righteousness and wickedness have in common? Or what fellowship can light have with darkness?"

They use this passage to argue that a Christian, therefore, can't have a demon. However, the passage is calling us to be holy, distinct, to consecrate ourselves to God. It is a call to separate ourselves from the behaviors and practices of non-believers.

Paul says, "Come out from them and be separate. . . . Therefore, since we have these promises, dear friends, let us purify ourselves from everything that contaminates body and spirit, perfecting holiness out of reverence for God" (2 Corinthians 6:17, 7:1).

It is a call for a church that has come out of a pagan society to live in the new Kingdom reality of Jesus' Kingdom culture. Paul doesn't say a Christian can't have a demon and be in need of deliverance. The idea that some people seem to believe is that if you come to Christ, all demons must leave the territory they have occupied in your soul because of the light of the Spirit. They must be driven out. But that isn't the way the rest of sanctification occurs. We have to cooperate with the cleansing process with our choices to give God access to our hearts. We have to surrender and yield ourselves to God so that we can overcome sin and darkness.

And is it true that light cannot dwell with darkness in the spiritual realm? Think about the book of Job. Do you remember where Satan appears at the beginning of the book of Job? He appears in the throne room of Heaven. If light forced out the presence of darkness, how can Satan be in the throne room? Here is the personification of evil in the very living room of God.

> This doesn't imply that God is confused about right or wrong, nor does He condone sin, but neither is He threatened by evil in any way.

Or think about Jesus' statement to us in Luke 11:13: "If you then, though you are evil, know how to give good gifts to your children, how much more will your Father in heaven give the Holy Spirit to those who ask him!" Jesus calls us evil, yet tells us that the Father will answer our prayers for the Spirit's presence in our lives. God apparently isn't as wigged out about evil as we claim. Satan can be in God's presence in Heaven, and the Spirit can dwell in evil people like us. This doesn't imply that God is confused about right or wrong, nor does He condone sin, but neither is He threatened by evil in any way. And his great love for us compels Him to deal with us in a patient, compassionate manner as we learn to yield our will to Him and overcome by His strength.

Sixth, Jesus tells a parable that indicates we shouldn't ever do deliverance on someone who is a nonbeliever. Luke 11:24-26: "When an evil spirit comes out of anyone, it goes through arid places seeking rest and does not find it. Then it says, 'I will return to the house I left.' When it arrives, it finds the house swept clean and put in order. Then it goes and takes seven other spirits more wicked than itself, and they go in and live there. And the final condition of that person is worse than the first."

Luke tells us that a person's soul is like a house, and if their house is swept clean from the demonic, but the Spirit of God is not dwelling there, they are not sealed off from further infestation. I won't do deliverance with someone unless I know the Holy Spirit lives inside the person and can keep him or her from greater demonization and a worse condition.

Finally, experience talks. Everyone I know who does deliverance ministry works with Christians to get them free. Jesus had a conversation with the Sadducees in Matthew 22. They were testing him, and they asked him a question about the Levirate law.

When a woman's husband dies, the Levirate law stated that the man's brother had to marry her so she would be provided for and his lineage would be continued. The Sadducees made up a story about a woman who married seven brothers, none of whom had any children with her, and they asked whose wife she would be at the resurrection. They didn't even believe in the resurrection, but they were testing Jesus.

Jesus made an astonishing statement; it ought to give us

all pause. He said, "You are in error because you do not know the Scriptures or the power of God" (Matthew 22:29). It is not astonishing that He said they didn't know the power of God. They didn't move in power, nor did they believe in a resurrection, so no surprise there. They had religion—a form of godliness, denying its power (2 Timothy 3:5). But what astonishes me is that Jesus says they were in error because they didn't know the Scriptures.

These leaders memorized huge chunks of the Old Testament. They were radically committed to the authority of the first five books of the Bible, the Pentateuch; they even memorized large portions of it. They spent a lifetime studying Scripture, memorizing Scripture, teaching Scripture. And yet Jesus says they are in error because they don't know the Scriptures!

When we deny the power of God, it is often because we don't know the Scriptures. We come to the Scriptures with our preconceived notions and our already made-up minds, and we don't give the Holy Spirit access to reveal to us the mysteries of the kingdom, the deeper things of God. We know about Scripture, but our worldview keeps us from receiving the revelation it has to offer. Let's be careful not to be in error and miss out on the power of God because of our worldview lens.

Let me give you one last image. Some people have a hard time believing that a Christian can have an indwelling spirit; that doesn't fit their theological box. Picture it this way. Rather than thinking about the demonic spirit inside of a person, or occupying a corner of their soul, think of the spirit as outside of the person but draped over the person's back and hanging on, slowing the person down, and creating spiritual bondage for them. They need someone to come and get that monkey off their back. They need someone to come and, with the power of God, set them free.

I was teaching a weekend class once at the seminary, and

a student came up to me on Friday night and said, "I used to be in a gang. I have demons, and I need help. I can feel things crawling inside of me while you are talking. I hear voices. They are blasphemous and condemning. I have done a lot of bad things in my lifetime. Can you help me?"

I said to him, "Tomorrow in class we will have a ministry time. When I ask for prayer, stand up, and we'll help get you free."

He said, "I am afraid." He was a huge guy, six-and-a-half feet tall, over 300 pounds. I poked him in the chest and said, "Look at the size of you! What are you afraid of? Jesus has this. Stand up." He straightened up and said he would stand for prayer.

The next day, I was introducing some demonization issues. I had two students who were arguing with me that Christians can't have demons. I didn't want to argue. I pointed out some of the things I just listed, but they continued to argue vociferously against me. Then I said, "You don't have to agree with me. That's fine."

What they didn't know was the guy who was right next to them was the guy who came to me the night before. I transitioned to prayer, and said, "If you want prayer, stand." This big man stood up. I prayed, "Come, Holy Spirit."

What took place next shocked me and everyone in the class. In all my years dealing with this stuff, it is the only time I've seen something like it happen. Most deliverances have a fairly low level of demonic manifestation; people may experience some anxiety, some confusion, and they may feel some discomfort, but generally I can command the manifestations of the spirits to stop. But this demonic spirit threw this giant man across the room. He flew through the air about four feet off the floor for about twenty feet until he hit a wall, and he landed at the feet of one of his fellow students, my friend Kelvin Walker.

I nodded to Kelvin and said, "You, cast that out." All the color drained from Kelvin for a second as he asked, "Me?" But he dove in, and with a little coaching from me, we got that big man free by the power of Jesus. And those two guys who vociferously argued with me had a dramatic worldview shift that day.

HOW SPIRITS ENTER

A demon, also called an evil spirit or an unclean spirit in Scripture, is a fallen angel. They have rebelled against God and seek to kill, steal, and destroy (John 10:10). They seek to indwell and control people, to wreak havoc in people's lives, and to enslave them to spiritual bondage.

How do spirits enter? How does one get demonized? The primary answer is sin. I am not saying that today, if you drive down the road and someone cuts you off and you give him or her the universal sign of disapproval, you will get a demon. But there are certain sins that tend to give the enemy ground.

For example, sometimes sexual sin leads to demonization. People who engage in promiscuity are susceptible to demonization. Demons can be transferred through sexual intercourse. Sometimes drug abuse can lead to demonization. I have known people who were promiscuous or who were addicts who did not have demons, but it is very common for people who have lived highly promiscuous lives or addictive lifestyles to need deliverance. Prostitutes often need deliverance. I have actually never seen an exception to this—everyone I know who has sold his or her body for money has needed deliverance.

Sometimes demons enter through abuse. Many times people who commit acts of violence and abuse have demonic spirits. But, sadly, often their victims end up with demons too. Satan isn't fair. Other people need deliverance because they have engaged in occult activity. People who practice witchcraft and other occult activity are giving Satan wide-open access.

Some demonic issues are passed from generation to generation. These generational spirits often enslave families to certain sin patterns, like occult activity, abuse, anger, and addiction. These are just some of the gateways to demonization: sin, abuse, occult activity, and generational demons.

When someone comes to me with a presenting problem that could be demonic, I ask these kinds of questions to help me discern whether their problem could be spiritual. Ask yourself these questions as you wrestle with whether you might need to experience deliverance:

Is there much addiction in your family tree? Is there a history of abuse? Was there physical, sexual, or emotional abuse? Have you been abused in any of these ways? Are there any mental hospitalizations, suicides, or suicide attempts in the family? Is there a lot of depression and suicide ideology? Has there been occult activity, witchcraft, ancestor worship, or other religious practices? Have you engaged in any occult activity?

These questions are indicators that there may be some demonic activity involved. It should be explored.

SYMPTOMS OF DEMONIZATION

It's important to be aware of the symptoms of demonization. First, some people who have demons hear voices. To be clear, some voices are rooted in psychological issues. But these voices have distinct personalities and say things that are blasphemous and destructive. They are dark, condemning, shaming voices.

Some people would not say that they hear voices, because the voices are not audible. Rather, they say that they have thoughts in their mind that don't feel like their own, that they can't control. The thoughts are dark, blasphemous, hurtful, condemning, or suicidal.

Another symptom is that some people with demonic spirits experience rage. This isn't simply a problem with their temper; this is a white-hot, supernaturally empowered anger. Rage. I've talked with many people who have grown up in homes of "rage-aholics," and they have a family name for the blinding rage that comes upon them. It is a generational spirit that is recognized by a name.

Many people who have demonic spirits feel tortured or tormented. It is a spiritual and psychological torment they feel. Sometimes it may involve physical pain as well. Jesus delivered a woman who had a spirit that caused her physical problems. I've seen cases where a demon attacked someone and they ended up with scratches or physical signs of abuse.

In some cases, people can be sexually assaulted by a demon. These spirits are called incubus or succubus spirits; they come in through rape or sexual molestation. These spirits victimize some people repeatedly. These people wake up in the night because it feels like someone is raping them, but no one is there. They feel all the physical sensations of sexual assault, but a demonic spirit perpetrates it. This is becoming increasingly common in our society because of sexual assault, abuse, and date rape. If I talk about this in a classroom of fifty people, I always have a handful of people come up to me afterward and, through tears, tell me their tale of horror.

Another common symptom is struggling with blasphemous thoughts. I've talked to older people who love God yet have struggled for years with blasphemous thoughts in the middle of worship. After doing deliverance with a person like that, the thoughts were gone forever.

Many people experience condemning thoughts. They suffer a constant barrage of the enemy's attacks, accusations belittling them, condemning them, judging them, shaming them, and telling them they are worthless. Sometimes the condemning voices come from their childhood—the spirits use the words that were spoken to them as children. Words like, "You are worthless. You are good for nothing." They can't get out from under the weight of it. They memorize verses like "Therefore there is now no condemnation for those who are in Christ Jesus" (Romans 8:1). They experience inner healing; they forgive their offenders. But it doesn't help. Yet on countless occasions I have done deliverance with someone crushed under the weight of condemnation only to have them report that they never struggled with those condemning thoughts again.

Another symptom of demonization is having suicidal thoughts. It isn't that these people are sad or have experienced great loss and heartache, and in a season of grief think, "I wish I wouldn't have been born." That could be the case, but often these people are driving down the street on a sunny day, they are listening to their favorite music, having a good day, and all of a sudden this thought comes to them: I should drive into a tree and take my life. When I mention this scenario to an audience, there is always a reaction—sometimes people burst into tears, others audibly gasp, and others come and talk to me privately, because this is an all-too-common occurrence.

Finally, some people struggle with self-harm. Think about the Gadarene demoniac in Mark 5. He is living among the tombs, and he is cutting himself with stones. Now, think about how many people in this generation are struggling with cutting. It is an incredibly common problem, and it is on the rise. If you talk openly with young people and they trust you enough to open up with you, you will see it is a problem of epidemic proportions.

These are some of the symptoms of demonization. Sadly, all too often Christians I have met all over the world have lived under the weight of these symptomatic expressions because they did not participate in a church that understood how to set them free. I think this is cosmic treason.

Sometimes people ask me how to discern if something is a demon or if it is a psychological issue. It's a great question. We need to be humble; it helps to work with professional counselors who also understand the spirit world. There are times in which I have worked with someone who had demons manifest with demonic voices speaking out loud, but after I finished casting out the spirits, there were still psychological issues that needed to be addressed with counseling.

For example, sometimes the person still had hallucinations that were connected to a past wound. I prayed with them that the wound would be healed, and the hallucinations would leave, but the hallucinations persisted, and I referred them to a counselor who could help them. However, the voices that manifested themselves were demonic, and they had experienced freedom from that. The soul is complex. We need to operate with compassion, humility, and wisdom.

There have also been a couple of times when a counselor called me because I was working with one of their clients, and the client gave them permission to talk to me. On one occasion, the counselor called and said, "You made more progress with this person in one session than I made in five years." That's because they had demonic spirits, and no amount of counseling could help alleviate the torture this person was experiencing in their soul—they simply needed a deliverance.

Jesus gave us authority to set people free; we must learn how to develop spiritual authority and help the captives get free.

BREAKING GROUND

Now that you're familiar with the symptoms of demonization, let's examine how to get rid of demonic spirits.

First, you have to break the ground. Ephesians 4:26, 27:

"'In your anger do not sin'; Do not let the sun go down while you are still angry, and do not give the devil a foothold."

Literally, a foothold means an inhabited place; the Greek word is *topos*, referring to ground. Some things in our lives give the enemy a stronghold, a place to inhabit, ground to firmly hold. We must break that.

Demons stay when ground is present. If you have gone through this book, and sincerely followed the principles—forgiving, repenting, and more—then you have already broken most of the ground. When I am doing deliverance, I try to have the person go through Soul Care before I do the deliverance so that I do not have to spend much time helping them break ground. I want to break as much ground up front, before the session, as possible; it makes the session much quicker and easier for the person.

There are three main things that constitute ground.

Unconfessed Sin Creates Ground

Unconfessed sin creates ground. You have to confess your sins; you have to bring it all into the light. The key is to make sure all your confessions are current. When you confess your sins, they are brought under the blood of Jesus (1 John 1:9), and all of the enemy's ground is broken. Jesus broke the ground on the cross; you must appropriate the work of the cross through confession. One of the most common forms of ground is bitterness. Ephesians 4:26, 27 warns you not to allow your anger to go unprocessed, not to let the sun go down on your anger, and to never give the devil a foothold.

If you forgive those who sin against you, if you pray blessings on your enemies, the ground is broken, and the demonic spirits will leave upon command.

Secrets Create Ground

Secrets create ground. Sometimes the person knows the

secret. It is a sin from their past, or it may be that they have confessed it before God, but they have kept it in the dark with others, and they need to bring it into the light with God and others to break the grip of the enemy. But most of the time the secrets are not known by the person, yet still give ground to the enemy. They are family secrets.

Years ago, I was teaching a Soul Care class at Alliance Theological Seminary. I woke up in the middle of the night and the Lord said to me, "This class is full of demonic spirits." My first thought was, *Really? You woke me up in the night to tell me that? That could have waited until 6 a.m.* But I said, "Full? What do you want me to do?" He said, "I want you to do a group test, and equip them to do deliverance. Get them all free."

I went to class the next morning and spoke to Dr. Martin Sanders, who is now head of the doctoral program at Alliance. I told him what the Lord said to me in the middle of the night. He said, "What do you want to do?" I told him I wanted to test the whole class at once, and see how many of them had demonic spirits. He said, "You lead, I'll follow." So we plunged in, over our heads.

I tested for demonic spirits (more on that later), and more than two-thirds of the class had demonic issues. Martin looked at me and said, "Now what, big guy?" The look said: "You got us into this, you get us out of this!"

We trained the class on how to do deliverance, and then we set them into small groups to work on getting each other free. Martin and I served as coaches.

One of the groups ran into a problem. They came running up to me pleading for help. I came over to the group only to discover that one of their classmates, Jeff, had a mute spirit. He was nearly frozen. It was like everything moved in slow motion, even his blinking, and he couldn't speak. I had not come across a mute spirit at that point in my life, but I knew

Jesus did in the gospels, and I figured Jesus would help.

Once again, I dove into the deeper waters, where dependence is a necessity and the power of God a must. Your next level with God lies beyond the boundaries of your current experiences. The only way you can get there is to risk more than you are comfortable with.

> Your next level with God lies beyond the boundaries of your current experiences. The only way you can get there is to risk more than you are comfortable with.

I tried what I knew how to do. I commanded the spirit to speak. Jeff opened his mouth, but nothing came out. I said, "I loose your tongue in Jesus' name." Again, the mouth opened, but there was no sound. I had no idea what to do. But when I don't know what to do, I know who does. Theology 101: God is smart, and He knows stuff I don't know, and He likes to tell me.

I waited on God. The Holy Spirit spoke: "He has a secret." I said, "The spirit?" He said, "Yes." I said, "That's legal?" He said, "Yes." I said, "Mute spirit, Jesus tells me you have a secret. Is that truth before God?"

A whisper came out of the man's inner being. He didn't even open his mouth, but a voice came from within him and hissed, "Yes." It was a creepy whisper. I commanded the spirit to step aside in Jesus' name. This allowed Jeff to come back to regular functioning.

I said, "Jeff, did you hear that conversation?" He said, "Yes." I said, "Do you know the secret?" He said, "No. I've confessed everything I know." I believed him. I had been with him, and he wasn't hiding. I said, "No; it isn't you. It is something from your past that you don't know about. Jeff, you are going to have to go home tonight and fast. Ask God to reveal the secret to you, and then we'll finish up tomorrow."

He did. The Lord showed him the secret by giving him pictures from his infancy. The pictures revealed that he had been molested when he was a baby. He saw the person who did it. It was a relative who was in prison for molestation. He called his mother and asked, "Mom, did he live with us when I was a baby?" She said, "Yes, he lived with us from the time you were 3 to 6 months old." Jeff came in the next day with this information that the Holy Spirit had revealed. I called the mute spirit back to attention, and instantly he resumed this catatonic-like state; once again, Jeff couldn't talk. I said, "Mute spirit, Jesus revealed to us that Jeff was molested by this family member when he was a baby. That's your secret. Is that truth before God?" The whisper came up out of his inner being again: "Yes." His ground was broken, and I commanded this spirit to leave in Jesus' name. The spirit left, and Jeff was free.

Jeff had wrestled with some perverse sexual temptations his entire life and couldn't find freedom from the temptations and images—until that day. Please don't misunderstand: not everyone who wrestles with sexual temptation does so because of demonization; mostly, that is not true. But this guy couldn't get rid of the pictures in his head until he got rid of the source of those pictures. He was dramatically changed. He ended up leading family members to Christ and helping them get free. It changed the course of his life.

Curses Create Ground

Finally, curses can give ground to demonic spirits. There are three types of curses. **First, there are religious curses.** If someone is praying for you, but to the wrong side—to dark spirits—then they are cursing you. Even if the person is praying for you, the demons don't bless; they only curse. If someone is praying against you, then that is a curse.

Second, there are behavioral curses. The book of

Deuteronomy talks about blessings and curses. Sins that are repeated from generation to generation lead to a curse upon a family. These become demonically reinforced family sin patterns. Sometimes there is a curse without a demonization. The curse still needs to be broken. Other times there is a curse that gives a demon ground to stay, and the curse needs to be broken in order to break the ground and make the demon leave.

Third, there are word curses. James 3 talks about two types of wisdom. There is wisdom from Heaven that is "pure; then peace-loving, considerate, submissive, full of mercy and good fruit, impartial and sincere" (James 3:17). But there is another form of "wisdom" that is a demonic curse.

James says, "But if you harbor bitter envy and selfish ambition in your hearts, do not boast about it or deny the truth. Such 'wisdom' does not come down from heaven but is earthly, unspiritual, demonic" (James 3:14, 15).

When we have a bitter root, or envy, we will often feel compelled to give someone a "word." I've met people who give angry words and called them "prophetic." Or I've heard them say, "I feel compelled by God to tell you this," and then they proceed to tell a person off. These "promptings of the spirit" feel very compelling, but they are not prophetic from the Spirit of God. They are demonically inspired. The person who gives this angry word does not always have an indwelling demon. The enemy uses them because of the bitter root or envy. But, regardless, the word they speak is a demonically inspired curse.

We need to break curses in Jesus' name. Galatians 3 tells us that Jesus died on the cross to become a curse for us and to break the curse of sin and Satan over us. He broke the curses against us by assuming our curses on the cross. We claim the blood of Jesus to break curses.

And we have to bless those who curse us. Blessing those who curse us is a spiritual weapon with the power to break curses. It prevents the curse from landing on us and sends back a blessing to the one who is cursing us, which gives them an opportunity to repent. Break it in Jesus' name, claim the blood, and pray blessings—if the curse doesn't lift, then get a team to pray and fast with you.

I can actually feel when I have been cursed. It feels like a lead blanket on my spirit. There have been mornings when I awoke and said to Jen, "Someone is cursing me today." She asks, "How do you know?" When it had happened, I could almost always feel it. Often I would wait, and God would tell me who it was. Then I would pray blessings on the person, and I would feel the curse lift. Later on someone would come to me and tell me that the person had been speaking ill of me and confirm what I already knew.

Years ago, I was in Nigeria on a trip with my friend Martin. On the first day of the trip, I preached a sermon to a group of leaders. The talk was anointed by God, and it resulted in one of the most amazing responses I have seen. Thousands of people literally ran to the altar to confess their sins. It was a God moment.

But the next time I preached, I felt blocked. I had no idea what it was. I went to see Martin and said, "I'm blocked, bud." He said, "It's little Rob stuff"—meaning he thought it was my Soul Care issues, some inner issue making me feel insecure. I said to him, "No, bud. This isn't little Rob stuff. I feel spiritually blocked." He said, "Did you sin?" I said, "I know what to do with sin. No. I feel blocked. It's like I can't get my words past the pulpit."

One of our friends, John Torres, who is a Presbyterian charismatic pastor, overheard our conversation and said, "Did you get cursed?" I had no category for curses—again, my Western worldview had messed up my biblical worldview. I knew curses were in the Bible, but I didn't have any category for that in my mind. I was running through the internal file cabinet in my mind, trying to find something under curses, and John said, "Think. This is Africa!"

I said, "I know that, John. I don't know. . . . Well, there was this lady who got mad at one of the guys I brought because he still smokes, and she saw him, and she spit on him and said, 'You and your pastor come from America with your weak spirits!'" John said to me, "You got cursed! Let me pray over you in tongues and it will break." I said, "Great." New experiences.

He prayed in tongues, and he had an interpretation. He said, "You've been cursed five times before, but you failed to recognize it. The Lord protected you from it, but He isn't going to protect you anymore, because He wants you to learn a new level of authority." The curse broke. I preached with the anointing again. And I learned a lot about curses. It became useful in deliverance and in life.

In that same class Martin and I were teaching at Alliance Theological Seminary in which we encountered the mute spirit, there was another distress call from a group of students. They came running up to me like their hair was on fire and said, "We need help!"

I went with them and saw a young Chinese man lying on the floor with a demonic voice coming out of him, speaking in some sort of demonic tongue. I asked another Chinese student if it was Chinese, but he said no. I commanded the spirit to speak in English, and it did.

Right away I sensed something was wrong. Something was amiss with this deliverance. I commanded the spirit to step aside so I could talk directly to Anson. I said, "Anson, have you been through deliverance before?" He said, "Yes. Five times. But they keep coming back." I said, "Really? Who did it?"

Sometimes people go through multiple rounds of deliverance, but the people doing the deliverance don't really know what they are doing, and the person doesn't get free. But when he told me the people who did his deliverance, I knew them by reputation. They knew what they were doing.

I said, "Anson, we have a problem. I don't know what it is. But I'm going to try to do what I know how to do, and if they come back, then we'll figure it out. God knows what to do."

I did the deliverance, and the demons left. I saw him three months later and said, "How are you doing?" He said, "Not good. They're back." I said, "Really? Did you talk to Martin about it?" He said, "Yes. He just said I must have let them back in." I said, "No. That's not it. We left a gate open." He said, "What does that mean?" I said: "I don't know. But God will show us."

We had a class with us that weekend at our church, and at the end of the weekend we tackled the deliverance. We had about thirty-five people there, students and people from my church who were praying, watching, and learning. We got into the deliverance, and once again, I was in over my head. But it wasn't over Jesus' head.

At one point in the deliverance I looked at Martin and said, "Do you know what to do?" He shook his head and said, "I have no idea. Do you?" I shook my head no. We have had a lot of experiences between us, but we were utterly stumped.

I looked up and saw the class had overheard our interchange, and their eyes were wide with disbelief and horror. I said, calmly, "It's OK. Don't worry. Jesus knows what to do. He'll show us."

As soon as I said it, I got a word from the Spirit: "Godfather." I thought: *Godfather, that can't be right. It must be grandfather.* So I said aloud to the spirit: "Grandfather!" He called back in his deep, dark, gravelly voice, "GODFATHER!" I said, "OK. That's what I thought I heard." I made the spirit step aside so that it was no longer in control, and then I addressed Anson. "Tell me about your godfather," I said.

He told me that he was born on a holiday in China that is called "the gates of hell." In order to protect him from the dark spirits and the gates of hell, his parents brought him to the temple, and his godfather dedicated him to the ancestor spirits. A dedication ceremony to a demonic spirit is a curse. And this curse had forced open the gates of hell, so that every time Anson underwent deliverance, the spirit would leave, but the gate was forced open, and the spirit would come back. Together we sensed that he had to stop calling this man godfather; this put his relationship with his parents at risk.

He prayed and fasted, called his parents, and told them that he would no longer call the man godfather. Fortunately, his parents were gracious. His deliverance was completed, and the spirits never came back because the curse was broken and the gate was closed. I learned a lot that day. And Anson experienced a tremendous breakthrough in his life.

I try to break as much ground as I can up front, before the deliverance, but some of these things you can't discover until you get into the deliverance itself. If you are leading the deliverance, it is best to have the person do as much preparation work as possible. Send them through a process like Soul Care to break the ground, and to prepare for the deliverance, and then do a spiritual test. Sometimes there will be things that come up during the session, and you will have to rely on the Holy Spirit for guidance and revelation.

THE PROCESS OF DELIVERANCE

I always encourage people when they start a deliverance to use a system. Some people try to do deliverance, but they leave spirits behind. They are not thorough and exhaustive. They don't break all the ground, and spirits remain, or they fail to close some gates, and spirits return. I have included an addendum, at the end of this book, that outlines a system and procedure I have personally used for years and have used to train and equip hundreds of others to do deliverance. I highly urge you to use this in the beginning when you are learning deliverance ministry.

Begin with a Spiritual Test

1 John 4:1 teaches, "Dear friends, do not believe every spirit, but test the spirits to see whether they are from God." When doing a spiritual test, you command the spirit to come to attention whom Jesus highlights or singles out; call that spirit to attention. Jesus stands at the center of every believer's soul, and if there is any demonization, He will force the demonic spirit to come into the light. If there is no demonic spirit, then the Holy Spirit will cooperate with the test, and He will answer the biblical questions that you pose.

To perform a spiritual test, you simply ask the spirit at attention to answer these biblical questions. The Holy Spirit always gets 100 percent. In the addendum, I have included a list of the questions you should ask. But here are some of the examples: Did Jesus Christ come in the flesh? Is Jesus Christ the Lord? Is Jesus Christ your Lord? Do you honor the blood of the Lord Jesus Christ? The Holy Spirit always says yes. Demonic spirits will say no. They may say yes to a few questions you ask, but they can't hold their contempt for Jesus for long. They show their true colors.

Break Any Ground, and Command the Spirits to Leave

After all the ground is dealt with, then you command the spirit to go where Jesus sends it. Demons come in hierarchical structures. Keep them in their hierarchies, and send the leader of a group out with those underneath him. See the addendum, following the final chapter, for more detailed instructions.

Don't Go It Alone

I always urge people who are starting out in deliverance ministry to develop a team around them. It helps to have discerning people who can pray with you and listen to the Spirit's promptings. In the beginning of my deliverance ministry, I always brought a team in with me, because I wanted the prayer support and the help. Now, after thousands of deliverances in all different cultures around the world, I still bring a team in because I want to equip others to do this ministry of God's kingdom.

Be Spiritually Prepared

It is important to come in spiritually prepared. If you are praying on the team, leading the team, or the one being delivered, make sure your confessions are current. If I suspect it is a particularly strong demonic infestation, I will pray and fast. I have been in sessions where a demonic spirit accused someone on the prayer team of sin that they had not yet confessed. It is a terrible thing to be called out by a demon in the middle of a deliverance session. Make sure you are spiritually prepared.

Exercise Spiritual Authority

The capacity to do deliverance is all about spiritual authority. Jesus gave His disciples authority to cast out demons (Matthew 10:1). I've seen some people try to cast out demons by yelling and screaming at the demon. It isn't about power. You don't need to yell or scream. I've seen other situa-

> I've seen some people try to cast out demons by yelling and screaming at the demon. It isn't about power. You don't need to yell or scream.

tions where a person with a demonic manifestation will get up and run, and the people on the prayer team will run after them and literally tackle them. This is closer to hand-to-hand combat than it is deliverance ministry!

You don't need to yell, scream, or resort to hand-to-hand combat. You have to exercise authority. Make commands in Jesus' name. If someone got up to run, I would simply command them to stop in Jesus' name. I've seen people yell at demons, "Come out! Come out! *Come out!!*" But, that doesn't cause the demon to leave. If there is ground, you can yell, scream, and pray at the top of your lungs, but it isn't going to matter. Break the ground, and use spiritual authority to command the demon.

Spiritual authority isn't static; it is dynamic. You can expand your spiritual authority; you can develop it. Think about this biblically with me. In Matthew 10, Jesus gave the disciples authority to drive out demons. They had success. They even came to him after one successful mission and said, "Even the demons submit to us in your name!" (Luke 10:17). But they didn't always have enough authority to deal with a demonic situation—they had to develop it and expand it.

For example, when Jesus came down from the Mount of Transfiguration, He found His disciples tangling with a sticky demonic situation. The disciples couldn't cast out a demon from a boy, and the spirit was manifesting and beginning to draw a crowd. Jesus simply cast it out and set the boy free.

The disciples asked him about it later: "Boss, why couldn't we cast it out?" They were stumped because they had success casting out demons in the past. So, what went wrong this time? In Matthew's version, Jesus tells them it was because their faith was so small. In Mark's version, He explains to them that this kind only comes out by prayer and fasting. But interestingly enough, Jesus neither prays nor fasts when He casts it out. He just commanded it to leave. So what was He saying?

I think the broader conversation may have gone something like this: On a scale of 1 to 10, you have cast out demons that were a 4 or 5. This one was a 6. In order to cast out this spirit, you need to expand your umbrella of spiritual authority. The way to do that is to expand your intimacy with me, and your faith in me, so you can trust me to handle the 6. But if your faith isn't at that level, and your authority can't cover this level of spirit, then you need to pray and fast. If you pray and fast, it will deepen your intimacy and increase your faith, expand your authority, and you'll cast out the 6.

Jesus didn't need to pray and fast because His authority had it covered. He just made the command, the spirit left, and the boy was free. When we run into a spirit that we can't handle, we need to increase our prayer coverage, increase the size of our team (we can combine umbrellas to increase coverage), and/or pray and fast.

On more than one occasion I have had to stop a session, which I usually only allow to go for two hours, and say to the person, "I'm going to pray and fast over this, and I'm going to bring in a few people who are experienced intercessors to pray and fast with us." Then I will come back to the situation a week later, after prayer and fasting, and the person will be set free.

You have to persist. Jesus always wins in the end. You can expand your spiritual authority through prayer, fasting, persistence, and teaming with other people.

Another important point about deliverance: it is not a cure all. People often come into a deliverance session hoping to make everything better in their life, even though they haven't done the hard work of the soul. That isn't the way it works. We have to be willing to repent, forgive, solidify our identity, heal our wounds, break family sin patterns, and overcome fears. Deliverance is a necessary part of the freeing work of Christ, but it is just one part, not the end all be all.

Let the Battle Come to You

Finally, don't go on a witch hunt. When I first started doing deliverance, I would have a conversation with someone, and I could tell they needed deliverance. I would say to them, "You might want to come for deliverance." I realized before long that Jesus never initiated this ministry. He initiated teaching, and He initiated healing, but deliverance was a reactive ministry for Jesus. Someone came to Him with a presenting problem; the presenting problem was not always known to be demonic. Sometimes the presenting problem was a physical problem, but they initiated, and Jesus dealt with the roots.

Now I always wait for people to approach me. They may come with anxiety, depression, addiction, the emotional pain of past abuse, or some other presenting problem that has its roots in some demonization. In other words, they don't always come saying, "I have a demon."

A few years back I was in New York City teaching a Soul Care conference. On Sunday morning, a young woman was standing next to me receiving prayer. I was praying for someone else, and suddenly the young woman fell over.

Sometimes someone will fall over because of the presence of God. The Old Testament word for glory was kabod. Its roots are similar to our English word heavy. The glory is the presence of God, and sometimes when God manifests His presence, His glory, it comes with a heaviness that actually can cause someone to fall.

John the apostle, the one who laid his head on Jesus' breast, falls over like a dead man when he encounters the glory of Jesus in His resurrected state in Revelation 1. This was kabod. Ezekiel encountered the glory (kabod) of the Lord and fell down on his face, too (Ezekiel 3:23).

Yet, when this young woman fell over next to me, I knew it was not God. It was demonic. I finished praying with the woman I was praying for and knelt down on the floor next to the woman who had fallen, and I began to address the demonic spirit that had presented itself.

This poor woman had suffered every kind of abuse. She had been dedicated to Satan in a home of occult activity. She had been physically abused and sexually abused. Just about every nasty thing that can happen to a person on this sinful planet had happened to this poor woman.

Many times when someone is abused, they have a bent will. The bent will in a deliverance will often cause the person to cower before the demonic spirit. The spirit bullies them, and they often crawl up in a fetal position on the floor and cry, wail, and the demon manifests, often loudly and strongly.

I stopped the manifestations and said to the woman, "I need you to fight with me. I know you have been victimized, but you are not a victim. You must fight. I need you to look to Jesus. Look to Jesus."

She sniffed and gasped for a breath and nodded. I could see her posture change, and she was looking to Jesus, ready to engage in the fight. And a fight it was. We broke ground. She had people to forgive. There were sins to confess. There were curses to break. The demons were strong, and she was tired. Near the end of the deliverance, she was so tired she cried out through a torrent of tears, "I can't go on. I can't go on. I can't go on." I knew she was tired, but I also knew I was leaving to go back home. I said to her, "Sweetie, I am going home today. I want to finish before I go. We are close. Look to Jesus."

She nodded, and through tears she started saying, "I kept coming for help. Why wouldn't anyone help me? I kept telling them it was darkness. Why wouldn't anyone help me? I knew it was demonic. Why wouldn't anyone help me?"

By the time she had finish saying this, she was shouting. There were over one hundred people in that room listening to her cry, "Why wouldn't anyone help me?" I will never forget that cry. It was haunting.

There are many times when I am doing deliverance and I hear the sounds of hell. Jesus talked about weeping and gnashing of teeth. I have heard the sounds of hell during deliverance—the screams, the weeping, and the gnashing of teeth. They are gut-wrenching, soul-stirring sounds. No one who hears them can remain the same.

Martin and I were in a class one day, and a woman cried out in a demonic manifestation; it was the sounds of hell. We got her free. Martin said to the class, "Never forget these sounds. This is why we do what we do. This is what it will be like for everyone who is not reached for Christ. This is what it is like for everyone who is not set free."

> If the church doesn't do deliverance, who will? If the church does not own her spiritual authority, who can? If the church does not set people free in the name of Jesus, where can these souls go for help?

If the church doesn't do deliverance, who will? If the church does not own her spiritual authority, who can? If the church does not set people free in the name of Jesus, where can these souls go for help? If the church doesn't do her job, then people are left with the sounds of hell echoing through their souls.

We finished the deliverance of that woman in New York City after two hours of exhausting battle. They don't usually take me that long anymore, but there was a lot of ground, and she was struggling mightily with the bent will. After two hours, all the demons were gone, and the presence of God came. In all my years of doing deliverance, I have never seen the presence of God come at the end of a session like that.

I was doing a final spiritual test with her to make sure she was free, and the Spirit of God began speaking to her. She relayed what He said. It came out in a first-person narrative, and as she spoke it out, the presence of God flooded the room.

She reported the Spirit saying, "I love her. She is my baby girl. I am so sorry for her pain." As the Spirit continued like this, I could feel tears hitting my arm. I looked up and saw one of the leaders of the church weeping in the presence of the Lord. I felt tears hitting my right shoulder, and I looked up and one of my intercessors who had come with me was weeping on my shoulder in the presence of God. I felt tears hitting my left shoulder and I looked up, and it was another of my intercessors weeping. I felt tears hitting my left hand, and I looked up and it was my daughter Darcy; at the time she was 13 years old.

We finished the deliverance, we said our goodbyes, and we got in the car to go home. We were all tired, and the car was pretty quiet, and then this soft voice came from the back seat. Darcy said, "Dad?" I said, "Yeah, baby?" She said, "That was the coolest thing I've ever seen. Can you teach me how to help people get free?"

> That's what the sounds of hell do to you—they give you courage to get involved in the King's business.

That's what the sounds of hell do to you—they give you courage to get involved in the King's business. I said, "Of course, baby. You didn't get a junior Holy Spirit."

We need more mighty warriors to step up at this hour of history and pick up their authority in Christ and help the captives be set free in Jesus' name, for Jesus' glory! May you be among their numbers!

SPIRITUAL ACTION STEPS

- Reflect on your worldview as it relates to demonic strongholds. Does it align with the biblical worldview?

- Ask yourself the list of questions related to how spirits enter. Is there a history of addiction in your family tree? Is there a history of abuse? Was there physical, sexual, or emotional abuse? Have you been abused in any of these ways? Are there any mental hospitalizations, suicides, or suicide attempts in the family? Is there a lot of depression and suicide ideology? Has there been occult activity, witchcraft, ancestor worship, or other religious practices? Have you engaged in any occult activity?

- Examine the symptoms of demonization. Do you experience any of these symptoms?

- If you feel like you might need a deliverance, get help from a trusted, spiritually mature friend, and walk through the steps in the addendum at the end of this book.

Prepare by making sure your confessions are current and doing the work outlined in each of these chapters first.

CONCLUSION

People often come to me with a presenting problem that has them in a complete state of desperation. They may be struggling with an addiction that has them by the throat, and they are gasping for relief. They may be battling with a depression that has them beleaguered. They may be rattled with an anxiety that feels overwhelming and debilitating. What they want above all else is to be fixed. They want this problem to leave.

You may have picked up this book with that sense of desperation in your soul. As you work on these principles of healing the soul, and help others find freedom, here are a few final thoughts to keep in mind.

Soul Care Is a Process

Remember the ongoing nature of the journey. It takes one day longer than a lifetime to finally get well. When you meet Jesus face to face, you will be like Him; in the meantime, you are on a journey. Along the journey there are ups and downs, there are victories and defeats, there are triumphs and tragedies. You

> Remember the ongoing nature of the journey. It takes one day longer than a lifetime to finally get well.

have to learn to be OK with your brokenness. You aren't going to get it perfectly right in this lifetime. You can get stronger, healthier, and more mature, but you will still wrestle with your human frailty. Yet God chose you in Christ before the foundations of the earth, and He did so out of a heart full of love

(Ephesians 1). He knew you were a mess, and He still chose you—flaws and all. Jesus isn't nervous today about your journey. Press in, and press through.

In order to press in and press through, you must process deeply. Too often people process enough to alleviate their suffering. They process their soul junk until they feel a little better, and then they stop processing. They don't press in and press through. They press in, find comfort, and stop pressing. But those who find the most freedom press in and press through. They keep pressing in to God, and they press through to intimacy. They keep pressing in to self-awareness, and they press through to deep self-knowledge that reflects understanding of the root issues of the soul, self-knowledge that connects all the dots between these various Soul Care principles. Self-awareness is the gateway to breakthrough.

I was desperate to get things fixed in my life at the beginning of my Soul Care journey. But some of that desperation was just driven by the fear that I might lose Jen. So often fear fuels our desperation. After a while, after I established the foundation of God's love more firmly set under my feet, I started to realize I was OK. I was still broken, and I was going to continue to struggle with broken parts and broken pieces all my days, but I was loved, and God was enough for me. I started to obsess less and feel more relaxed on the spiritual journey toward Christlikeness. We all need to take ourselves a little less seriously and enjoy the journey. Celebrate the good things in life, including the victories along the way, and the love of God every day. David Benner said, "You are not simply a sinner, you are a deeply loved sinner."[10] And that is that. God is with you. God is for you. God loves you. And nothing can

---

10. David G. Benner, *The Gift of Being Yourself* (Downers Grove: InterVarsity Press, 2015), pp. 62, 63.

take that away from you. That is enough.

God is close to the brokenhearted. God is irresistibly attracted to the contrite of heart. God draws near to the humble, but the proud walk alone.

Keep Walking in the Light

As you continue your Soul Care journey, keep walking in the light. Always. Walk in the light with God and others. I have friends who have struggled with some dangerous addictive behavior. I have known people who died from drug overdose. The biggest mistake people make isn't just going back to a drug once they are off of it; the biggest mistake they make is when they feel the pull but aren't honest about it.

I have had some vitally important friends over the years, and we have been committed to walking in the light with God and each other. That one commitment has saved me untold amounts of darkness in my life. God is close to the brokenhearted. God is irresistibly attracted to the contrite of heart. God draws near to the humble, but the proud walk alone. Don't be too proud to get help. Don't be too proud to be honest. Make a steely resolve in your heart to die with no secrets and to live in the light with God and others. It is a powerful thing to be honest. There is no healing where there is pretending.

Prioritize Your Time with God

Another key is to make time with God a nonnegotiable in your life. Only God can heal the soul. God can do more healing in five minutes than a counselor can do in twenty years. That isn't a knock on counseling; it is a testimony to God's healing grace.

Most life change occurs alone with God. You need to be

with Him; you need to give Him access to your heart. Learn to sit in His presence and welcome His healing love.

I think the secret of success is simply to find what God wants and to do it. This is true on the journey toward inner healing, too. I often didn't know what to do, but I knew who did. I kept coming to Him, and He kept showing me what to do. I kept saying "yes" to God and surrendering. He never outlined the big picture up front; He led me through in a trusting walk, hand in hand, one step at a time. He is faithful, and He will see you through.

I made an unbending resolution to spend time with God when I was in my twenties. I have changed my approach to God over the years, varied my spiritual disciplines, and adjusted my rhythm, but I never neglected my fundamental commitment to be alone with God. And that commitment to be with Jesus, to know Him, pursue Him, access his presence, has made all the difference in my journey.

Go for the Roots

You also want to go for the roots and not the leaves. Fight the disease and not the symptoms. One of my favorite little phrases in life is this: The issue is not the issue. We get fixated on the wrong things and become desperate to make these side issues right. We end up battling symptoms and never diagnosing and treating the disease.

One of the most important questions to ask about the soul is, "Why?" Why do I do what I do? What is underneath that? Get to the roots. Once again, God knows. Theology 101: God is smart, He knows stuff we don't know, and He likes to tell us. Walk with other wise and discerning friends who are continuously seeking to understand the deeper things of the soul.

Be Patient

Another key: be patient with yourself, and wait on God.

Life change is hard, and it takes time. Psalm 37:7 says, "Be still before the Lord and wait patiently for him." We all have things in our life that we want to change, problems we want to solve, answers to prayer we long to see, and character traits we seek to alter. David did, too. He learned to wait on God.

The Lord told David he'd be king, but that launched him into a decade of agonized waiting. He didn't strive to make it happen. He stood still before the Lord. He rested in God's trustworthy promise. But don't get the wrong idea: this was not a serene, peaceful resting. The waiting was painful, difficult, hard, agonizing.

The root word for wait here is to dance, whirl, writhe. There is a tension. You wait for God to deliver you. But you wait for God's answers in a whirling dance of emotions, disappointments, doubts, and agony, writhing in prayer and coming to a place of surrender, trust, and obedience. Resolve to keep coming, keep trusting, keep surrendering, and keep obeying. You fail. You fall. You flop. But you get up, and you turn your eyes to Jesus once again.

> There are some things God can accomplish with His tenderness over time that He cannot accomplish with His power in a moment.

This is the deep life of faith. This is where Christ is formed in you and where you are made ready for the answer to your prayers to come forth. This is where you come to realize character and intimacy are more important than the answer itself, and that your relationship with God is more important than being fixed by God. This is where you learn to give God access to the deep places in your heart. Stand still, waiting in the writhing dance of faith, and discover that God is good. There are some things God can accomplish with His tenderness over time that He cannot accomplish with His power in a moment. Embrace the process-oriented nature of change.

Remember that God isn't interested in fixing you; He wants a relationship with you. God is far less concerned about your behaviors than you think He is, and He is far more concerned with your heart than you'll ever know. I'm not condoning sin. But I am saying that the heart is the issue—if you get the heart in right alignment with God, the behaviors follow.

Out of the overflow of the heart, a person speaks and acts. And God addresses the issues of the heart in the context of relationship. It is relationship that He is after. It is relationship for which He paid the price of his blood. It is relationship that heals our soul. It is relationship that forms Christ in you. He doesn't want you to *behave*. He wants you to *love Him,* and when you love Him with all your heart, and your heart is healed, redeemed, and formed in His loving presence, your behaviors will come around too.

THE CULTURE OF THE KINGDOM

I put my faith in Christ more than forty years ago. I surrendered my life to Christ and experienced a transformational encounter with God more than thirty years ago. I have been following Him wholeheartedly ever since. And it has been twenty years since I started this Soul Care journey. It has helped me immensely to become a better man, a better husband, a better father, a better leader, and a better Christ-follower. But I haven't arrived. I'm not even close. I'm not the man I want to be, but I'm not the man I used to be, either, nor am I the man I am going to be. I'm on the journey, and these principles have been critically important to making the journey more peaceful, more loving, more fulfilling, and more Christlike.

These seven Soul Care principles are not principles to be

used once and then forgotten. These are principles of the kingdom of God; these are part of Kingdom culture. You have to constantly renew your mind and make sure your identity is rooted deeply in the love of Christ.

I established this firm foundation under my feet in the midst of a marriage struggle, but when others attacked me publicly, I needed to go back to this foundation. Once again I needed to stand on the truth that the issue of my value was settled on the cross. My value was not dependent on the size of the church I led or the opinions others held about me. In those days, I went back to the foundation.

Once again, I also had to forgive people who sinned against me. I blessed those who cursed me, and if I died tonight, I would still die with no enemies. If you consistently learn to bless those who curse you, and forgive those who sin against you, you will grow into a gracious, magnanimous person. But this doesn't happen overnight. It is a developmental process that results from applying this kingdom principle over and over again in our lives. This is how we grow, and how Christ is formed in us. There were new wounds to be healed and new fears to be overcome. I didn't outgrow the need to apply these principles. I've had to apply them over and over again in my life. And therein lies the path to freedom.

Jesus said, "If you hold to my teaching, you are really my disciples. Then you will know the truth, and the truth will set you free" (John 8:31, 32). You have to hold to the truth, and that means you have to renew your mind with it, and you have to appropriate it at the appropriate time over and over again in your life. You have to live into it. Knowing the truth will not set you free. But holding onto the truth will.

Life change happens in an atmosphere conducive to change. You need anointed truth that is received into an open heart receptive to the light. You need true community that is open, honest, confessional, and grace-filled. You need the power and presence of God for healing, freedom, and transformation. And you must press in and press through.

So often people press in to God, and into the healing journey of the soul, just long enough to feel better. Once they feel some relief from their current presenting problem, they stop pressing in. Press in, and press through. Don't settle for good enough. Don't settle for some alleviation of the symptoms. Go for the roots, and hold on to God until deep life change comes. Unpack the suitcase of the soul from all the junk that is in there. The more you unpack it, the more room you will have for God to fill you. Don't settle for a little bit more of God in your life. Press in and press through and discover the freedom and fullness of God in Christ.

SOUL CARE PRINCIPLES

These seven Soul Care Principles are essential principles to life change; these are building blocks to a healthy soul.

You must build a healthy foundation, an identity that is established not on what you do or what you have, but on who you are in Christ. The issue of your value is settled at the cross.

You must walk in the light with God and others through repentance. You will never rise above your level of self-awareness. Self-awareness is the gateway to transformation. It doesn't guarantee it, but you can't get there without it.

Light is a gift, not an intrusion. You must welcome it and continually walk in the light with God and others. You must experience the release of forgiveness, not just the cognitive understanding of it, or your soul will be diseased.

You have to overcome the pull of your family sin patterns. You must deal with these sins severely before they deal severely with you.

You have to forgive those who sin against you. The greatest mark of the Father's love in your life is the capacity to love your enemies. Jesus said even the pagans can love their friends—to do so is no credit to us. But to love our enemies? Now *that* is a mark of the Father's love. Bless those who curse you. Forgive those who sin against you.

You need healing for your wounded places, for the bruises of your soul. Jesus is the Healer. There is no soul too wounded for His healing touch to repair. There are no irreparable people in the presence of God.

You have to conquer your fears. The number one command in Scripture is "Fear not," and the fact that it is the most-often-used command is no accident. The people of God make more mistakes in the time of fear than at any other time. But His perfect love can cast out fear.

You have to break the demonic strongholds of the enemy. You have an enemy, but he has been defeated. Jesus can free you from the strong man's grasp.

I believe Soul Care is going to be the gateway to evangelism in this generation. I think people are going to come to faith in Christ today more because they know they are broken and in need of a healer than because they know they are sinners in need of a Savior. That doesn't mean we shouldn't speak of sin and a Savior.

One of the principles of a healthy soul is that we must repent of sin. We must speak of sin. We must speak of our Savior. But I think people are going to come to Jesus because He is a Healer frequently in our day and age. People know they are broken, and they are looking for help. And Jesus is a Healer. Don't just become a healthy person so you can live a healthier life; become a healthy person so you can help others find Jesus the Healer who can set them free!

Let me close with a final story. I was in Redding, California at a conference in February 2014. I was there with my friend Ron Walborn, who is the dean of the seminary. We took a group of students with us that we were teaching together. Ron had to leave early, so he called me on his way out and said, "Can you go meet with one of our students? She is a Vietnamese woman named Ruth." I said, "Sure. What do you want me to do?" He said, "She's stuck. She is completely shut down." I said, "Sure. I'll meet with her."

I walked into the lounge where she was sitting, and she said, "Oh, no. It's you." I laughed. "What's that mean?" I asked. She said, "Your reputation has preceded you." I said, "Do you want me to help?" She said, "I guess." I said, "Tell me your story."

The most important part of her story was this: as a little girl, her mother used to say to her, "Women are oppressed. That's just the way it is. There is nothing you can do about it."

Ruth learned to stuff all of her emotions. She thought: *No one cares. No one will love me. No one will nurture me in my pain.* So she just stuffed it. When something bad would happen, she would go into her room and sit quietly. She didn't pray, she didn't listen to music, she didn't journal. She just sat there alone in her room and stuffed her pain.

She didn't allow herself to feel anything. Not anger. Not sadness. Not grief. There were no tears; she just swallowed her disappointments, heartaches, and grief. She didn't talk to anyone about her pains, her hurts, or her disappointments. Not even God; she figured He didn't care either. She just shoved it all down into the basement of her soul.

But as she shut down her negative emotions like fear, rejection, hurt, and anger, all the positive emotions shut down with them, emotions like joy, peace, and love. Ruth was just numb.

She told me her story, and an image came to my mind. I said to her, "Ruth, it is like you are sitting in a steel room. There are no windows. And you can't get out. You are in this dark and lonely place. But Jesus stands outside at the door, and He knocks. He wants you to open it and let Him in."

She said, "Why doesn't he just open it Himself? He can come in if He wants to."

I said, "He is a gentleman. He won't force himself upon you. He is not an oppressor. You must choose to let Him in."

I could see she was reluctant, so I said to her, "I won't force you, either. We have one more service tonight. If you want prayer after this service, if you're ready to open your steel-box soul, then come up to me, and I'll pray with you."

She nodded, but stiffly. At the end of the service, she came up to me and said, "I'm ready." I laid my hand on her head and said, "Just picture yourself in that steel room, and open the door to let Jesus in. I'll pray."

I simply prayed, "Come in, Lord Jesus."

The presence of God was so strong upon her that she just collapsed under the weight of His presence; she fell over. She stayed down on the floor for about 45 minutes. When she got up, she was radically changed. Jesus did soul surgery; He accessed the deep recesses of her soul. Over the next several months she experienced many long overdue tears and much joy. She experienced grieving and healing. Most importantly, she experienced God's loving presence.

Today she no longer lives in a little box. She has a full range of emotions. She can feel sadness, anger, and hurt, but she can also feel love, joy, and peace. Every time I see her, she comes running up to me and throws her arms around me. But it wasn't me. I can't open up the box in someone's soul. I can't heal the human heart. I was just pointing her to Jesus. Only the love of a once blood-stained and now risen Savior can redeem a life marked by pain. When someone comes to me for soul help, my goal is never

> Only the love of a once blood-stained and now risen Savior can redeem a life marked by pain.

to meet with the person. My goal is to get the person to meet Jesus. He is the Healer, and in Him there is hope.

I pray God may help you on your journey toward wholeness. May you know the tender affections of our heavenly Father. May you experience His transforming presence on your Soul Care journey. May the abundant life of Jesus be yours to live. May you live life free and full!

ADDENDUM:

DELIVERANCE HELP SHEET

We recommend using the following procedure for deliverance ministry, especially as you begin. For more practical help with the process of deliverance, consider attending or viewing a Deliverance Training Workshop at www.DrRobReimer.com

Preparation

Make sure you do not go into this alone. Bring other mature spiritual people along who can pray. Make sure your confessions are current. Obviously, you must be a follower of Jesus. (Remember Acts 19 and the incident with the seven sons of Sceva.)

Remember, it is best, as preparation, to have the individual go through a Soul Care process before the deliverance session. Have them walk through this book with you and apply the principles of each chapter. If that is not feasible, at a bare minimum you should ask them to confess their sins, create a list of people they need to forgive, and begin praying blessings on all of them while making a decision to develop the will to forgive them.

Deliverance Procedure

1. Explain the Process

Begin by explaining deliverance to the person. Explain that there are good spirits and bad spirits. Bad spirits are fallen angels that seek to indwell and control people. Explain that God, and demons, speak to us directly. As someone going through a deliverance, their job is to report what they are hearing, feeling, experiencing, sensing, and "seeing."

God (and demons) speak to us in the following ways. (Note: For a more detailed explanation, see my book *River Dwellers*.)

1. They can speak in an audible voice;
2. They can speak through your thoughts;
3. They can speak through your feelings;
4. Sometimes spirits speak through pictures;
5. They can communicate through a "cartoon caption"—this is a word that people can see in their mind's eye. Often a demon will confuse the letters, mix them up, and move them around, but you can command them to be straightened out so that they are readable.
6. Finally, the Holy Spirit can speak to our "knower": You just know something. This is Spirit-to-spirit communication.

Explain to the person that they should not filter responses; this is a common problem. Instruct them to report whatever they sense, see, hear, and feel.

Sometimes the demon will communicate to everyone present in an audible voice that is dark and gravelly, but that isn't very common. If it doesn't communicate directly, then the person being delivered also serves a role like a reporter. They need to report whatever communication they are receiving from the spirits.

Different people receive from the spirit realm in different ways, and different spirits communicate in different ways. This is why it is important to report everything. One time I did a group test and my wife was present, and she came to me afterward because she said she wasn't "hearing" anything. So I did a spiritual test with her one on one, but I coached her to tell me what she was seeing. My wife gets about 90 percent of her communications from the Spirit as pictures; she is a seer. She said, "I see a picture of a cross. It is glowing white." I said, "That's good. Tell me what you feel." She said, "I feel peace." I gave her a thumbs-up and smiled, and said, "That's the Spirit of God. That's good. Now I'll do the rest of the questions, and if you see any dark things there in that picture, let me know, or if you start feeling anxious, tell me." She went through the whole test with the glowing cross and the peace of God. Clean test. Helping people report well and thoroughly is vital to the process.

Sometimes they are getting the right answers, but they are feeling resistance, anxiety, or some other indicator that something is not right. You have to coach some people through the reporting process so they do not hold back what they are receiving.

2. Pray

Pray for protection, wisdom, discernment, and the power of the Spirit of God. Ask the person to pray a prayer of surrender to Christ. Don't pray fear-based, magic-type prayers. Keep your eyes on Jesus, and pray with confidence and peace. You do not need to be afraid. Jesus isn't nervous, and He is greater still than any other spirit (Ephesians 1:18-23).

You can also make a series of commands in this prayer time; this is to limit the demons' activity in the session. You will have to reinforce it during the session at times.

Make the following commands in Jesus' name:

- "Stay in the hierarchy that you are in."
  Demons come in hierarchical structures, like a pyramid with a leader at the top. It is quicker and easier to do deliverance if you keep them in their hierarchy.

- "You will cause no harm to anyone here, nor to their families."

- "No throwing up."
  Once in a while, demons can make a person feel sick, but you can command them to stop.

- "No undue physical manifestations, no confusion, no deception, no condemnation."

- "No anxiety."

- "No choking."
  Sometimes demons give people a choking sensation, but you can command them to stop.

- "No dividing or hiding. No fleeing to escape this session."

When some manifestation starts, you can try to command it to stop. For example, there is usually some low level of anxiety that is felt, but if it intensifies, you can usually limit it by commanding it to stop. This is why it is important that the person reports whatever is happening. For example, sometimes they will feel a pain in a part of their body as a demon manifests, but you can command it to stop in Jesus' name.

3. Do a Test
After prayer, call the spirit to attention. Say something like, "Now the spirit whom Jesus calls to attention, come to attention. Jesus is at the center of this person's soul, and there is all light and no darkness. Come stand in the light next to Jesus. Now, spirit at attention, answer these questions in Jesus' name."

Now ask the series of questions listed below. A wrong answer is an indication of the likely presence of an evil spirit. Go through each question until you hit a wrong response. When you get a wrong answer, STOP, and move to the second list of questions in step 4 below.

- Is Jesus Christ the Lord? Is Jesus Christ your Lord?

- Did Jesus Christ come in the flesh?

- Do you honor the blood of the Lord Jesus?

- Did Jesus Christ die on the cross and rise again?

- Is it through faith in Christ alone that we can be saved? Is there any other name under Heaven by which people may be saved?

- Do you testify that this person is a child of God through faith in Jesus Christ?

- Is Jesus Christ accursed? (This is a bad thing; the answer should be NO.)

- What is your purpose in this person?
  When the Spirit of God is present, the answers will be things like love, light, peace, joy, etc. When a demonic spirit is present, the answers will be dark things. Often they will state their name or function here: destruction, rage, hatred, bitterness, anger, sexual immorality, lust, depression, anxiety, etc.

- Is it your desire to pour out the love of God in this person's heart?
  Occasionally you will deal with someone who has toxic shame, and they will get all positive responses except this one. They don't get a negative response. They just don't hear anything. That is more than likely not demonic. It is just toxic shame. You must always divide soul and spirit. This is most often not a demonic spirit; this is just a soul issue. The person is struggling to believe and receive the love of God.

- Do you produce the fruit of the Spirit in this person? Love, joy, peace, patience, kindness, goodness, gentleness, faithfulness, and self-control?

- Does the Scripture say that the Holy Spirit proceeds from God the Father?

- Do you proceed from God the Father?

- Does the Scripture say that the Holy Spirit is an eternal Spirit?

- Are you an eternal spirit?

- Do you love this person?

- Are there any remaining indwelling spirits? Any hiders?
  I only ask this question if every other question received
  a correct response, and it is clear that it is the Holy Spirit
  who is communicating. Sometimes there is another hiding, and the Holy Spirit will show that. If so, ask the name,
  and deal with the spirit.

- Is there anything you would like to say to this person?
  This question is also reserved for the Holy Spirit at the
  end of a clean test. When you get to the end of a positive
  test, the Holy Spirit is often recognizably present, and this
  can be a very powerful time for the individual to hear
  from God.

4. Ask the Spirit at Attention These Key Questions

If a demon is present, ask the following important questions. After each question, verify the answer by asking, "Is that
the truth before God?"

- What is your name?

- What is your function?
  Ask this if the name isn't an obvious function. For example, if the spirit's name is Hatred, its function is implic-
  it in the name. Also, sometimes one of the intercessory
  team members will hear a name. Test it with the spirit
  to make sure that name is accurate. I suggest having the
  team members write things down and hand them to the
  leader. It is best if only one person is the point leader; it
  makes it less confusing and quickens the process.

- Do you have any ground to stay?
  Ground must be specific. It has to be unconfessed sin;
  it cannot be something that the person has confessed in

their past. That is already under the blood of Jesus, and the spirit is simply trying to accuse and condemn the person. Do not allow the demons to accuse or condemn people and hold old sins over their head. This isn't ground; this is just an attack. Don't let them. It has to be specific, unconfessed sin.

They will also try to say things like, "I want to stay." That's not ground. Ground is specific, unconfessed sin—like the person is bitter toward their spouse. They simply need to confess that to the Lord, and agree with God to forgive them, and the ground will be broken.

- Do you have any spirits under your control? If so, how many? Do any of those spirits have ground to stay?
  You don't necessarily need the names of these underlings. But I do need to know if they have any ground to stay, and if they do, the ground must be broken.

- Do you have a leader within this person?
  Sometimes a spirit does not have a leader; one spirit is the leader of all the rest—that top leader is usually the last spirit to come forward and be cast out. If you move from leader to leader, it makes the process much quicker.

- Do you see any gates, windows, or portals open? Are there any secrets or curses that give you any right to return?
  If there are any gates open or secrets or curses, they must be dealt with to break the ground. If you have an open gate, ask the spirit to name it. Often it is a generational curse. Break curses in Jesus' name.

5. Command the Spirits to Leave

Once the needed information is acquired from the spirit, and ground is broken, command that group of spirits (the leader and those under him) to "go where Jesus sends them," and do so in Jesus' name. Then, deal with the next leader by starting over with Step 4.

Always try to keep spirits in groups. Move up the hierarchy from one leader to the next leader, and cast them out by groups. For example, imagine I am dealing with a spirit named Anger, and Anger has three spirits under him. During my questions, I find out that Anger has a spirit above him named Rage. Neither Anger, nor any of the three under him, have any ground; the ground is broken, and there are no secrets or curses or gates left. I send Anger and the three under him to wherever Jesus sends them. Then I call Rage to attention. I verify the spirit's name by saying, "Rage, is that your name?" If yes, then I go back to the questions in Step 4 with this new group of spirits. Keep repeating this process until you cast out the last group.

6. Repeat the Test

Once the last group of spirits is cast out, go back through the test questions from Step 3 and make sure there are no "hiders." Keep going through the process until you come up with a clean test, where all questions from Step 3 are answered correctly, and all spirits are gone.

7. Invite the Holy Spirit to Speak

When the test finishes clean, and the Spirit of God is answering the questions, end by asking the Holy Spirit if there is anything further He would like to say to the person. (Many very cool God-encounters take place during this time!)

8. End with Prayer and Final Instructions

The demons will sometimes come back on the outside and threaten. The person needs to take their stand in Christ, submit to God, and tell the enemy to flee (James 4:7). It is helpful for the person to "renew the mind" (Romans 12)—and to replace the lies the demons have been speaking with the truth of Scripture.

There is often some follow-up Soul Care work that needs to be done to help the person on their journey to wholeness. Jesus is a Healer, Savior, and Redeemer. He came to set the captives free. No one is irreparable with Jesus.

ABOUT THE AUTHOR

Rev. Dr. Rob Reimer is the founder of Renewal International, which he began to fulfill his call to advance the Kingdom of God through personal and corporate spiritual renewal. His books *Soul Care, Spiritual Authority, Deep Faith, River Dwellers, Pathways to the King* and *Calm in the Storm* have sold worldwide. Rob mentors Christian leaders, and his conferences have helped thousands of Christians to find freedom and fullness in Christ. Personally transparent, Rob relates lessons learned as he has walked with God, responded to His Word, and processed pain in marriage and ministry. These lessons are not only taught, but participants actively begin the process of incorporating them into their lives, walking in the light, practicing hearing from God, and accessing His power for ministry.

Currently, Dr. Reimer is the Professor of Pastoral Theology at Alliance Theological Seminary in NY, where he earned his Master of Divinity degree. He also holds a Doctor of Ministry in Preaching from Gordon-Conwell Theological Seminary.

To access eCourse, live, or video teaching on *Soul Care*, or to explore more of Rob's work, view his itinerary, or to invite him to speak, please visit www.DrRobReimer.com

ALSO BY DR. ROB REIMER

River Dwellers
Living in the Fullness of the Spirit

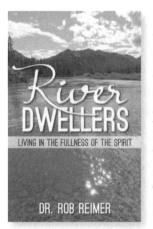

Did you ever wish there was more to your Christian life? Too often the Christian life is reduced to going to church, attending meetings, serving God, and doing devotions. But Jesus promised us abundant life – a deep, intimate, satisfying connection with the living God. How do we access the abundant life that Jesus promised? The key is the presence and life of the Holy Spirit within us.

Jesus said that the Spirit of God flows within us like a river – He is the River of Life. But we need to dwell in the river in order to access the Spirit's fullness.

In *River Dwellers,* Dr. Rob Reimer offers a deep look at life in the Spirit and provides practical strategies for dwelling in the River of Life. We will explore the fullness of the Spirit, tuning into the promptings of the Spirit, walking in step with the Spirit, and developing sensitivity to the presence of the God in our lives. This resource will guide you toward becoming a full-time river dweller, even in the midst of life's most difficult seasons when the river seems to run low.

Together let's become River Dwellers, living where the fullness of God flows so that we can carry living water to a world dying of thirst!

Pathways to the King

Living a Life of Spiritual Renewal and Power

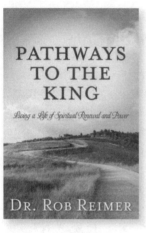

We need revival. The church in America desperately needs revival. There are pockets of it happening right now, but we need another Great Awakening. About forty years ago, the church was impacted by the church growth movement. The goal of the movement was to get the church focused on the Great Commission— taking the Good News about Jesus to the entire world. The church was off mission, and the movement was a necessary course correction. But it didn't work. Many people came to Christ as a result of this outreach emphasis, and I am grateful for that. More churches are now focused on evangelism, helping people come to know Jesus, than they were before the movement. But we have fewer people attending church now (percentage wise) than ever before in the history of the United States. We need revival.

This book is about how we can usher in revival and also about the price that we must pay to experience it. I believe we have a part to play in seeing the next great spiritual awakening. God wants us to be carriers of His kingdom. He wants us to experience the reality and fullness of His kingdom, and he wants us to expand the kingdom to others – just like Jesus did. In order to do that, I believe we must follow 8 Kingdom Pathways of Spiritual Renewal: Personalizing our Identity in Christ, Pursuing God, Purifying Ourselves, Praising, Praying Kingdom Prayers, Claiming Promises, Passing the Tests, and

Persisting. These 8 pathways are discussed in great detail, are securely rooted in biblical truths, and are illustrated by compelling examples from Scripture and from my life, the lives of believers in my community, and in the lives of great Christians throughout history.

Available at www.DrRobReimer.com

Deep Faith

Developing Faith that Releases the Power of God

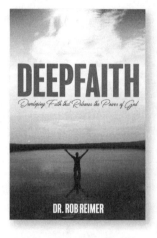

Jesus said, "Very truly I tell you, all who have faith in me will do the works that I have been doing, and they will do even greater things than these" (John 14:12). The extraordinary promise of Jesus is that we can do Kingdom works that He did - cast out demons, heal the sick, save the lost and set the captives free.

Jesus wants to advance his Kingdom through us. But this promise comes with a condition: the level of our Kingdom activity is dependent upon our faith.

There are promises in Heaven that God wants to release, but they cannot be released without faith. There are miracles that God wants to do that cannot be done without faith. There are answers to prayer that God wants to unleash that cannot be unleashed without faith. There are works of the Kingdom that God wants to accomplish that cannot be accomplished unless the people of God develop deeper faith. But there is hope for all of us, because faith can be developed.

Faith opens doors and creates opportunities for accessing God's power against all odds. Faith is a difference maker, a future shaper, a bondage breaker, a Kingdom mover. In his latest book, Dr. Rob Reimer challenges readers to develop deep faith that can release the works of the Kingdom. Faith is not static; it is dynamic. We can and must take an intentional path toward developing our faith if we want to see the works of the Kingdom in greater measure.

Spiritual Authority

Partnering with God to Release the Kingdom

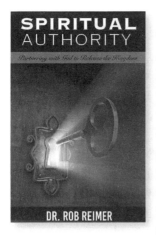

Jesus gave his disciples authority to preach the good news of the kingdom of God and to cast out demons, heal the sick, save the lost and set the captives free. Everywhere Jesus went, the kingdom came with power. There was no proclamation of the gospel without a demonstration of power. It was the authentic demonstration of Jesus' power through his followers that ignited the greatest spiritual movements in the first century. Today, we are becoming more like the spiritual climate in the first century then like 1950 America. In a pluralistic, syncretistic society where all deities are considered equal, only the unequal display of Jesus' power will convince people of the supremacy of Christ. The key to demonstrating the power of the King is Authority and authority is not just positional; it is developmental. Spiritual authority is rooted in identity, expanded in intimacy and activated by faith. This book takes an in depth look at how we can grow in identity, intimacy and faith so that we can develop our authority and release the kingdom.

Also available in Spanish (Autoridad Espirituald).

Calm in the Storm

How God Can Redeem a Crisis to Advance His Kingdom

There is nothing like a crisis to reveal the cracks in the walls of our soul. But God promises to redeem all things that come into our lives to make us more like Jesus. We are experiencing a unique crisis in our day and age, COVID-19. It has created fear, death, and will leave economic disaster in its wake. In this book, I don't just want to talk about how we can survive this crisis, or how we can access the peace of God in tumultuous times. I want to talk about how God can redeem a crisis in our personal lives to take us deeper into maturity and intimacy with Christ. And how this particular crisis could potentially lead to revival if the church processes it well. We stand on the precipice of an unprecedented opportunity to be purified and mobilized on mission to advance the Kingdom of God in our generation.

The Tenderness of Jesus

An Invitation to Experience the Savior

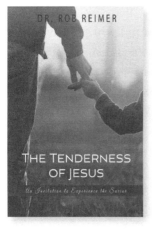

The world is a broken place marred by evil, and evil's influence impacts us all. It is often difficult for people to grasp what God is like in a world such as ours. Jesus shows us the heart of God in a world of heartache. He is the most beautiful, compelling, tender person who has lived.

Jesus is the radiance of God's glory. He shines forth what God is like; He is a beacon of light that cuts through the darkness of evil and radiates the goodness of God. He is the exact representation of God the Father. If you want to know what God is like, look to Jesus. Don't look through the lens of evil or the lenses of either the church or religion. Look to Jesus. That is why He came. The world is not an exact representation of God. The church is not an exact representation of God. Jesus is. He came to freshly present what the Father is like to those of us who are spiritually impaired by a world of suffering.

The Tenderness of Jesus, in many ways, is my most personal book to date. I invite you to listen in as I write to my four young adult children about the tenderness of Jesus Christ. Come sit with us around the dinner table. May this fresh glimpse of Jesus heal your broken heart and reignite your spiritual fervor.

The Soul Care Leader

Healthy Living and Leading

How do we live a healthy life and lead others into spiritual, emotional and relational health and wholeness? That is the focus of this book.

Trying to help others find freedom and wholeness is draining work. What do we do to become healthy and maintain our well-being? What are the practices and rhythms we need to engage in to be effective Soul Care practitioners? How do we create a culture where life-change flourishes? How do we minister in the power of the Spirit so that we can lead others into breakthroughs?

Too often people are talking about the same problems that they were talking about several years ago but they aren't finding a path to freedom. We need to help people get to the roots and not merely manage their dysfunction and sin. These are the questions and topics that this book will seek to equip you in as you seek to live and lead people into freedom and fullness in Christ.